The Ba
Fan's Guide to
Spring Training

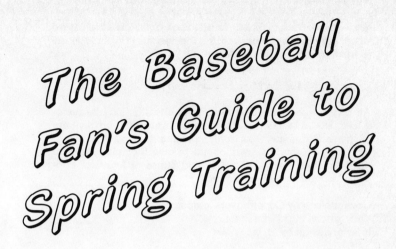

# The Baseball Fan's Guide to Spring Training

## Mike Shatzkin and
## Jim Charlton

**Addison-Wesley Publishing Company, Inc.**

Reading, Massachusetts     Menlo Park, California     New York

Don Mills, Ontario     Wokingham, England     Amsterdam     Bonn

Sydney     Singapore     Tokyo     Madrid     San Juan

Cover design by Copenhaver Cumpston
Illustrations by Sandie Brecher
Interior design by *In the Can*

Photographs are reproduced with the kind permission of:
National Baseball Hall of Fame – pages 9, 17, 18, 20-1, 29;
Associated Press – page 24-5;
Mike Mumby – pages 8, 11, 13, 14, 15, 22, 23, 28;
Mike Mumby/AP – page 10 top;
LA Dodgers – page 10 bottom;
Ron Scherl – pages 30, 31.

We have made every effort to ascertain the ownership of all copyright holders. In the event of any inadvertent omission of credit, we will be pleased to make the necessary correction in future printings.

Set in 10½ on 12pt Memphis

Library of Congress Cataloging-in-Publication Data
Shatzkin, Mike.
The baseball fan's guide to spring training/Mike Shatzkin and Jim Charlton.

ISBN 0-201-13234-6
1. Baseball — United States — Training — Miscellanea. 2. Baseball — United States — Clubs — Directories. I. Charlton, James, 1939 — II. Title
GV875.6.S53 1988          87-28798
796.357'07 — DC19

ABCDEFGHIJ – FG –898
First printing, January 1988

# Contents

# Introduction and Acknowledgments

CO-AUTHORS MIKE SHATZKIN and Jim Charlton and their editor for this book, George Gibson, have been enjoying the magic of Spring Training for a long time. Charlton started visiting Florida to watch his college roommate, Jim Bouton, compete for a job with the Yankees in the early 1960s. Shatzkin and Gibson began making the migration on a regular basis in the mid-1970s. They could see the annual increase in interest from baseball fans all across America in what had been a pretty private party for most of the first 100 years of its existence.

Although Shatzkin and Gibson missed connections and went to Florida separately in the spring of 1985, both came back with the same conclusion: fans going to see Spring Training games needed *help*. Although the settings and ballparks are intimate and proximate once you get there, the critical information about schedules, tickets, ballpark locations, and other logistical considerations is scattered, requiring a fan to seek answers to basic questions from a number of sources. Out of the perceived need for that information grew this book.

Shatzkin and Charlton got a lot of help in gathering the information to add to their years of personal observation. Rich Friedman, referred to them after a pressbox conversation with

*Sport* editor Barry Shapiro, hit the phone. The help of the people who answered for the ballclubs was indispensable in preparing this book: Jim Schultz, Atlanta Braves; Ned Colletti, Chicago Cubs; Don Fuller, HoHoKams; Brad Del Barba, Cincinnati Reds; Debbie Atchison, Tampa Tarpons; Linda Black, Tampa Sports Authority; Chuck Pool, Houston Astros; Pat O'Conner, Osceola Astros; Charlie Blaney, Dodgertown; Monique Giroux, Montreal Expos; Kevin McHale, West Palm Beach Expos; Dennis D'Agostino, New York Mets; Joe McShane, Port St. Lucie; Mike Ryan; Larry Shenk, Philadelphia Phillies; John Timberlake, Clearwater Phillies; Greg Johnson, Pittsburgh Pirates; Bob Carter, Pirate City; John Henry, Bradenton Public Works; Brian Bartow, St. Louis Cardinals; Mike Bertiani, St. Louis Cardinals; Linda Prince, St. Louis Cardinals; Jim Altaffer, St. Petersburg Public Works; Kip Ingle, St. Louis Cardinals; Bea Barnes, San Diego Padres; Mary Cordery, Yuma Chamber of Commerce; Dennis Donnelly, Yuma Parks and Recreation; Duffy Jennings, San Francisco Giants; Larry Gunning, Scottsdale Charros; Rick Vaughn, Baltimore Orioles; Red Morecroft, Orioles Florida Ticket Manager; Dick Bresciani, Boston Red Sox; Dick Radatz, Winter Haven Red Sox; Jan Newton, California Angels; Kevin Hulich, California Angels; Pete Richert, Palm Springs Angels; Tim Clodjeaux, Chicago White Sox; Ed Smith, Sarasota White Sox; Rick Minch, Cleveland Indians; Marty Hoppel, Tucson Toros; Connie Piotrowski, Detroit Tigers; Lew Matlin, Detroit Tigers; Ron Myers, Lakeland Tigers; Dan Pearson, Boardwalk and Baseball; Jeff Coy, Kansas City Royals; Tim Skibosh, Milwaukee Brewers; Frank Pezzarano, Compadres Stadium; Tom Mee, Minnesota Twins; Lou D'Ermillo, New York Yankees; Mark Zettlemyre, Ft. Lauderdale Yankees; John Mazzola, Ft. Lauderdale Stadium; Kathy Jacobson, Oakland Athletics; Dave Smith, Phoenix Firebirds; Bob Porter, Seattle Mariners; Dave Niehaus, Seattle Mariners' broadcaster; Jay Miller, Gulf Coast Rangers; Gary Oswald, Toronto Blue Jays; Ken Carson, Dunedin Blue Jays.

Mike Mumby and the Hall of Fame (librarian Tom Heitz and photo collection assistant Theresa Booan, in particular) gave the book critical background information and interesting photographs. Jane Charnin-Aker helped develop the historical perspective.

Barry Gross checked our spelling, punctuation, and consistency of style.

Gary Slochowsky hit a lot of typewriter keys and helped organize the team-by-team information.

Shep Long and Jessica Rosenthal did invaluable work in pulling all the various pieces of the project together and making sure they fit into a cohesive whole.

A special thanks is due Louise Kennedy for her organizational assistance, especially in compiling the lists of nonbaseball activities in each area, and for the inspiration for the cover design, and Robert Rosiak for Spring Training site information.

The development of this project also gave rise to another: Shatzkin has joined with other partners to form SUNBALL Spring Training Tours, a company that will offer complete package tours to every team, every week, from anywhere in the world beginning with Spring Training 1988 (1–800–I LUV SUN). SUNBALL will cut through the extensive planning that this book makes clear is necessary to avoid disappointments over sold-out ballgames or missed opportunities to get close to the action, though it can't duplicate the historical and statistical detail in these pages. Baseball fans visiting Spring Training — alone or on tour — will see more if they know what is in this book.

In the spring of 1988, as has been the case increasingly for spring after recent spring, hundreds of thousands of fans will make the trip to Florida or Arizona to watch their favorite team (or to watch no particular favorite at all). SUNBALL or not, most of them will do it on their own. *The Baseball Fan's Guide to Spring Training* is for them, and for the hundreds of thousands of others who might not make it this spring but someday will.

Mike Shatzkin and Jim Charlton

September 1987

# CHAPTER 1

## Why You Need, and How to Use, This Book

BASEBALL CHALLENGES AND stimulates the senses and the intellect: it is green fields and bright sun, grace and power, immediate action and a historical context, muscular exertion today and concise statistics tomorrow. *The Baseball Fan's Guide to Spring Training* has — in the spirit of the game itself — many things to offer. Both a travel guide and a baseball book, it provides specific travel advice, much of which has never been made available in one source, while offering a wealth of historical and statistical detail that will please any baseball buff.

Rare is the baseball fan today who has not heard firsthand about the wonders of Spring Training. Friends, relatives, and co-workers return from Florida and Arizona with irresistible tales of small, intimate stadiums where the Gods of Summer are as close to you as your next-door neighbor; and of Major League games played under a near-tropical or desert sun while most big-league fans are still shoveling snow.

In 1986 over 2 million tickets were sold to the Spring Training games of the 26 Major League teams. Surveys — including one conducted by the city of Orlando to demonstrate the economic impact of the Twins' facility — indicated that more than 70 per cent of the tickets went to out-of-state fans, more than half of

1

whom had traveled specifically to see baseball. That's a major league migration, by anyone's standards.

The fans travel to see something special and different. Spring Training is unlike the everyday big-league environment in very specific ways:

**Intimacy.** The ballparks are smaller than Major League parks; the players live close together and among the writers, announcers, and executives; the daily practice sessions (often unfenced and unpoliced) are open to the public. And many of the marketing functions of big-league baseball — TV networks doing specials, baseball card photographers getting their shots, and reporters covering the games — are in plain view as they never are during the regular season.

**Spontaneity.** Because the games don't count, pitchers run in the outfield while play goes on; a Class AA catcher can find himself playing shortstop in the late innings to give a Major League starter a break from the afternoon sun; the DH from one team might spend an inning or two in his opponents' bullpen, chewing the fat with a former teammate from a third club; the managers might decide by mutual consent to play a few extra innings to create some work for pitchers and bench players.

**Proximity.** Not only are the fans closer to the players and the players closer to their management and media, the teams train close to each other. Many fans catch a Braves game in the afternoon and a Yankee game at night; or watch the Phillies take batting practice before going to see a Blue Jays game; or watch the first four innings of the Giants and the last four innings of the Athletics. A player from the Pirates, given a day off, might show up at a Dodgers-Tigers game to visit some friends. And, of course, lots of former ballplayers make the rounds of the camps visiting old buddies or looking for work.

Indeed, Spring Training for the baseball fan is like a vast, unorganized amusement park without signs to most of the rides. Getting the most out of it requires *knowledge* and *planning*. Providing the knowledge to direct the planning is the purpose of this book.

In *The Baseball Fan's Guide to Spring Training* you will learn how to get the schedules for Grapefruit and Cactus League games (not as simple as one might think) and how to order tickets (specific information is provided for each team). We give you the essentials for mapping a travel plan: which teams are close together and how close; where the tickets are tough to get and where they are readily available; what other attractions exist near the various groups of teams; which airports to use; and which team hotels offer an intimate glimpse of the players, and where you are most likely to get autographs at the ballpark. Then we show you how to take your special team and player interests, your relative willingness to commit in advance to destinations and games, and your appetite (or tolerance) for time in the car to help you shape the Spring Training plan that makes sense for you.

Each team section includes a narrative on the hottest rookies each spring since 1960 that is filled with facts and statistics, followed by a listing of each year's top Spring Training rookie, and a suggested list of prospects to watch for in the spring of 1988. The rookie listings are not a statistically inspired compilation, though they have been carefully researched. Most teams have kept only casual Spring Training records, at best, until very recently. The perspective continues that Spring Training's many functions — trying players out in new positions, changing batting stances, experimenting with new pitches and new players — undercut the validity of the statistical record. Some prospects have great springs but get sent down; others do poorly and stick with the Major League club. The Rookies of the Year were voted by the Baseball Writers' Association of America, the official judge, and we have made mention in the narratives of other awards won by individual players.

It is fascinating to watch the fortunes of teams ebb and flow as rookies arrive, are traded, exceed expectations, or don't pan out. Indeed, the history of each team's rookies is in many ways a history of the team itself.

The rookie lists for each team omit players of the caliber of Steve Carlton, Dave Winfield, and Bob Horner. A variety of circumstances create these oddities: a player overlooked in training camp or spending his spring with the minor leaguers or (like Winfield and Horner) stepping out of college ball directly to a Major League position. Some players spend two or three years working their way into the lineup, and it is difficult to say when their days as a hot prospect ended and their status as a veteran began.

The top rookie and hot prospects lists come from an amalgamation of observations, opinions, awards, statistics, arguments, and articles. Several publications — *The Sporting News, Sport,*

*Sports Illustrated, Baseball Digest, Baseball America,* and
Zander Hollander's annual guides — generally make preseason
predictions or offer postseason awards. We have deferred to
contemporary opinions wherever possible but have employed
the blessings of hindsight to throw in some proper objections.
For the Yankees, Mets, and Dodgers, the three teams that have
rookie awards for Spring Training performance, we have gone
with their choices for each year with an addition or two they
may have overlooked at the time.

Finally, at the back, you will find tables comparing Spring
Training results with the regular-season record of every team
since 1960, which will doubtless fuel debate over whether
there is a connection.

You may enjoy reading through *The Baseball Fan's Guide*
from cover to cover. By doing so, you will surely augment your
baseball knowledge as you experience Spring Training vicari-
ously or in person, for there are facts and statistics here you
will not find elsewhere. You can also use the book as an efficient
travel reference tool by following these guidelines:

*1.* Decide where you want to go (that is, which teams you
want to see) and how much time you have to spend.
Chapter 3 and the introductions to each of the team group
listings will tell you which teams are where and how far
apart they are, while suggesting a central base and other
things to do in the area.

*2.* Refer to the entries for specific teams to get the information you need to obtain schedules and order tickets.
Pay careful attention to the situations in which advance
purchase is advisable and where it is *essential.* The entries
also provide descriptions of and directions to each stadium,
the best spot for autographs, the players' favorite night spots,
and other details important to the fan.

*3.* If you will need to rent a car, do it early since the college
breaks and increasing numbers of Spring Training fans
can deplete the available autos.

*4.* Get a competent travel agency to secure a hotel or motel
room for you. We have omitted a listing of suggested
places to stay from this book, since the choices (price,
quality, location) are extremely varied in the warm-weather
tourist locations where Spring Training takes place. You
won't end up on a park bench if you don't reserve in advance
— there are a lot of hotel rooms in Florida and Arizona —
but you may spend more time than you want looking for

lodging and more money for less satisfaction than you could with advance reservations made by someone with expertise.

**5.** We have listed the addresses and telephone numbers of local Chambers of Commerce; if you feel you want more extensive tourist information than we have in the book (about restaurants and lodging, or concerning nonbaseball tourist attractions), they'll be glad to give it to you.

**6.** Bring *The Baseball Fan's Guide* with you to give you essential, on-the-spot information about parking, radio broadcasts, maps and directions to stadiums and practice fields, numbers to call to locate B games, and guidance on which team hotels to hit and which to skip.

As you use this book, keep one very important thing in mind: Spring Training is a changing, dynamic experience. Teams move each spring. (In 1988 the Mets, Royals and Reds are in new locations, and there will be more changes in 1989.) New facilities are built, old ones are improved, and often the "improvements" tend to reduce fan access. B games and extra innings are often scheduled spontaneously on 24 hours' (or less) notice at the request of a manager or general manager. Undoubtedly, a practice field or two will have moved and a section of stands will have been added or taken away between the time we checked our facts and the time you visit a site. To get the most out of your visit to each camp, follow a very simple rule:

Walk completely *around* the stadium *before* you walk in to take your seat for a game. That way, you will be sure that you aren't missing an opportunity to get close to a batting cage, a practice session, or a few players lounging in the sun.

# CHAPTER 2

## Rites of Spring Training

SPRING TRAINING IS such a civilized and pleasant ritual that it seems perfectly natural it should have preceded the formation of the Major Leagues. Today's fans, attending games in Florida and Arizona, or reveling in the first box scores that signal the arrival of spring, may be interested in an overview of Spring Training's history, to more fully appreciate its magic.

The first foray south took place in the late 1860s, when owners observed that many of their players were showing up out of shape, "looking like aldermen," as one owner put it. In 1869, the notorious William "Boss" Tweed of Tammany Hall fame sent his New York Mutuals south to New Orleans to prepare for the season by playing local teams. In February of 1870 the Cincinnati Red Stockings, the champions and winners of 56 straight games in 1869, and the Chicago White Stockings made Spring Training trips to New Orleans as well. The Cleveland Forest Cities went to Washington, D.C., in 1883, and the Boston Red Stockings also traveled to ever-popular New Orleans in 1884.

Hall of Famer Cap Anson is sometimes given credit for holding the first Spring Training camp. In 1886 Anson took his Chicago White Stockings to Hot Springs, Arkansas, to have them work the winter kinks and beer out of their systems. Here, far from the winds of Lake Michigan, he had his band of generally low-paid roughnecks walking 20 miles a day and living in a dollar-a-day boarding house. One of those players was a young outfielder, Billy Sunday. He went on to fight powerful forces in the Windy City as an anti-liquor evangelist — without much success — and Chicago is still remembered in song as "the town that Billy Sunday could not shut down."

*1934: White Sox manager Lew Fonseca (2nd from left) instructs 4 never-known hurlers in Pasadena.*

Also in 1886 another future Hall of Famer, manager Harry Wright, put his Philadelphia club on a train headed for Charleston, South Carolina. *The Sporting News* reported that the Pittsburgh club was leaving for St. Louis and other relatively southern towns for its spring workouts. Pittsburgh, Louisville, and Detroit all did some training in Charleston that year. Anson, Wright, and managers and owners of other clubs saw the advantages of going south to get into shape early, and from 1886 on Spring Training was an annual ritual.

In 1887 Wright turned down an offer from a Florida town to bring his team there to train. Wright contended that the distance was too great and chose Savannah, Georgia, instead. In 1888 he retreated farther north, taking his Phillies to Cape May, New Jersey, then a fashionable coastal resort. March is a chilly month in New Jersey, but Wright had his squad up at 6 A.M. for a douse in the surf and a pre-breakfast run on the beach, a routine that, Harry said, "made them look pretty sick."

Teams adopted the practice of training for a short time in warmer climes and then making their way north, stopping along the way to play exhibition games. Minor league teams welcomed the Major Leaguers because fans would flock to the contests to see the locals do battle with the stars, and the Major League teams were able to recoup some of their training expenses. One year the Southern League even delayed opening its season until May 1 to allow time for exhibition games against the Major League clubs. In the spring of 1887 the Detroit team broke camp in Macon, Georgia, and barnstormed for two months, covering 4,000 miles and traveling as far north as St. Paul, Minnesota.

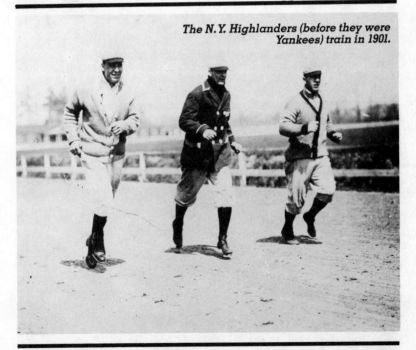

*The N.Y. Highlanders (before they were Yankees) train in 1901.*

The year 1888 marked the first appearance of a team in Florida, when the Washington Statesmen (later the Senators) took a 15-man squad, including young catcher Connie Mack, to Jacksonville. Mack recalled how hotel after hotel refused them rooms until, finally, one agreed to take them in — but only on the condition that the players not mix with the other guests or eat in the dining area. Ballplayers, it seems, suffered the same

*1937: San Diego Padres (PCL) feature the young Ted Williams (3rd from left).*

*Holman Stadium (Vero Beach, Florida) — the Dodgers' spring home*

indignities as did the actors of the day. The cautious hotel owner was probably correct in his assessment of baseball men, for those early players were a rough bunch indeed. Connie Mack also reported that when the Senators rented two shacks from a woman on the outskirts of town, "there was a fight every night, and they broke a lot of her furniture." Harold Seymour confirms this image in his *Baseball: The Early Years*; when fans were astonished to learn that the hard-bitten members of the 1878 Buffalo team had joined the YMCA, he reports, they were assured that it was the only way the team could get to use the Y's gym.

*Professor Stengel conducts spring class at the Boston Braves' Wallingford, CT camp for Tony Cuccinello, Phil Masi, Manny Salvo, Lefty Gomez, Jim Tobin.*

It wasn't until 1908 that the first permanent Spring Training site was established, in Marlin Springs, Texas, where John McGraw took his New York Giants. They had finished the previous season in second place, a game behind the Chicago Cubs; maybe McGraw figured a little better conditioning might bridge the gap. It didn't, as the Giants lost a tie-breaking playoff to the Cubs, made possible by Fred Merkle's infamous base-running blunder. But Texas had been established as an attractive Spring Training location, and so it remained through World War I, with as many as seven teams practicing there in one season.

In 1914 Branch Rickey took the St. Louis Browns to St. Petersburg in the Sunshine State. Their training site — "Coffee Pot Field," also known as "Coffee Pot Grounds" — marked the arrival of baseball on Florida's west coast. But it was Al Lang who earned the title of "father of Florida baseball" from *Baseball* magazine for his efforts in bringing the game south for the spring. Lang had moved in 1911 from Pittsburgh to St. Pete, where he became a successful businessman and was eventually elected mayor. He loved baseball and set about attracting Major League teams to Florida, with such energy and influence that by 1929, 10 of the 16 teams trained there. His legacy, the field built in 1946 and named for him, is today the spring home of the St. Louis Cardinals.

One spring Lang read that snow had halted training for the Pirates for three straight days. Lang wrote to Bucs owner Barney Dreyfuss, a friend from his days in Pittsburgh, and urged him to relocate to St. Petersburg — then a small fishing hamlet of 3,000. Dreyfuss resisted. In 1922 Lang built Waterfront Park, a stadium overlooking the harbor, and the Boston Braves moved their training headquarters there from Galveston, Texas, that spring. The Braves liked their new home: they returned for five springs, signed a contract for an additional five-year commitment, and stayed through 1937. The New York Yankees, then baseball's most popular team, had been spending their springs in New Orleans, where the lifestyle was perhaps a little wild for effective training. They arrived in the more subdued St. Petersburg in 1925, setting up shop at Crescent Lake Park. One spring, the story goes, Babe Ruth hit a legendary home run out of that park and onto the front porch of the West Coast Inn, in deep right field.

Lang didn't stop at the St. Pete city limits. In Tampa he found a spot for the Washington Senators, while the Dodgers (or Robins, as they were still sometimes called) moved to Clearwater in 1923. With Lang's encouragement, Sarasota issued an invitation in 1923 to the Giants, a team with a reputation for being finicky about accommodations. The Giants were satisfied in Sarasota, although sportswriter Sam Crane noted at the time that "nearly the whole team has had to buy real estate in order to get rid of the salesmen long enough to play a little baseball." Everybody got in on the Florida land boom, including Giants manager John McGraw, whose Sarasota real estate dealings eventually went sour. But as long as McGraw was selling, the Giants stayed in Sarasota. Rube Marquard of the

Braves and the Yankees' Bob Shawkey also pitched plots of land when they weren't hurling baseballs.

In 1929 the Tigers and their new manager, Bucky Harris, decided that its dry moderate climate made Phoenix the ideal training site. Under their previous manager, Ty Cobb, the Bengals had done all their training from 1922 through 1924 in Augusta, since the Georgia Peach preferred to stay close to home. The move to Phoenix made the Tigers Arizona's first Spring Training team, but they stayed only that year. It would be close to two decades before the Indians, under manager Lou

*1940: Indians manager Vitt with ace Bob Feller.*

Boudreau, set up in Tucson in 1947. They won their only postwar World Series championship a year later, and they've stayed

**13**

in Tucson ever since. The Giants, too, moved to Arizona in 1947, taking the Tigers' lead and settling permanently in the Phoenix area — save for the curious spring of 1951. That year the Giants and their interborough rivals, the world champion Yankees, switched Spring Training sites: the Yankees moved to Phoenix, the Giants to St. Petersburg. The Yankees may have left a little magic behind, for the Giants won the National League title in 1951, only to lose the Series to the Yanks. The Indians, Giants, and soon-to-arrive Chicago Cubs have been the anchors of the Arizona contingent.

4 great Yankee outfielders running for the '49 pennant in St. Pete: (l to r): DiMaggio, Keller, Bauer, Henrich.

Al Lang couldn't persuade Phil Wrigley to come to Florida. Wrigley owned not only the Chicago Cubs, but also Catalina Island off the southern coast of California, where the Cubs began training in 1922. With a magnificent home in nearby Pasadena and a lush training site, Wrigley had no interest in moving his team; the Cubs trained at Catalina Island for 26 of the next 31 years. They moved to Mesa in 1952 and have been an Arizona fixture ever since — except, like the Giants, for a one-year out-of-state fling, theirs in 1966 in California.

The rest of the permanent Arizona group has, with one exception, been composed of the more recent West Coast teams; Seattle, Oakland, the California Angels, and San Diego have all obviously found it more convenient to stay closer to home. The one exception is the Milwaukee Brewers, but they have a West Coast legacy: born as the Seattle Pilots in 1969 when the Major Leagues expanded into divisions, they moved to Milwaukee the following year. They took with them their Arizona training roots.

Not everyone believed that having many of the clubs in close proximity was a good thing. Owners didn't like their players mingling with those on other teams because they were afraid their employees would trade salary figures. And one scribe, reporting in the 1927 spring season for *Baseball* magazine, raised a competitive concern: "Is it not possible that too friendly relations develop between players who get to know each other so well in the pre-season, and this familiarity diminishes the real rivalry between clubs? Goodness knows that the promoters and fans have to work overtime in these days of payroll supremacy to keep the spirit of competition aflame without the dampener, if it is such, of having every player in both leagues trade dinner dates with each other."

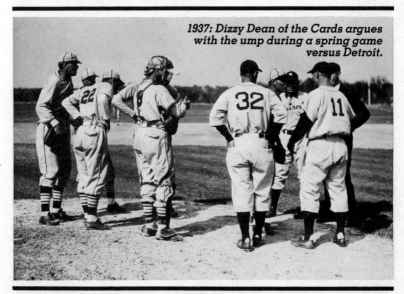

*1937: Dizzy Dean of the Cards argues with the ump during a spring game versus Detroit.*

American League President Ban Johnson, perhaps sensitive to this type of criticism, high-handedly instituted a rule prohibiting American League teams from playing each other in the spring. The rule was not in effect for long, since a number of AL teams protested, arguing that the ban hurt them in the pocketbook. The teams that played the immensely popular Ruthian

Yankees in Florida and during the swing north could make enough money to pay their expenses for the entire spring, so Ban's ban ended up profiting the rival National League clubs. A particular beneficiary was the Brooklyn Dodgers. In 1926 they played the Yankees in 14 straight games on their way north. The Dodgers were eager to have a go at their cross-town rivals, having played in their shadow for some years. To shake up his complacent veterans, who had finished seventh the year before, Yankees manager Miller Huggins brought in rookies at shortstop and second base, Mark Koenig and Tony Lazzeri. They helped galvanize the Bronx Bombers, who annihilated the Dodgers 14 games to none, launching a reign of dominance of the boys from Flatbush that would end only in 1955, when Brooklyn finally beat the Yankees in a World Series.

One other way financially strapped teams could recover their Spring Training expenses was by leaving behind a rookie as payment. In 1908 the Red Sox trained in Little Rock, Arkansas, and compensated the minor league team there by leaving a young outfielder who had been up briefly the year before, with the understanding that, if the player developed satisfactorily, the Red Sox could buy him back. Good thing for the Bosox they had that stipulation, because the rookie hit .350 for Little Rock. His name was Tris Speaker, and his contract was bought for $500. Speaker stayed in the Major Leagues for twenty-one more seasons; in 1937 he and his .344 lifetime batting average found a permanent home in Cooperstown.

But the majority of rookies offered in kind were doubtless unknowns like Buzzy Wares. His team, the lowly St. Louis Browns, trained in Montgomery, Alabama, in 1913. When it came time to break camp, they couldn't pay the rent for the minor league field they had been using. Wares, a rookie infielder, was given to the Montgomery team as payment. The Browns later repurchased him for 91 games in 1913-14; he managed to hit .220 before being sent down, possibly to Montgomery once more.

As Spring Training games gained larger audiences, teams found it easier to foot their bills; by the mid-1920's rookies no longer found themselves being left behind like chattel. Intracity rivalries were a logical, and regular, source of income. The Browns' and Cardinals' two-game series in the "Mound City" drew 75,000 fans, enough to pay most of the teams' expenses for the spring. The intra-city series between the Phillies and Athletics in Philadelphia was popular and profitable as well, while the Yankees and Giants, too, drew big crowds for their games in New York.

Florida would remain the most popular choice as a training site, though some teams found homes on foreign shores. The Giants ventured to Havana, just 90 miles from Miami, in 1937. The Dodgers were also in Cuba for three springs in the 1940s and managed to get into some trouble in Havana. One night, several Dodgers got drunk and found their way to Ernest Hemingway's estate. The writer talked pitcher Hugh Casey into donning boxing gloves, and the two battered each other about. Little wonder the Dodgers thereafter had detectives following their players around the island. The Pirates were the last team to train in Cuba, in the spring of 1953.

The Yankees have, over the years, been the most international of teams. In 1913 they traveled to Hamilton, Bermuda. Hal Chase, the Yanks' first baseman, fell off a bicycle there and broke his leg. The pinstripers finished in seventh place that year, 38 games out, and chose to train within the United States the next spring. While based in St. Petersburg, though, they did travel abroad again: to the Panama Canal Zone in 1946 and to Puerto Rico in 1947.

World War II brought an abrupt shift in Spring Training plans. Judge Kenesaw Mountain Landis, baseball commissioner, ruled that teams had to forgo their annual trek south

*In 1939, sage manager Bill McKechnie (glasses) prepares the Reds for the pennant.*

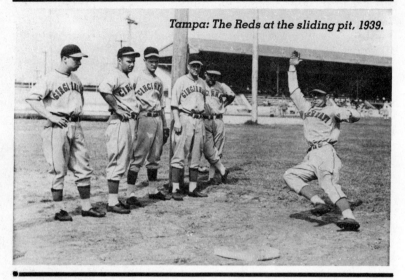

*Tampa: The Reds at the sliding pit, 1939.*

and instead practice close to home, because of wartime travel restrictions. For the springs of 1943, '44 and '45, Indiana replaced Florida as the most popular Spring Training state. Seven teams — the Browns, Tigers, Reds, Indians, Cubs, Pirates, and White Sox — trained in such Indiana towns as Muncie, Terre Haute, and French Lick. Fans could watch their favorite players trying to get in shape in the nippy outdoors or in heated armories and fieldhouses. The Red Sox trained at Tufts College in Medford, Massachusetts, while the Braves went just a tad farther south to the Choate School in Wallingford, Connecticut. The Brooklyn Dodgers went north, to Bear Mountain, New York — where, after one March blizzard, the pitchers threw snowballs as well as baseballs.

The Giants and Yankees, meanwhile, were in New Jersey, which wasn't all that bad. The Giants' Spring Training headquarters was the grounds of the old John D. Rockefeller estate, in Lakewood. In 1945 they lived in the county-owned Rockefeller mansion, complete with 47 plush, color-coordinated rooms, 17 baths, oriental rugs, and glassed-in porches. They trained on a nine-hole golf course. But this was not totally new to the Giants; they had trained at Lakewood in 1895 and 1896. The Yankees trained one year at Asbury Park and then moved 60 miles south to Atlantic City for '44 and '45. Their ballpark was Bader Field, named for Mayor Ed Bader, who was quite a baseball fanatic. This was a vast parade ground that the army used as a drill field. Its dimensions: 450 feet to left, 560 to center, 390 to right. Babe Ruth and Lou Gehrig had long retired and Mickey Mantle hadn't yet arrived, so it's doubtful any Yankee hit one out of Bader Field.

One could only imagine where the Blue Jays, Expos and Twins would have found themselves training had they existed during World War II. Baseball heaved its own sign of relief when the war ended, allowing the sport to resume its love affair with Florida in the spring of 1946.

In 1947 the great innovator, Branch Rickey, was approached by a Vero Beach executive. Bud Holman suggested that the Dodgers transfer their Spring Training operation from Pensacola to an unused U.S. Navy training base at Vero Beach. The site — 109 acres with two huge barracks-like buildings that could accommodate up to 1,000 ballplayers — had been a center for training small bombers. After the war the U.S. government deeded the facility to the city. Red Barber, the Dodgers' legendary radio announcer, recalls that Rickey had used the Pensacola Naval Air Station as a "minor league factory," and that may have predisposed him to the Vero Beach set-up.

Rickey sent young Buzzie Bavasi to meet with the Vero Beach officials, who told him they wanted the Dodgers to pay $20,000 a year in rent for the facility. Bavasi dutifully reported the $20,000 demand to his boss, but Rickey was not about to pay that kind of rent — and he knew full well that Holman was eager for the publicity a Major League facility would bring to the town. Bavasi had pointed out to Holman that 14 writers traveled with the team, would be spending their expense money in town, and would "have a Vero Beach dateline every day." Rickey, the consummate negotiator, countered Holman's figure with a nominal offer, which the town fathers accepted. The Dodgers finally bought the facility in 1960.

From the day of their arrival in Vero Beach in 1949, the Dodgers changed the face of Spring Training. For the first time, an organization had all its players, from every level, in one camp, a practice that has eventually been copied by most other clubs. This was the beginning of the "Dodger way of doing things", and since 1949 the Dodgers have won more National League pennants than any other team.

When Branch Rickey and the Dodgers broke the color barrier with Jackie Robinson in 1947, they brought about a new Spring Training complication. Florida was hospitable to white players, but their black teammates in the pre-Civil Rights era

St. Pete: Cards stretching with fans in the stands.

were not greeted with the same enthusiasm. Whether clubs stayed at posh hotels or humble motels, black ballplayers were required to find lodging elsewhere. They generally found it with local black families. This deplorable situation persisted into the 1960s.

Not only was finding a place to stay in Florida a problem for the black player, but so was getting down there in one piece. Before the days of the superhighway, the road to Florida wound through many small Southern towns. For a black man driving a nice car, this was not a safe way to travel. Black players reported spending their days sleeping in ramshackle "colored only" motels and their nights driving, so as not to be spotted or, worse, stopped, in a hostile Jim Crow county.

1940: In Sarasota, the Red Sox show off 6 future Major League pitchers. (l to r): Mickey Harris (lost 2 in the '46 series), Earl Johnson (won 1 in the '46 series), Al Brazle, Randy Heflin, Bill Butland, Herb Hash.

With the expansion of the two leagues in the 1960s, Spring Training became even more popular with the fans. The expansion teams gained immediate followings and even showed some pre-season success. The "expansion" 1961 Washington Senators, who replaced the team that Calvin Griffith took west to Minnesota, finished first in the Grapefuit League in its initial try but, predictably, wound up last in the American League standings. The first-year Mets were just shy of a .500 spring record in 1962, when the new Houston Colt .45s came out ahead at 14–11, but they finished tenth and eighth respectively in the realigned 10-team National League.

Such reversals should not surprise anyone who has followed Spring Training over the years. It's clear from comparing Spring Training and regular-season records (see appendix for those figures, 1960-87) that there is little correlation between the two. Between '60 and '87, 16 teams went from the top of the Grapefruit and Cactus League standings to win pennants — but 15 did the same thing after a last-place spring finish. And it goes the other way, too: 11 teams thrilled their fans with a first-place spring record, only to sink to the bottom by the end of the year, while 17 end-of-season cellar-dwellers had been stuck there in the spring standings, too.

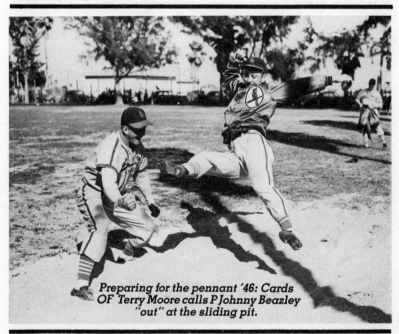

*Preparing for the pennant '46: Cards OF Terry Moore calls P Johnny Beazley "out" at the sliding pit.*

Many of today's ballplayers argue that Spring Training is too long. In the early days, six weeks were usually needed for the athletes to whip their overweight, hibernating carcasses into shape. Players now arrive in much better condition because, unlike their predecessors, most make enough money playing baseball to avoid having to take jobs during the winter to support themselves. Instead, many spend the off-season working out, using sophisticated conditioning programs, or playing winter ball.

*Feb '62: Casey leading the first charge of Mets pitchers and catchers, including Roger Craig (under the bat).*

"Any team can get into shape in a month or three weeks if the players are in decent condition when they come down," observed Cleveland pitching great Bob Feller. This idea is not new. In 1913 AL President Ban Johnson stated that "the training season has developed in recent years beyond the stage where it is working to the best interests of the game and the greater efficiency of the players engaged." Johnson echoed the feelings of Ty Cobb, who had a notorious disdain for Spring Training. As if to prove its insignificance, Cobb held out the entire 1911 pre-season over a salary dispute. Because of the public clamor, the argument was settled a day before the regular season started, and Cobb, without benefit of any practice, went on to hit .420 that year. Tim Raines emulated Cobb in 1987 by electing for free agency, missing Spring Training, and then playing well enough not only to make the All-Star Team but also to win the midsummer classic for the National League.

Cobb and Raines are, of course, gifted exceptions. But if clubs didn't need to evaluate dozens of players in the team system, they could probably break camp in a month or less. It is possible some Spring Training injuries could have been averted with shorter camps, though mishaps are so perverse and unpredictablle that one can never guarantee avoiding them.

Some celebrated spring injuries have occured away from the ballpark. While the Giants were training in Cuba in 1937, pitcher Freddie Fitzsimmons fell asleep in a rocking chair, rocked over his hand, and broke a finger. Fitzsimmons had pitched for New York 13 years, but the Giants saw fit to trade him to the Dodgers a few months after that incident.

For some, Spring Training has been season-ending; for others, career-threatening. Dodger slugger Pedro Guerrero missed the 1986 season with a knee injury suffered toward the end of Spring Training. Most baseball fans were able to see the replay of his sliding accident at third base dozens of times. Broken legs sustained during spring practice shortened the careers of Hall of Famers Walter Johnson and Rabbit Maranville, as well as of the Yankees' Billy Martin.

There was a different kind of casualty in the Cubs' Spring Training camp of 1954. Owner Phil Wrigley replaced player-manager Phil Cavarretta with another longtime Cubbie, Stan Hack, making Cavarretta the only manager ever to be fired during Spring Training. After he was spurned by the Cubs,

Cavarretta, a Chicago native, played for the White Sox during the 1954 and '55 seasons.

The worst Spring Training victim, however, was Red Sox manager Chick Stahl. One morning during the spring of 1907, in West Walden Springs, Indiana, he finished breakfast at the team hotel, returned to his room, and drank four ounces of carbolic acid. He left a suicide note: "Boys, I just couldn't help it. You drove me to it." Stahl had apparently been contemplating the act for some time, but it is not known what might have sealed his decision. He died with a lifetime managerial record of 5–13.

But if the spring season were shortened, the fan would be the loser, for the real joy of attending or following Spring Training lies not in the outcome of the games but rather in watching the pitchers working on new grips and pitches, a fringe player battling for a spot on the team, or the veteran battling to keep his job despite the challenge from a rookie, celebrated or unknown.

Nothing is as symbolic of the hope and anticipation of Spring Training as the rookie. In earlier days the rookies had little help making the squad. Ty Cobb would never forget the veterans sawing his bats in half during his first Spring Training in 1905, and Casey Stengel didn't fare much better when he hit the scene a few years later. "When I was breaking in," Stengel recalled, "you'd come to camp with a letter of recommendation from someone. Then you'd say to yourself, 'I think I'll go up to the batting cage and hit.' 'Whoa,' some regular would say. 'Who are you and who sent you?' So you'd whip out your card and show it to him. If he thought your recommendation was OK, he'd step aside and let you hit — maybe as much as three times."

Billy Herman remembered his first days with the Cubs of 1931. "Breaking in was rougher back in those days than it is today. The veterans resented you because you were after their jobs; and the coaches ignored you unless you made a mistake. There was very little instruction back then. They figured you'd had good seasoning in the minors and left you on your own."

One wonders, then, how another Cub, player-manager Johnny Evers of Tinker-to-Evers-to-Chance fame, could make the following contradictory statement about veterans in *Baseball* magazine in 1913: "Another feature that has made the modern training trip more effective is the attitude of the regulars toward the new men. This has resulted from the fact that the baseball player nowadays is an entirely different individual than he was in the so-called old days. He is fair-minded and intelligent, and with few exceptions, gives the younger man a square deal. They do not show any jealous feelings toward the newcomer. They rather welcome him and take pains to teach him the rough and rocky road which they have traveled themselves. When he finds he can no longer keep pace he meets his release with calmness, knowing that he has outlived his little day and it is time for him to leave the stage and give up his place to a younger player." Do Evers's observations prove that everything is relative, or that he was taken out a few too many times by incoming runners at second base?

*1939 or 1940: Cubs manager Gabby Hartnett teaches hitting with a fishing pole*

Today Spring Training bears a much greater resemblance to Evers's vision than to that of Cobb and Stengel, though rookie hazing remains an enduring ritual. Veterans give tips to the younger players, a process that continues throughout the year, even as the older players recognize that the rookies may well replace them down the line. But Spring Training can also produce other magical professorial moments. Stars from years past occasionally attend camp, especially in the early weeks, specifically to work with younger players. On a given day, Ted Williams will be on an outer field at Chain O'Lakes Park giving batting advice, while Whitey Ford may be on a distant mound in Fort Lauderdale watching a prospect's delivery and follow-through.

Indeed, much of the history of Spring Training has grown out of the annual emergence of new talent, as the rookie narratives in each team entry of this book illustrate. There is something magical about seeing, for the first time, a gifted young player striding to the plate or to the mound, in one of his first appearances in a Major League uniform. Those who saw the Yankees train in Phoenix that one spring, 1951, when they traded sites with the Giants, may remember a nineteen-year-old shortstop who had led his class C Joplin team in everything (including errors) the year before. Casey Stengel invited Mickey Mantle to his preliminary camp that year, and Mantle didn't escape Stengel's notice for long. As the inimitable Art Daley wrote: "At first sight of him the Ol' Perfessor froze to the point like a retriever dog which has just flushed a covey of priceless quail." Mantle made the Yankee squad in 1951, launching one of baseball's legendary careers.

*1965: Champion Cards Groat, Musial (retired), and Gibson are served spring training eggs by manager Schoendienst.*

Pete Reiser, the Dodger outfielder, must have prompted similar reactions from those who saw him as a youngster in camp more than a decade earlier. Reiser, whose career was shortened and almost certain stardom eclipsed by a series of disabling injuries, was a rookie wonder in his first spring, in 1940. He homered his first time at bat, walked the next, then slashed singles in his following two turns. The next day he hit two more home runs and added two singles. Before the Yankees' Lefty Gomez finally retired him, Reiser had eight hits and three walks. He still went down to Elmira to begin that year, but he led the National League in hitting in 1941, his first full season.

*A Pirate awaits the arrival of a Red Sox baserunner. The clubs haven't met outside of spring training since the 1903 World Series.*

The chance to see a new talent unfolding for the first time in Major League competition is one of the beauties of the spring season, one of the magnets for the ex-players and coaches, the youngsters with bubble-gum cards to be signed, the retirees who flock to the day games to compare this year's crop with those of seasons gone by. For baseball is, more than any other sport, a generational game, linking the past to the present through statistics and records, photos, and memories. The overlapping of decades is the glorious aspect of Spring Training. When baseball begins again, it reassures and renews. As Dodger manager Tom Lasorda declared, "I love Spring Training. I wish they'd play baseball 365 days a year."

*The 1987 White Sox limber up in Sarasota.*

# CHAPTER 3

## Choosing Time and Place

AFTER YOU'VE DECIDED to go to Spring Training, you must decide *where* (which of the *four* principal locations you want to visit) and *when*. Visiting more than one of the groups is reserved for those who (a) can take a week or more for this sort of adventure and/or (b) enjoy spending large parts of vacation time in motorized conveyances.

Spring Training, start-to-finish, is a six- to seven-week event. Most fans go during the first four weeks, for the daily regimen of exhibition games. These generally begin on the first weekend in March and end (depending on that year's calendar) on the last weekend of March or the first in April. The last games are played the day before Opening Day, which is always the first Monday in April.

Pitchers and catchers report to camp three weeks ahead of the rest of the squad. This schedule gives a pitcher's valuable arm time to loosen up before he must face a batter. Once the "regulars" join the batterymen for the ten days before the games start, intrasquad games — open to the public — are played most days. Pitchers start out working an inning or two in intrasquad games, with most able to go about three innings when the exhibition season begins.

When the regulars report, the forty-man roster — the entire squad of players protected from the draft of other Major League teams — is in camp. Since teams play the season with twenty-four- or twenty-five-man rosters, fifteen or sixteen of the forty will end up in the minor leagues. Nonroster invitees, minor leaguers, and players trying to hook on with a new club are also present. Often, extra nonroster catchers are brought to the Major League camp because so many are needed to warm up pitchers and help execute drills.

At about the time the exhibition schedule begins, the minor leaguers — those players who are under contract but not on the forty-man roster — report to camp. At that time, the Major Leaguers may move from what is actually the minor league training ground to the stadium, yielding the bigger training ground to the large number of minor leaguers. Since the Major Leaguers play a game every day, these games, in effect, become the practices.

In games played during the first ten days to two weeks of the exhibition season pitchers go three innings or less, and veterans at the other positions usually play no more than five innings and seldom more than three days in a row. This, consequently, results in liberal use of substitutes from the legions of players in camp who will not make the Opening Day roster. These early weeks are the perfect time to see young phenoms who may not make the Majors right away and, in general, to see *many* ballplayers in each game.

The games played over the last two weeks of exhibition are taken more seriously and are more like regular-season contests. Normal starting lineups open most home games and stay in for seven innings or more; starting pitchers go five innings or longer.

The kind of Spring Training experience you'll have depends heavily on *when* you go. Before the exhibition season starts, a fan can get the most intimate glimpse of the Major Leaguers, but the "competition" is only intrasquad. Early in the exhibition season, a fan sees a lot of ballplayers being evaluated by a management not really trying to win each game. Later, the games more closely resemble regular-season competition.

But even more important than *when* is *where*: which of the groups of teams you visit. There are four.

**1. The Southeast Florida group.** The Orioles, Yankees, Braves, Expos, Mets, and Dodgers have their home stadiums along a 130-mile stretch of I-95 from Miami to Vero Beach. The Braves and Expos share the same stadium at about the midpoint, with the others strung out to the north and south.

**2. The Theme Park Florida group.** The Twins, Astros, and Royals are the core of the group, based in Orlando and Kissimmee, the homes of Disney World/Epcot Center, Boardwalk & Baseball, Sea World, and a host of other amusement centers. The Twins, Astros, and Royals are within a half-hour of each other. The Red Sox and Tigers are 90 minutes west in Winter Haven and Lakeland, exactly half-way between Orlando and Tampa. As they are inland teams, we have included them in the Theme Park Group, although they are certainly accessible to anyone visiting the Gulf Coast group. The Dodgers in Vero Beach and the Reds in Plant City are similarly accessible to Theme Parkers.

**3. The Gulf Coast Florida group.** The Blue Jays, Phillies, Cardinals, Pirates, and White Sox are close together, encircling Tampa Bay from Dunedin in the north to Sarasota beyond the southern tip, and are within an hour of each other. The Rangers require a short hop further down the coast to Port Charlotte, and the Reds lie 20-odd miles east of Tampa, in Plant City. Again the Red Sox and Tigers lie inland towards Orlando, interstate drives of one to one and a half hours.

**4. The Arizona group.** The Cubs, Brewers, Mariners, Giants, and Athletics all train within a half hour of each other in and around Phoenix. The Indians are a couple of beautiful desert hours south, in Tucson. The Padres are headquartered in Yuma, which is two miles northwest of the middle of nowhere. The Angels spend the early weeks and the first two weeks of the exhibition season at their Gene Autry complex in Phoenix, though it has no stadium. They eventually head to a facility in Palm Springs, a short commute from the eastern suburbs of their regular-season home in Anaheim. The Padres and Angels both spend the first two weeks of Spring Training in Phoenix, playing "road" games, after which the other teams journey to Yuma and Palm Springs.

When you pick any Florida group, you will see teams from other Florida groups as the visitors. But star players tend to remain at home during the longer road trips, and you'll want to take that into account if you're planning to see your favorite team on the road. Also remember that teams within a group tend to play each other often, so the games you see will be heavily dominated by them.

A final reminder of anomalies in the setup of the teams.

*1.* There are four teams – the Dodgers, Tigers, Reds, and Red Sox – that could be considered to be in *two* clusters. The Dodgers, at the northern end of the Southeast Florida group, are closer to the Theme Park teams than they are to teams in the southern end of their own group. The Tigers and Red Sox literally straddle the line between the Theme Park and Gulf Coast groups. The Reds' new Plant City home is nearer to the Tigers than to Tampa.

*2.* The Angels and Padres are really not in a group at all; their home sites are near no other team, including each other. If you want to catch the Angels or Padres and get the

**Minnesota Twins** *Orlando*
**Boston Red Sox** *Winter Haven*
**Detroit Tigers** *Lakeland*
**Houston Astros** *Kissimmee*
**Kansas City Royals** *Orlando*

**Los Angeles Dodgers** *Vero Beach*
**New York Mets** *Port St. Lucie*
**Atlanta Braves** *West Palm Beach*
**Montreal Expos** *West Palm Beach*
**New York Yankees** *Ft. Lauderdale*
**Baltimore Orioles** *Miami*

**Toronto Blue Jays** *Dunedin*
**Philadelphia Phillies** *Clearwater*
**Cincinnati Reds** *Plant City*
**St. Louis Cardinals** *St. Petersburg*
**Pittsburgh Pirates** *Bradenton*
**Chicago White Sox** *Sarasota*
**Texas Rangers** *Port Charlotte*

*GRAPEFRUIT LEAGUE*

full Arizona Spring Training experience, it's best to see them in Phoenix, where they spend most of the first two weeks of the exhibition schedule as a "road" team (although the Angels actually have a practice facility and "host" some B games) before going "home" to Palm

Springs and Yuma, respectively.

**3.** The Indians are also a fair distance from their nearest neighbors (the Brewers at the southern end of the Phoenix

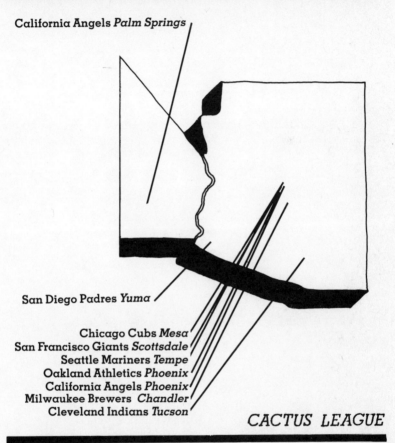

California Angels *Palm Springs*

San Diego Padres *Yuma*

Chicago Cubs *Mesa*
San Francisco Giants *Scottsdale*
Seattle Mariners *Tempe*
Oakland Athletics *Phoenix*
California Angels *Phoenix*
Milwaukee Brewers *Chandler*
Cleveland Indians *Tucson*

*CACTUS LEAGUE*

group), and even some very devoted Indians fans might choose to base themselves in Phoenix and "commute" to Indians home games in Tucson. This provides them with a greater choice of "local" games each day.

**4.** The Texas Rangers in Port Charlotte and the Orioles in Miami are an hour or so from their nearest neighbor.

# CHAPTER 4

*Southeast Florida Group*

Los Angeles Dodgers *Vero Beach*
New York Mets *Port St. Lucie*
Atlanta Braves *West Palm Beach*
Montreal Expos *West Palm Beach*
New York Yankees *Ft. Lauderdale*
Baltimore Orioles *Miami*

*W PALM BEACH*

*FT LAUDERDALE*

*MIAMI*

MIAMI, THEY SAY, is losing its luster as a tourist attraction. Even the college kids have abandoned Ft. Lauderdale for Daytona Beach (where there is no Major League team.) So much the better for baseball fans. This is the star-studded group of Spring Training teams: the Yankees, Mets, *and* Dodgers; the powerful Orioles; the nationally televised Braves; and the French-flavored Expos.

This is the best of the destinations in which to live out two of the purest Spring Training fantasies: "beach-in-the-morning-and ballgame-in-the-afternoon" and "it's-a-beautiful-day-and-night so-let's-see-two."

All the ballparks in this group are located within 10 minutes of I-95, and the highway itself is never more than 20 minutes from the uninterrupted beach heaven that ribbons Florida's Atlantic coast. The Yankees and Orioles schedule frequent night games, the others occasionally, providing fairly regular opportunities to see two complete games in one day.

If you visit this group as a neutral fan looking for maximum baseball action with minimum travel, you'll certainly want to stay in West Palm Beach. It has a major airport (as do Ft. Lauderdale and Miami, of course), and its ballpark has a Major League game every day the sun shines, since the Braves and Expos share the facility. Less than an hour down the road are the Yankees in Ft. Lauderdale, which you approach from the north side of town (avoiding the Ft. Lauderdale airport on your way in and out). It takes about an additional 40 minutes to get to the Orioles' home near Miami Airport.

The drawback to West Palm Beach as a base of operations is that flights and hotels are somewhat less plentiful than in Ft. Lauderdale or Miami. The northern end of Ft. Lauderdale — near the Yankees' camp and avoiding the need to drive through the city to reach the four teams to the north — is a good second choice.

North of West Palm Beach, in a much less developed part of southeast Florida, are the Mets' new facility in Port St. Lucie (40 minutes from West Palm Beach) and the Dodgers' long-established home at Vero Beach (90 minutes from West Palm Beach).

Miami Beach — less than 20 minutes east of the Orioles' ballpark — is loaded with beautiful Art Deco buildings, a wide price and luxury range of beach hotels, and lots of nighttime entertainment. Ft. Lauderdale has great beaches near the ballpark, big-city night life, and some real hotel bargains (particularly on weekends) in the "business travelers' strip" on I-95, which is (remember) a 15-minute hop from the beach.

Basing yourself near Port St. Lucie (*in* is hard, since the town is largely in the process of being built) or in Vero Beach makes sense only if you're looking for a very peaceful beachfront setting or are madly devoted to the Mets or Dodgers. Under either of those circumstances, each is a beautiful choice. But it's a bit of a haul to the next nearest team or to a large airport.

*Dodgertown* in Vero Beach is uniquely charming among all the Spring Training facilities in Florida or Arizona, and is definitely worth a visit if you're headquartered anywhere in the Southeast Florida group, except Miami. The Orioles', Expos', and Braves' practices are every bit as accessible as those in Dodgertown, with all the informal opportunities for getting autographs, pictures, and conversation with the players. But the overall integrated setting of the Dodgers' facility, where ballplayers literally "stroll" in uniform from their bungalow on Jackie Robinson Way or Don Drysdale Drive across open fields to the stadium, is unmatched.

## SOUTHEAST FLORIDA DISTANCES

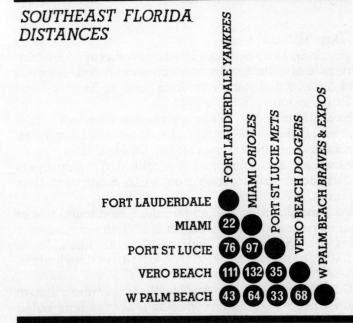

|  | FORT LAUDERDALE YANKEES | MIAMI ORIOLES | PORT ST LUCIE METS | VERO BEACH DODGERS | W PALM BEACH BRAVES & EXPOS |
|---|---|---|---|---|---|
| FORT LAUDERDALE | ● |  |  |  |  |
| MIAMI | 22 | ● |  |  |  |
| PORT ST LUCIE | 76 | 97 | ● |  |  |
| VERO BEACH | 111 | 132 | 35 | ● |  |
| W PALM BEACH | 43 | 64 | 33 | 68 | ● |

## Batting Cages

West Palm Beach: Grand Slam, 1500 North Florida Mango Road, (305) 686-2255, three baseball cages, two softball cages.

Ft. Lauderdale: Grand Slam U.S.A. Sports Complex, across the street from Ft. Lauderdale stadium, (305) 776-4487.

Port St. Lucie: The Batter's Box, 865 Biltmore, five baseball cages, four softball cages (under construction as book went to press).

## SOUTHEAST FLORIDA AIRPLAY

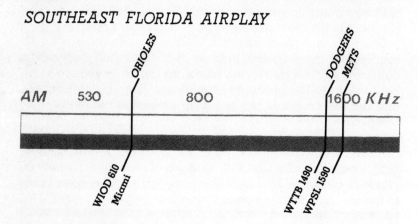

## Sunny-Day Alternatives

***Miami Beach Art Deco National Historic Preservation District:*** A square mile of restored '20s and '30s resort hotels, between Jefferson Avenue and the beach from Sixth to Twenty-Third Street. Saturday tours. (305) 672-2014.

***Parrot Jungle,*** Miami: Nation's only natural subtropical jungle; exotic birds fly free in lush setting. 11 miles south of downtown at 11000 Southwest 57th Avenue, Miami. (305) 666-7834.

***Monkey Jungle,*** Miami: Most complete collection of monkeys in the United States, all running free. 14805 Southwest 216th Street, Miami. (305) 235-1611.

***Motorized gondola tours,*** Ft. Lauderdale: Hire a tour guide or pilot your own six-seat boat by the hour, half-day or full day.

***Gondolas of America, Inc.*** Bahia Mar Yacht Basin, South Docks, 1007 Seabreeze Boulevard (Route A1A), Ft. Lauderdale. (305) 522-3333.

***Jungle Queen cruises,*** Ft. Lauderdale: River tour and a stop at an Indian village for alligator wrestling. Leaves from Bahia Mar Yacht Basin (see above). (305) 462-5596.

***Flamingo Gardens,*** Ft. Lauderdale: 60 acres of botanical gardens, petting zoo, Everglades museum. 3750 Flamingo Road, Ft. Lauderdale. (305) 473-0010.

***Morikami Museum of Japanese Culture,*** Delray Beach: Bonsai gardens, exhibits about tea ceremony and other cultural artifacts. 4000 Morikami Park Road, Delray Beach. (305) 499-0631.

***Cruises,*** Port St. Lucie: Assorted tours including Jupiter Island, Lake Okeechobee, St. Lucie River. Tours leave from Stuart on U.S. 1, just north of the Roosevelt Bridge; contact Hy-Line of Florida, P.O. Box 105, Stuart, 33495. (305) 692-9500.

## Rainy-Day Activities

***Cloisters of the Monastery of St. Bernard de Clairvaux,*** Miami: Built in 1141; shipped from Europe by William Randolph Hearst; oldest building in this hemisphere. 16711 West Dixie Highway, North Miami Beach. (305) 945-1462.

***Museum of Art,*** Ft. Lauderdale: Controversial collection of twentieth-century art; free tours. One East Las Olas Boulevard, Ft. Lauderdale. (305) 525-5500.

***Discovery Center,*** Ft. Lauderdale: Hands-on science and art exhibits. 231 Southwest Second Avenue, Ft. Lauderdale. (305) 462-4115.

***King Cromartie House,*** Ft. Lauderdale: Filled with antiques and artifacts of pioneer days; next door to Discovery Center. 229 Southwest Second Avenue, Ft. Lauderdale. (305) 764-1665.

***Henry Morrison Flagler Museum***: Ultra-posh showplace of the nineteenth-century entrepreneur's hoard of treasures. Whitehall Way (off Cocoanut Row), Palm Beach. (305) 655-2833.

***Norton Gallery of Art***: Fine small museum with strong holdings in modern French and American paintings, Chinese jades; free. 1451 South Olive Avenue, West Palm Beach. (305) 832-5194.

***Burt Reynolds Dinner Theatre,*** Jupiter: Evening performances; 1001 Indiantown Road. Box office, (305) 746-5566. Burt's horse range, western store, and petting zoo are all near by, two miles down Jupiter Farms Road off Indiantown Road; ranch information, (305) 746-0393.

***Driftwood Inn,*** Vero Beach: Waldo Sexton's eccentric architectural masterpiece, built of flotsam and filled with jetsam. 3150 South Ocean Drive, Vero Beach. (305) 231-9292.

***Gilbert's Bar House of Refuge,*** Hutchinson Island: Built in the nineteenth century to rescue shipwrecked sailors, now a lifesaving museum and turtle aquarium. Follow signs from Stuart through Indian River Plantation; entrance is south of plantation. (305) 225-1875.

## Day Trips

From the southern part of this region: ***Everglades National Park.*** 1½ million acres of the country's largest remaining subtropical wilderness. Main park entrance and visitor information center is on U.S. 27, about 10½ miles southwest of Homestead. For canoe tours, contact Everglades Canoe Outfittters, 39801 Ingraham Highway, Homestead 33034. (305) 246-1530.

From the northern part of the region: ***Kennedy Space Center***, Cape Canaveral, offers frequent guided tours. Disney World and Epcot Center are also within reach, two to three hours by car from Vero Beach and Port St. Lucie.

# ATLANTA BRAVES

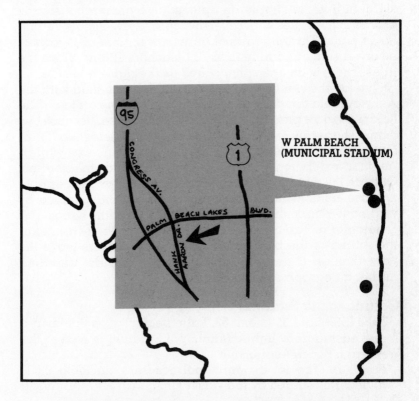

W PALM BEACH
(MUNICIPAL STADIUM)

■ **Current site:**
Municipal Stadium
715 Hank Aaron Drive
West Palm Beach, FL 33401
(305) 683-6100
■ **Dimensions:**
330' left and right;
400' center
■ **Seating:** 4,392
■ **Built:** 1962
■ **Off-season use:**

West Palm Beach Expos;
Florida State League
(Class A): also Winter In-
structional League teams
from the Braves, Expos,
Orioles practice there.
■ **Practice site:** At the
stadium daily at 10:00 A.M.
■ **Game time:** 1:35 P.M.
■ **Most convenient airport:**
West Palm Beach.

Municipal Stadium was built in 1962 in preparation for the Braves' move from Bradenton to West Palm Beach. The Braves share the complex's six fields with the Montreal Expos.

Municipal is one of the most convenient and accessible of the Spring Training sites, located less than a mile from an exit of I-95 and surrounded by ample free parking lots. The stadium itself is simple and pleasant. Symmetrical stands extend to the bases with cover over the reserved seats behind home plate. Thirteen rows of boxes are in front of 14 rows of reserved seats and nine rows of bleachers extend down the lines. There is an open picnic area on the right-field side.

Outside the center-field fence is a duplicate field with the same outfield dimensions and bleacher seating for fans. The field is used for practices and intrasquad games. Because two teams share this facility, there is often an interesting "B" or intrasquad game being played on that diamond, even while a "regular" exhibition game is being played inside the stadium. Outside the right-field fence is another large and accessible practice field, which is often used for batting practice by visiting teams coming in to play the Braves or the Expos.

Autographs can be garnered before and just after games at the railing of the box seats or bleachers; players leave the park through a doorway on the first base side, affording further autograph opportunities.

## Getting to the Stadium

Take **Interstate 95** to exit **53**, Palm Beach Lakes Boulevard. Travel east for four lights. Municipal Stadium is next to the West Palm Beach Auditorium.

*Parking:* The lot at Municipal Stadium can hold 2,300 vehicles. It is shared by the West Palm Beach Auditorium.

## Tickets

Atlanta Braves
Municipal Stadium
P.O. Box 2619
West Palm Beach, FL 33401
(305) 683-6100

The team's exhibition schedule is available from this address in late December. Season and single-game tickets go on sale January 1. Tickets ordered by phone may be paid for using MasterCard, Visa, or American Express. If the phone order is placed the day before the game, the tickets will be held at the "will-call" window. The Braves sold out eight times in 1987.

*Prices:* Reserved box $7; grandstand $6; general admission $3.

## Team Hotel

Hyatt Palm Beaches
630 Clearwater Park Road
West Palm Beach, FL 33401
(305) 833-1234

Two local radio stations broadcast from the lobby. Bob McCann hosts a show on WGST and Dave O'Brien is on WSB.

## Players' Favorite Leisure Spots

The Braves often attend the jai-alai matches at the Palm Beach fronton and the dog races at the Palm Beach Kennel Club. The most frequented restaurant is Manero's, a steak and seafood place in West Palm Beach, only a mile from the stadium, which proudly calls itself "a Braves spot." Other establishments popular with the players are Tony Roma's, for ribs, MacArthur's Vineyard, a bar and restaurant that serves steaks, ribs, and fish, and a Mexican restaurant called Plata Grande.

## Previous Spring Training Locations

*Boston Braves (1901–52)*
*Milwaukee Braves (1953–65)*
*Atlanta Braves (1966–present)*

| | |
|---|---|
| 1901 | Norfolk, VA |
| 1902–04 | Thomasville, GA |
| 1905 | Charleston, SC |
| 1906 | Jacksonville, FL |
| 1907 | Thomasville, GA |
| 1908–12 | Augusta, GA |
| 1913 | Athens, GA |
| 1914–15 | Macon, GA |
| 1916–18 | Miami, FL |
| 1919–20 | Columbus, GA |
| 1921 | Galveston, TX |
| 1922–37 | St. Petersburg, FL |
| 1938–40 | Bradenton, FL |
| 1941 | San Antonio, TX |
| 1942 | Sanford, FL |
| 1943–44 | Wallingford, CT |
| 1945 | Washington, DC |
| 1946–47 | Ft. Lauderdale, FL |
| 1948–61 | Bradenton, FL |

1962        Palmetto, FL
1963–present   West Palm Beach, FL

## Hottest Prospects

When the Braves opened Spring Training in 1960, it was their eighth year in Milwaukee, after having spent more than three-quarters of a century in Boston. They would spend five more seasons in Wisconsin before packing the tepee and heading for Atlanta.

The Braves had a veteran team in 1960, one that had finished no lower than third — and that but once — in every year in Milwaukee. The 1960 season would be no different: the Braves finished second behind the Pirates.

To augment their experienced lineup, the Braves were looking for mound help from a trio of young pitchers: Terry Fox, Don Nottebart, and Ken MacKenzie. Only Nottebart won any games for the Braves, and all three were with other teams within two years. To catch the group in 1960, the Braves gave a two-game trial to the 19-year-old brother of their first baseman, Frank Torre. Joe Torre would lock up the job in 1961. He got little competition from another rookie catcher in 1962 who has gained most of his fame off the diamond, on camera: Bob Uecker.

Despite another cadre of promising young pitchers in camp in 1964, the best of the prospects was hard-hitting Dominican outfielder Rico Carty, one of the first gifts from the little town of San Pedro de Macoris, which has since gained such prominence for the talented players it has produced. As a naïve youngster in 1960, Carty had signed 10 pro contracts; when the mess was sorted out, Carty ended up with the Braves, who converted him from a catcher into an outfielder. Carty had hit .327 at Austin in 1963, improved that to .330 with 22 home runs in his rookie year and might have won the batting title if he'd had enough at-bats to qualify. His effort would, under normal circumstances, have won him the top rookie honors, but the Phillies' Richie Allen also debuted in 1964 and had even more impressive statistics.

In retrospect, however, the 1964 camp was most notable as the beginning of one of the most remarkable careers in baseball history. Phil Niekro, although a nonroster pitcher, was impressive enough to stick with the Braves for a short while. He was soon sent to Denver, where he posted an 11–5 record. By 1965 he was ready for the Majors. He has been there ever since, and has won more than 300 games, employing perhaps the most famous knuckleball of them all.

Eight-year minor league veteran Walt Hriniak looked ready when the Braves brought him up at the end of 1968, but he was injured late in Spring Training the following year and spent the first part of the season on the disabled list. Hriniak's long stint in the minors may be one reason he developed his coaching skills; he is now the esteemed batting and baseline coach of the Boston Red Sox.

In 1971 the Braves had two outstanding young hitters, both of whom had come up briefly the year before. Earl Williams had hit .318 at Shreveport, and Ralph Garr was the International League's batting leader with a .386 mark. Williams, the big catcher, had his moments in a brief career; but Garr really left his mark as a hitter, batting .343 his first year, winning the batting title in 1974 at .353, and compiling a career average of .306.

Dusty Baker was considered ready in 1972, after two .300-plus seasons at Richmond. But he was hurt in Spring Training, leaving the Braves short of outfielders. Rowland Office was summoned from the minor league camp and hit a grand slam in a win over the Orioles. It was a brief moment of glory; Baker hobbled back to claim his spot and was a National League stalwart in Atlanta, Los Angeles, and San Francisco over the next 13 years. Office made it to the majors in 1974.

The outstanding player in 1973 was a relief pitcher, Tom House, whose subsequent flashes of brilliance were overshadowed by one moment in the limelight. House, now the Texas Rangers' pitching coach, caught Hank Aaron's record-breaking 715th home run in the Atlanta bullpen, April 8, 1974.

The Braves' leader in the past decade, Dale Murphy, played 19 games at the end of the 1976 season, hitting .262, five points under his best average with four minor league clubs. But the potential was there, as all the scouts could see. Murphy started the 1977 season at Richmond, leading the International League in RBI with 90; the Braves brought him up at the end of the year, and he was the top prospect in the '78 camp. The 6'5" Murphy was clearly miscast as a catcher, and first base suited him no better. Moved to the outfield, he blossomed into one of the finest all-around players in the 1980s, winning Gold Glove as well as home run awards and two consecutive MVP trophies, in 1982 and 1983.

Murphy was joined midway through his first season by another rookie gem. Bob Horner had never seen Spring Training, having signed in June 1978 after graduating from Arizona State, where he broke Reggie Jackson's school home run records.

Named NCAA player of the year, Horner jumped straight to the Majors, compiled some magnificent rooke stats with the Braves, homering in his first game, and won Rookie of the Year. Contract disputes and injuries marred his years in Atlanta; the last dispute caused Horner to seek his fortune in Japan in 1987.

In 1980 Dominican shortstop Rafael Ramirez, one of the many from San Pedro de Macoris, had a fine spring to earn a spot with the Braves, but he started on the bench when manager Bobby Cox decided to go with the more experienced Luis Gomez, acquired from Toronto. Gomez responded by hitting .191. Nonroster pitcher Rick Camp, who had pitched well for the Braves in 1977 and '78, regained his position and went on to save 22 games during the regular season; he became one of the Braves' more reliable pitchers on pitching-weak teams during the next few years. The Braves hoped their pitching woes would be soothed by the 1983 arrival of Craig McMurtry, considered their best pitching prospect in years. He actually exceeded expectations with a fine 15–9 rookie record. But he never recovered from the dreaded sophomore jinx and was traded to Toronto in 1987.

High expectations also plagued the Braves' two brilliant 1984 prospects: outfielder Brad Komminsk and first-baseman Gerald Perry. Komminsk had hit .334 with 103 RBI at Richmond, causing Hank Aaron to call him one of the most promising players he had ever seen. Perry's .314 International League average also suggested great things to come. Both were given their shot in Spring Training, and Komminsk responded with a team-high 11 RBI to go with a .295 average. And both struggled miserably in the Majors, spending more time in Richmond than in Atlanta. Komminsk was eventually traded to Milwaukee for Dion James; Perry finally established himself in 1987 and became the first first-baseman in a decade to steal more than 30 bases.

## Top Rookies Each Spring

1960   Don Nottebart, pitcher
1961   Joe Torre, catcher
1962   Howie Bedell, outfield
1963   Dan Schneider, pitcher
1964   Rico Carty, outfield
1965   Phil Niekro, pitcher
1966   Ron Reed, pitcher
1967   Marty Martinez, shortstop; Jim Britton, pitcher
1968   Felix Millan, second base

1969   Walt Hriniak, catcher
1970   Oscar Brown, outfield
1971   Ralph Garr, outfield
1972   Dusty Baker, outfield
1973   Tom House, pitcher
1974   Leo Foster, shortstop
1975   Biff Pocoroba, catcher
1976   Jerry Royster, infield
1977   Brian Asseltine, second base
1978   Dale Murphy, catcher
1979   Rick Matula, pitcher
1980   Rafael Ramirez, shortstop
1981   Terry Harper, outfield
1982   Brett Butler, outfield
1983   Craig McMurtry, pitcher
1984   Brad Komminsk, outfield
1985   Zane Smith, pitcher
1986   Paul Assenmacher, pitcher
1987   Steve Ziem, pitcher

## NL Rookies of the Year
1971   Earl Williams, catcher
1978   Bob Horner, third base

## Prospect to Watch in 1988
*Pete Smith,* pitcher. The righthander was acquired from
Philadelphia when Steve Bedrosian was traded to the Phils. He
was brought up at the end of 1987 and, though he didn't win
many, was impressive in his few starts.

# BALTIMORE ORIOLES

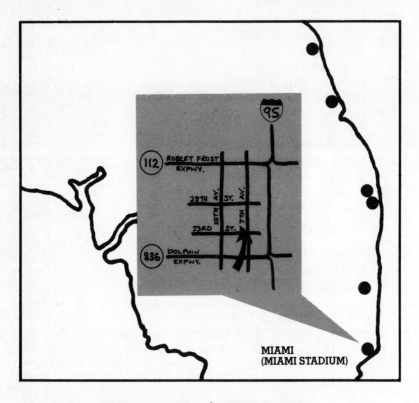

MIAMI
(MIAMI STADIUM)

■ **Current site:**
Bobby Maduro Miami
Stadium, 2301 Northwest
10th Avenue, Miami,
FL 33127
(305) 635-5395
■ **Dimensions:**
335' left and right;
400' center
■ **Seating:** 9,548
(record attendance:
12,464, March 14, 1965,
versus the Yankees)

■ **Built:** 1948
■ **Off-season use:**
Miami Marlins,
Florida State League
(Class A, independent
team formerly owned
by the Orioles)
■ **Practice site:** At the
stadium daily at 10:00 A.M.
■ **Game times:** 1:30 P.M.
(day), 7:30 P.M. (night)
■ **Most convenient airport:**
Miami.

The Orioles have played in Miami since 1959. The current playing field was renamed Bobby Maduro Miami Stadium in honor of the Cuban who served as Bowie Kuhn's liaison between the Major Leagues and Cuba.

The stadium is one of the most charming and nostalgic of the Spring Training ballparks. It is tucked away in a warehouse neighborhood not far from the Miami airport. The area is not threatening but is somewhat off the beaten path for the typical Florida tourist. The park was built just after World War II but has a real art deco flair, more like the '30s. The lobby is graced by schmaltzy full-color murals of baseball and Americana. This year, the City of Miami is spending a considerable sum to renovate the stadium.

An interesting feature of the park is that there is a full-sized infield with no outfield tucked into foul territory along the outfield line beyond the third-base stands, which extend only to the edge of the dirt down both foul lines. Sometimes, even during a game, Oriole infielders will be working on pickoffs or rundown plays on what is literally a diamond without a setting.

The 36 rows of stands that arc the field are fairly divided: the first 12 rows are box seats, the next 12 rows are reserved, and the last 12 rows are general admission. Only the boxes aren't covered by the tin overhang that gives the stadium its distinctive appearance.

## Getting to the Stadium
Come off **Interstate 95** heading east on **Route 836** then north on Northwest 10th Avenue to 23rd Street and to the stadium.

*Parking:* The stadium parking capacity is only 600–700, and it fills up early. There is room for another 1,200 cars within a few blocks of the stadium. All parking is near a monorail stop, a unique and delightful way to travel to a day game.

## Tickets
Spring Training Ticket Manager
Bobby Maduro Miami Stadium
2301 Northwest 10th Avenue
Miami, FL 33127
(305) 635-5395

The Orioles offer an "Early Bird" ticket schedule in December, but the final schedule is not printed until early February. The revised edition has only a few minor corrections, so you can easily make plans from the early edition.

The Orioles do not sell season-ticket packages. Only single-game tickets are available. Mail-order ticket sales begin on January 10. Tickets go on sale at the Bobby Maduro Miami Stadium box office on February 9. Mail payment must be made by check, telephone orders by credit card. Sellouts occur at most once or twice a spring.

*Prices:* Field box $7; terrace box $5; general admission $4; children's and seniors' admission $2.

## Team Hotel

Hyatt Regency
400 Southeast 2nd Avenue
Miami, FL 33131
(305) 358-1234

Only a few of the players stay here, but many of the media people do. There are often remote broadcasts from the hotel.

## Players' Favorite Leisure Spots

The English Pub, Key Biscayne, and the Hollywood Race Track are all popular with Orioles' players.

## Previous Spring Training Locations

*St. Louis Browns (1901–53)*
*Baltimore Orioles (1954–present)*

| | |
|---|---|
| 1901 | St. Louis, MO |
| 1902 | French Lick, IN |
| 1903 | Baton Rouge, LA |
| 1904 | Corsicava, TX |
| 1905–06 | Dallas, TX |
| 1907 | San Antonio, TX |
| 1908 | Shreveport, LA |
| 1909–10 | Houston, TX |
| 1911 | Hot Springs, AR |
| 1912 | Montgomery, AL |
| 1913 | Waco, TX |
| 1914 | St. Petersburg, FL |
| 1915 | Houston, TX |
| 1916–17 | Palestine, TX |
| 1918 | Shreveport, LA |
| 1919 | San Antonio, TX |
| 1920 | Taylor, AL |
| 1921 | Bogalusa, AL |
| 1922–24 | Mobile, AL |

| | |
|---|---|
| 1925–27 | Tarpin Springs, FL |
| 1928–36 | West Palm Beach, FL |
| 1937–41 | San Antonio, TX |
| 1942 | Deland, FL |
| 1943–45 | Cape Girardeau, MO |
| 1946 | Anaheim, CA |
| 1947 | Miami, FL |
| 1948 | San Bernardino, CA |
| 1949–52 | Burbank, CA |
| 1953 | San Bernardino, CA |
| 1954 | Yuma, AZ |
| 1955 | Daytona Beach, FL |
| 1956–58 | Scottsdale, AZ |
| 1959–present | Miami, FL |

## Hottest Prospects

Since 1960 the Orioles have developed some of baseball's finest rookies, certainly one of the reasons they have been a dominant force in the American League in this era. No fewer than five Orioles have won AL Rookie of the Year honors since 1960.

The slugging John "Boog" Powell crashed Spring Training homers in 1960 but was deemed too raw to bring north that year. Two years later he was ready and fulfilled his promise, belting 339 round trippers in 17 years. The O's had another fine 1960 rookie, shortstop Ron Hansen, who showed that his 1959 average of .256 at Vancouver was no fluke when he hit the same figure for the O's and was voted AL Rookie of the Year. Hansen's fielding, in particular, earned him plaudits and left a legacy: though he and his glove soon moved on to the White Sox, his successors, Luis Aparicio (for whom he was traded) and Mark Belanger, were two of the finest fielders ever to play the position.

Sam Bowens was the best newcomer in camp in 1964, according to *The Sporting News*, but it was a 19-year-old pitcher named Wally Bunker, off a glittering 10–1 year in his only season in the minors, who went on to post a 19–5 record that year, by far his career best. Rookie outfielders in that 1964 spring camp included defensive genius Paul Blair and Lou Piniella, who would spend five more years in the minors and then surface as the AL's top rookie in Kansas City in 1969.

The 1965 crop included the aforementioned Belanger, Davy Johnson (who would unexpectedly set a single-season home run record for second basemen in 1973 by hitting 43 for Atlanta, one-third of his entire 13-year career total!), and Curt Blefary, who had hit 31 home runs at AAA Syracuse in 1964. During Spring Training, Blefary complained to manager Hank Bauer about not getting enough playing time. Bowens' pulled muscle opened the door for Blefary and he made the most of the opportunity, playing in 144 games and hitting 22 homers to win AL Rookie of the Year honors, the second Oriole in five years to do so. Also in camp was a young pitcher destined for stardom, who had posted an 11–3 mark with the Aberdeen Pheasants in the Northern League: Jim Palmer.

In 1967 pitcher Tom Phoebus had a fine spring and went 14–9 to earn the AL top rookie award from *The Sporting News*. That spring, the highly touted Mike Epstein, a baseball all-American and MVP in two minor leagues, appeared to have the first-base job sewn up but was replaced by Powell eight games into the season. Traded soon after to the Washington Senators, he could never approach his minor league success in the Majors. A curiously similar fate befell 1970's top rookie prospect, first-baseman Roger Freed, who would play only four games for the O's after a celebrated minor league career. Two other prospects in that 1970 camp were Bobby Grich and Don Baylor. Baylor was sent to Syracuse and would be the International League Rookie of the Year in 1970 while batting .327. He and Grich were Oriole stalwarts for several seasons before linking up again in California with the Angels, in 1977. Baylor has since brought his leadership skills to New York, Boston and Minnesota.

The cascade of talent continued in 1973 with the coming of Doug DeCinces and the "can't miss" Al Bumbry, who led the International League in hitting at .345. After hitting .309 during Spring Training, he hit a team-high .337 during the regular season and was named AL Rookie of the Year, with teammate Rich Coggins finishing second in the voting.

In the 1976 camp was another International League top rookie and MVP, Rich Dauer, along with future pitching stars Scott McGregor and Dennis Martinez. All of them contributed mightily to the excellent teams of the late '70s and early '80s, though their considerable accomplishments were overshadowed by those of a virtual unknown in camp in 1977. Eddie Murray got his chance when the Birds lost three players as free agents. His 11 homers the previous year in the minors gave no indication he would break Hansen's team rookie home run mark with 27 and would be one of his era's most prodigious sluggers. Like Powell, he has had a gift for hitting grand slams. Murray was the fourth Oriole since 1960 named AL Rookie of the Year.

In 1981 *Sport* magazine tabbed infielder Cal Ripken, Jr. as the "phenom of the year," but he spent most of it at Rochester, hitting .288. The following winter, the O's traded third-baseman DeCinces, making room for Ripken, who responded by hitting .264 with 93 RBI, winning the AL Rookie of the Year award and embarking on one of baseball's longest ironman streaks. His streak of consecutive innings played ended at well over 8,000 in September 1987. He added the loop's MVP award in 1982.

Ripken was to have been the solution to the Orioles' one long-term weakness: a third baseman to succeed the incomparable Brooks Robinson, who retired after the 1977 season. But Ripken preferred shortstop, so the search continued. Fritz Connally's fine 1985 spring debut made him a viable candidate: he opened the season for the Birds, and his two early grand-slam home runs suggested he might be the answer. But his career was meteoric: by midseason he had been sent to the minors, and two years later was out of baseball completely. The Orioles have tried numerous players at third since Robinson's retirement without finding a regular, and one wonders if Brooks didn't cast a spell when he departed.

The Orioles' farm system has come up a little dry in the past several seasons, coinciding with the general decline in the team's fortunes.

## Top Rookies Each Spring

1960   Boog Powell, first base
1961   Jerry Adair, second base
1962   Boog Powell, first base
1963   Bob Severine, outfield
1964   Sam Bowens, outfield
1965   Curt Blefary, outfield
1966   John Miller, outfield
1967   Dave May, outfield
1968   Merv Rettenmund, outfield
1969   Terry Crowley, outfield
1970   Roger Freed, first base
1971   Don Baylor, outfield
1972   Rich Coggins, outfield
1973   Al Bumbry, outfield
1974   Dave Johnson, pitcher
1975   Bob Bailor, shortstop
1976   Rich Dauer, second base
1977   Eddie Murray, first base

1978 Sammy Stewart, pitcher
1979 Wayne Krenchicki, third base
1980 Mark Corey, outfield
1981 Mark Corey, outfield/Cal Ripken, Jr., third base
1982 Cal Ripken, Jr., third base
1983 John Shelby, outfield
1984 Mike Young, outfield
1985 Fritz Connally, third base
1986 John Habyan, pitcher
1987 Ken Gerhart, outfield

## AL Rookies of the Year
1960 Ron Hansen, shortstop
1965 Curt Blefary, outfield
1973 Al Bumbry, outfield
1977 Eddie Murray, first base
1982 Cal Ripken, Jr., third base

## Prospects to Watch in 1988
*Jeff Ballard*, *pitcher*. Lefthander Ballard was the ace of the Rochester staff in the International League, posting an 11–4 mark through the end of August before being called up by the Birds.
*Pete Stanicek*, *second base*. Only Billy Ripken, who spent the first half of the year in AAA, kept Stanicek at AA-Charlotte, but the former Stanford speedster is rated one of the top minor league infielders.

# LOS ANGELES DODGERS

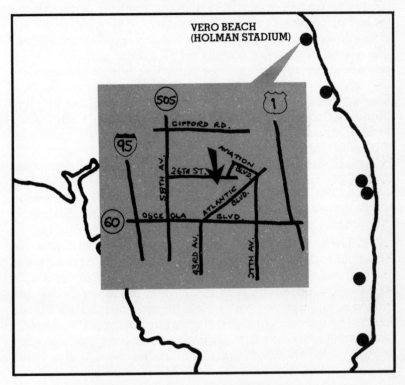

■ **Current site:**
Holman Stadium
Dodgertown
4001 26th Street
Vero Beach, FL 32961
(305) 569-4900
■ **Dimensions:** 360′ left
and right; 410′ center
■ **Seating:** 6,000
plus seating on grass
beyond outfield
(record attendance: 8,200,
March 19, 1979, versus

the Yankees)
■ **Built:** 1953
■ **Off-season use:**
Vero Beach Dodgers,
Florida State League
(Class A)
■ **Practice site:**
At Dodgertown daily
at 10:00 A.M.
■ **Game time:** 1:30 P.M.
■ **Most convenient airport:**
West Palm Beach
or Orlando.

With a population of 16,000, Vero Beach is among the smallest communities hosting a Major League team for Spring Training. Dodgertown stands at the site of a training base that the U.S. Navy turned over to the city after World War II. The Brooklyn Dodgers, then without a permanent Spring Training home, were invited to Vero Beach by Bud Holman, the local businessman for whom Holman Stadium is named.

The Dodgers' facility combines the organized practicality of the newer facilities, such as Port Charlotte and Kissimmee, with the charm of the older ones and offers unmatched intimacy. In the years since the Dodgers bought this land from the city, they have built an enormous and beautiful facility including living and meeting quarters, baseball diamonds galore, and twenty-seven holes of golf designed by the late Dodger owner Walter O'Malley.

Holman Stadium offers no shade (except to the press corps behind home plate), even to the ballplayers. There are no dugouts; the players sit on benches in the hot sun. The permanent stands extend further down the foul lines than in most Spring Training parks. A unique attraction at Holman Stadium — available only if the permanent seats are sold out — is the opportunity to sit on a grass embankment under a palm tree in the outfield. There is no outfield fence; a tree line in the middle of the embankment delineates an "over the fence" home run. Nowhere else can you watch Major League baseball under the shade of a tree with no fence separating you from the players.

Autograph opportunities abound at Vero. The players practice on the many diamonds sprinkled around the complex (walk away from the stadium behind the first-base line to find them), and the Dodgers' locker room is about a quarter-mile walk across these open fields. It is easy to catch players on their way into the stadium before a game or on their way back to the locker room afterwards. Players not being used in that day's game are often hard at work on other diamonds in plain sight.

## Getting to the Stadium
Take **Interstate 95** to **Route 60 East**, which is Walker Avenue. Travel east for seven miles to 43rd Avenue. Take a left on 43rd Avenue for half a mile to 26th Street, then turn right and follow on to the entrance.

*Parking:* According to Charlie Blaney, the director of Dodgertown, "The lots are never full. There is plenty of parking on golf courses."

## Tickets

Los Angeles Dodgers
Dodgertown
P.O. Box 2887
4001 26th Street
Vero Beach, FL 32961
(305) 569-4900

The printed schedule is available in late November. Season tickets are on sale from December 1 through March 1. They may be ordered by mail with a personal check or purchased at the stadium. Checks received before December 1 will be held. Single- game tickets may be purchased at the stadium beginning March 1. Reserved seats sold out eight times (out of eleven games) in 1987.

*Prices:* Boxes $6; standing room $4.

## Team Hotel

The players stay at Dodgertown. No one else may stay there and there are no fan-oriented activities.

## Players' Favorite Leisure Spots

The players' favorite night hangout is Bobby's Cafe & Lounge, located on the beach. It is the town's main sports lounge. The players also make use of the Dodger Pines Country Club and the Dodgertown Golf Club, both at Dodgertown, where they play golf after workouts. Both courses are open to the public.

## Previous Spring Training Locations

*Brooklyn Dodgers (1901–57)*
*Los Angeles Dodgers (1958–present)*

| | |
|---|---|
| 1901 | Charlotte, NC |
| 1902–06 | Columbia, SC |
| 1907–09 | Jacksonville, FL |
| 1910–12 | Hot Springs, AR |
| 1913–14 | Augusta, GA |
| 1915–16 | Daytona Beach, FL |
| 1917–18 | Hot Springs, AR |
| 1919–20 | Jacksonville, FL |
| 1921 | New Orleans, LA |
| 1922 | Jacksonville, FL |
| 1923–32 | Clearwater, FL |
| 1933 | Miami, FL |
| 1934–35 | Orlando, FL |

1936–40    Clearwater, FL
1941–42    Havana, Cuba
1943–45    Bear Mountain, NY
1946       Daytona Beach, FL
1947       Havana, Cuba
1948       Ciudad Trujillo, Dominican Republic
1949–present   Vero Beach, FL

## Hottest Prospects

The only team to produce more Rookies of the Year than the Orioles since 1960 is the Dodgers, who have had, until recently, the finest farm system in the Majors. With its support, they have won more NL pennants than any other team in the last three decades.

The Dodgers opened their 1960 spring camp in Vero Beach with a veteran team, one that had finished first or second seven times in the '50s. It would take a big man to break into the lineup, and the Dodgers had the biggest, 6' 7" Frank Howard. The former Ohio State basketball star had been up briefly with L.A. in his first two seasons; he would stay the year in 1960 and hit 23 homers, some of them of prodigious length, on the way to 382 in his 16-year career. Howard was named the NL's Rookie of the Year. The other first-year starter for the Dodgers was Tommy Davis, all-everything the previous year in the Pacific Coast League. Davis hit .276 in 1960 and would lead the league at .346 two years later.

The Dodgers thought they had a rookie repeater the next year in another Davis, Willie. He, too, had demolished Pacific Coast League pitching, hitting a point higher than Tommy's .345. In 1961 he was picked by *The Sporting News* as the Dodger's most likely top rookie. He hit a solid but unspectacular .254 in his first season in Dodger blue. The best of the new pitchers in 1961 was Ron Perranoski, who went 7–5 with a 2.65 ERA and blossomed into one of the dominant relief pitchers of the decade.

The Dodgers were singing the praises of Al Ferrara in the 1965 camp. Ferrara had sung selections from *La Traviata* at Carnegie Hall when he was 16, but he never reached such high notes in baseball. Jim Lefebvre was overlooked as that year's camp opened because he had spent the previous year in the military. He quickly made his mark, stepping into the second-base job and hitting .250; he was hot down the stretch in the Dodgers' tight pennant victory and was named the National League's Rookie of the Year.

Joining Don Drysdale and Sandy Koufax in the Dodger rotation in 1966 was another future Hall of Famer who was destined to win many more games than either of his Cy Young award-winning mound-mates. Don Sutton had won 23 games while striking out 239 batters the previous year in Triple-A. He was 12–12 for the champions in 1966 and was named the NL's top rookie pitcher. Though a 20-game winner only once, Sutton nonetheless won more than 300 games in a career spanning the better part of three decades.

Ted Sizemore arrived in 1969, playing two infield positions while hitting .271. The opening-day shortstop, the steady Sizemore was named the rookie of the Year in 1969 but was traded to St. Louis after the 1970 season as the Dodgers compiled their infield of the '70s. Sizemore's arrival initiated an extraordinary rookie era for Los Angeles, whose starting lineup would soon be transformed. Outfielder-to-be-shortstop Bill Russell also made the 1969 squad.

In 1969 the Dodgers initiated the Jim and Dearie Milvey Award for the top rookie each spring, named in honor of two long-time Dodger stockholders. Sizemore won it the first year, and Bill Buckner was the winner the following spring, hitting .283. Another infielder, first-baseman Steve Garvey, led the team with 21 RBI in the spring of 1970 and filled in at third and second that year and the three following, before Buckner moved to the outfield and Garvey could claim first.

In 1971 the Milvey Award went to Bob Darwin. Darwin had come to the Dodgers as a pitcher and then pitched seven more years in the minors, making a one-game appearance for L.A. in 1969. His 9.82 career two-game ERA prompted a switch to the outfield and to the American League, where his slugging statistics in Minnesota far outdistanced his mound performance. The best of the rest in 1971 was pitcher Doyle Alexander, who was 6–6 for the Dodgers, before being traded with some cannon fodder to Baltimore for Frank Robinson and Pete Richert.

Dodgertown was filled with good rookies in 1973. Tom Paciorek, coming off three straight 100-RBI seasons in the Pacific Coast League, was eager for a shot. Ron Cey, who had prompted the Dodgers to move Garvey off third base the previous spring, was also up from the PCL to claim a spot, thus completing the Dodgers' infield of the '70s. But the brightest hope was pitcher Eddie Solomon, the Milvey Award winner that year, whose arm was as good as his concentration was erratic.

Rick Sutcliffe won the Milvey Award in 1977 but spent the year in Albuquerque, posting a 3–10 record. By 1979 he had put it all together and was 17–10 for the Dodgers, the most wins by a Dodger rookie since Don Newcombe in 1949. He was named the National League Rookie of the Year. Also contributing in 1979 was Pedro Guerrero, whom the Dodgers had picked up in 1973 from Cleveland for now-forgotten reliever Bruce Ellingsen, one of baseball's most lopsided trades. Yet another prospect from San Pedro de Macoris, Guerrero was coming off two seasons of .337 and .333 at Albuquerque, leading the PCL in RBI both years and previewing the contributions he would make in years to come.

In 1980 the Dodgers were looking at Mickey Hatcher, the 1979 PCL batting champ at .371. He hit .261 in camp but just .226 for the year and was shipped to Minnesota at the end of Spring Training in 1981. Rudy Law was the Milvey Award winner in 1980, but the regular-season sensation turned out to be a non-roster surprise. Steve Howe won seven games and saved 17 more, a Dodger rookie record, and was named the NL's Rookie of the Year.

The Dodgers not only had another Rookie of the Year winner in 1981, but a Cy Young winner as well in the amazing Fernando Valenzuela. The chunky Mexican won his first eight starts, five by shutouts. He was 13–7 during the regular season with a 2.48 ERA, then won Game 5 of the League Championship Series and Game 3 of the World Series.

The Topps and *The Sporting News* Minor League Player of the Year in 1981 was Mike Marshall, the triple-crown winner in the PCL. He hit .355 with seven RBI in 16 spring games in 1982 but was sent back to Albuquerque. He punished PCL pitchers, hitting .388 until June, when he was called up to replace the injured Derrell Thomas; he has starred in Los Angeles since then. But Marshall had help at Albuquerque in 1982. This was undoubtedly one of the best minor league teams of all time, featuring Jack Perconte (.346), Candy Maldonado (.335, 104 RBI), Ron Roenicke (.316, 94 RBI), pitchers Ted Power (18–3), Brian Holton (16–6), and Rick Wright (14–6), among others. None of them, however, cracked the starting lineup for long, and their careers advanced in other cities.

Meanwhile, Steve Sax took over for Davey Lopes at second in 1982, the first change in the great infield of the '70s, which would be thoroughly dismantled the following year. Sax hit a solid .282 while stealing forty-nine bases, a Dodger rookie record. He was the only rookie on the All-Star team and was named the National League's Rookie of the Year, the fourth consecutive Dodger to win the award.

Orel Hershiser was the top rookie in camp in 1984, his talent obvious despite his 0–2 record that spring. When moved into the starting rotation, he went 11–8, finishing third in the Rookie of the Year voting. Both Sid Bream and R.J. Reynolds were considered quality prospects in 1983 and 1984, but they went to Pittsburgh for Bill Madlock the following year. The 1984 Milvey Award winner, German Rivera, was sent to Houston. Tracy Woodson was the top spring rookie in 1987, hitting .364 to lead the team.

Like the Orioles', the Dodgers' farm system has sustained the team for years but has recently produced a leaner crop. It is no coincidence that the Dodgers have also fallen on harder times, looking to bolster the team with trades instead of depending on the influx of young talent.

## Top Rookies Each Spring

| | |
|---|---|
| 1960 | Frank Howard, first base; Tommy Davis, outfield |
| 1961 | Willie Davis, outfield |
| 1962 | Larry Burright, second base |
| 1963 | Nate Oliver, second base |
| 1964 | Wes Parker, first base |
| 1965 | Al Ferrara, outfield; Jim Lefebvre, second base |
| 1966 | Don Sutton, pitcher |
| 1967 | Tommy Dean, shortstop |
| 1968 | Mike Kekich, pitcher |
| 1969 | Ted Sizemore, second base |
| 1970 | Bill Buckner, outfield |
| 1971 | Bob Darwin, pitcher |
| 1972 | Steve Yeager, catcher |
| 1973 | Eddie Solomon, pitcher |
| 1974 | Jerry Royster, third base |
| 1975 | Rick Rhoden, pitcher |
| 1976 | Glenn Burke, outfield |
| 1977 | Rick Sutcliffe, pitcher |
| 1978 | Bob Welch, pitcher |
| 1979 | Pedro Guerrero, outfield |
| 1980 | Rudy Law, outfield; Steve Howe, pitcher |
| 1981 | Fernando Valenzuela, pitcher |
| 1982 | Mike Marshall, outfield; Steve Sax, second base |
| 1983 | Orel Hershiser, pitcher |
| 1984 | German Rivera, third base |
| 1985 | Sid Bream, first base |
| 1986 | Reggie Williams, outfield |
| 1987 | Tracy Woodsen, second base |

## NL Rookies of the Year

1960   Frank Howard, first base
1965   Jim Lefebvre, second base
1969   Ted Sizemore, second base
1979   Rick Sutcliffe, pitcher
1980   Steve Howe, pitcher
1981   Fernando Valenzuela, pitcher
1982   Steve Sax, second base

## Prospects to Watch in 1988

*Shawn Hillegas*, pitcher.  One of the top prospects in the Pacific Coast League at 13–5 at Albuquerque, he beat the Braves in his first start in the Majors when brought up in August 1987.

*Brad Wellman*, third base.  He was named the Pacific Coast League All-Star third baseman and is given a chance to start for the Dodgers in 1988.

# MONTREAL EXPOS

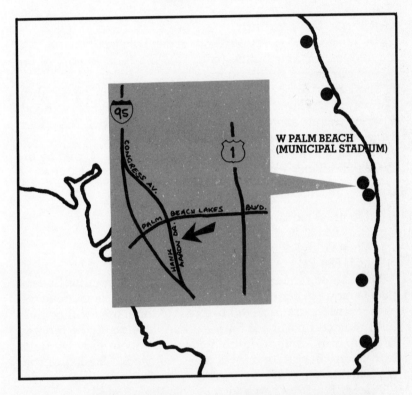

**W PALM BEACH (MUNICIPAL STADIUM)**

■ **Current site:**
Municipal Stadium
715 Hank Aaron Drive
West Palm Beach, FL 33401
(305) 683-6100
■ **Dimensions:**
330' left and right;
400' center
■ **Seating:** 4,392
■ **Built:** 1962
■ **Off-season use:**

West Palm Beach Expos; Florida State League (Class A): also Winter Instructional League teams from the Braves, Expos, Orioles practice there.
■ **Practice site:** At the stadium daily at 10:00 A.M.
■ **Game time:** 1:35 P.M.
■ **Most convenient airport:** West Palm Beach.

**67**

The Expos share Municipal Stadium in West Palm Beach with the Atlanta Braves. The stadium was built in 1962 in preparation for the Braves' move from Bradenton, and the facility accommodates both teams well with a total of six fields, two of which have ample seating for large crowds. For full-squad exhibition games, both teams use the main stadium. See Atlanta Braves for more complete description.

## Getting to the Stadium

Take **Interstate 95 to exit 53**, Palm Beach Lakes Boulevard, and travel east for four lights. Municipal Stadium is next to the West Palm Beach Auditorium.

The Expos' minor leaguers train 10 miles to the south of Municipal Stadium. To get there, take **I-95** to Hypoluxo Road. Proceed two miles west to Santa Lucas High School. The minor-league complex is adjacent to it.

*Parking:* The Municipal Stadium parking lot, shared by the West Palm Beach Auditorium, has a capacity for 2,300 cars.

## Tickets

Montreal Expos
P.O. Box 2546
West Palm Beach, FL 33401
(305) 689-9121

The printed schedule is available in early December. Season tickets may be ordered as soon as the schedule is made available. If orders are received before that time, they will be held until they can be filled. Single-game tickets may be ordered beginning in January. In both cases, payment may be made using a credit card or a local personal check. The Expos sold out five times in 1987.

*Prices:* Box $7; reserve $6; general admission $3.

## Team Hotel

Holiday Inn
4431 PGA Boulevard at I-95
Palm Beach Gardens, FL 33403
(305) 622-2260

There are no activities scheduled for fans. In fact, most coaches and players have condominiums in the area, and only the rookies and minor leaguers stay at the hotel.

## Players' Favorite Leisure Spots

You'll find the Expos on the golf links, although they also enjoy the local jai-alai at the Palm Beach fronton and the racing action at the Palm Beach Kennel Club. Their favorite eating establishments are MacArthur's Vineyard, a bar/restaurant serving steaks, ribs, and fish, Plata Grande, serving Mexican fare, and Tony Roma's, a place for ribs.

## Previous Spring Training Locations

1969–72   West Palm Beach, FL
1973–80   Daytona Beach, FL
1981–present   West Palm Beach, FL

## Hottest Prospects

The Expos came into existence in 1969, when the National League added Montreal and San Diego while Seattle and Kansas City joined the American League. With expansion came the splitting of the leagues into Eastern and Western divisions. This created league playoffs and more opportunities for teams to reach the World Series. But this was academic for the expansion Expos, who matched the Padres' record of 52–110 the first year, and finished deep in last place.

There were a few gems among the veterans that first year. Bill Stoneman, given up on by the Cubs, won 11 games, including an April no-hitter against the Phillies, and popular Rusty Staub cranked out 29 home runs hitting behind Coco Laboy. Laboy, a 10-year minor-leaguer, was not expected to do much when the Cards let him go to Montreal, but he hit a surprising 18 home runs with a .258 average, and was selected by *The Sporting News* as the NL's top rookie player. Laboy slipped under .200 the following year and soon disappeared; and the Expos, for the next few years, suffered the lot of the expansion team with a new farm system, struggling to find useful rookie candidates.

*The Sporting News* rookie award went to another Montreal freshman in 1970. Carl Morton, with a sparkling 18–11 record, was the recipient. Morton was signed by the Braves as an outfielder and didn't take up pitching until his third year in the pros. He returned to the Braves in 1973 for Pat Jarvis, in an exchange of pitchers. Another converted outfielder, Ernie McAnally, who played six positions in the minors, was counted on to deliver in 1971, and he came through with eleven victories his first year, but slumped thereafter. Jimmy Qualls, picked up from the Cubs, never quite blossomed. The Expos were still looking for shortstop help in 1972 and hoped Rich Hacker, nephew of former Cub pitcher Warren Hacker, might help. Again, they were disappointed, but they were about to hit the jackpot the next five years, as they built the contending team of the late '70s and early '80s.

Steve Rogers was a nonroster player in the 1973 camp, and even though he was impressive, the Expos sent him down. Wisely, they brought him up in June, and he finished the year with a nifty 1.54 ERA and a 10–5 record. *The Sporting News* named him the top rookie pitcher in the NL.

Two players promoted from Peninsula in the Carolina League, Jim Cox and Barry Foote, were expected to contribute in 1974. Foote had been an All-Star in every league he played in, and the predictions in Spring Training were that he'd be the Expos' regular catcher. He was, but only for a short time. That's because Gary Carter, the International League's top catcher in 1974, was the Expos' best prospect ever and could not be kept out of the lineup, playing three positions his first year. His play earned him a spot on the All-Star team.

Montreal had three young outfielders in 1977 — Bombo Rivera, Gary Roenicke, and Andre Dawson. Dawson had punished AAA pitching in 1976, hitting .350, and by June had won a starting position, joining two other rising stars — Ellis Valentine and Warren Cromartie — in what was, arguably, baseball's finest young outfield. Dawson finished the season at .282 and was named the National League's Rookie of the Year.

Bill Gullickson was the Expos' top pitching prospect since Rogers, but they brought him along slowly. After starting the 1980 season in the minors, he came up to Montreal to post a 10–5 record, the same as Rogers seven years earlier. In 1980, Tim Raines was voted the minor league Player of the Year and with good reason. He hit .354 at Denver and finished third in the MVP voting behind teammates Randy Bass and Tim Wallach. He was named Rookie of the Year at Denver and almost did the same his first year in the Majors, finishing second behind Fernando Valenzuela in 1981. *The Sporting News* named Raines the NL Rookie Player of the Year. In a season interrupted by the players' strike, he had 71 steals in 88 games.

Terry Francona, son of Tito Francona, came up at the end of 1981 and filled in for Raines when he was hurt. Francona always played well but never did crack the Expos' starting line-up. Dave Hostetler, with some impressive stats, was expected to make the jump to the Majors in 1982, but he did it with Texas, not Montreal. He was included along with regular third-baseman Larry Parrish in a most propitious trade for Al Oliver, who produced perhaps his finest year, hitting .331 for Montreal to lead the league.

Ken Phelps had some remarkable AAA stats when he came to camp in 1983 — a .354 batting average, 46 homers, and 141 RBI in 137 games. But he hit a disappointing .204 in the Grapefruit League, and the Expos sold him to Seattle before the season started. The best performer among the 1983 prospects was pitcher Dick Grapenthin, who posted a 1.80 ERA in the spring. This earned him a ticket to Montreal, but he was soon after farmed out for more seasoning.

By the end of the 1984 season, the Expos had skidded back under .500, and moved to shake up the team. Gary Carter, the All-Star catcher, was dangled in front of the Mets, who sent Montreal four young players who have since played major roles in the team's renaissance: Hubie Brooks, Mike Fitzgerald, pitcher Floyd Youmans, and Herm Winningham. The latter was named top rookie in the 1985 camp and was used mostly as a defensive outfield replacement during the year. But in 1986 he became a starter.

Andres Gallaraga was the 1985 American Association Rookie of the Year, and *Baseball America* tabbed him a top prospect. Indeed, he was. He came to 1986 Spring Training with high expectations but managed to hit just .107, with no extra-base hits in Grapefruit League play. Optioned out, he came back to hit .271 for the Expos, and in 1987 he and Raines challenged for the batting title.

## Top Rookies Each Spring

1969  Don Hahn, outfield; Coco Laboy, third base
1970  Marvin Staehle, second base
1971  Ernie McAnally, pitcher
1972  Rich Hacker, shortstop; Balor Moore, pitcher
1973  Pepe Frias, shortstop; Steve Rogers, pitcher
1974  Jim Fox, second base; Barry Foote, catcher
1975  Gary Carter, catcher
1976  Ellis Valentine, outfield
1977  Andre Dawson, outfield
1978  Dan Schatzeder, pitcher
1979  Bob James, pitcher
1980  Bill Gullickson, pitcher

1981   Tim Raines, outfield
1982   Dave Hostetler, first base
1983   Dick Grapenthin, pitcher
1984   Mike Fuentes, outfield
1985   Herm Winningham, outfield
1986   Andres Gollaraga, first base;  George Riley, pitcher
1987   Alonzo Powell, outfield

## NL Rookies of the Year
1970   Carl Morton, pitcher
1977   Andre Dawson, outfield

## Prospect to Watch in 1988
*Luis Rivera*, *shortstop*. A good fielder, Rivera has finally started to hit the ball well. He hit over .300 for Indianapolis in 1987 and was named the League's All-Star shortstop. After two short stays with Montreal, he is expected to make his third opportunity permanent.

# NEW YORK METS

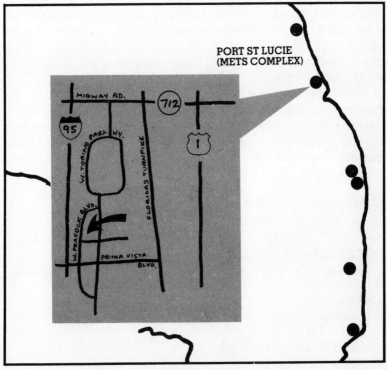

PORT ST LUCIE
(METS COMPLEX)

■ **Current site:**
St. Lucie County
Sports Complex
West Peacock Street
Port St. Lucie, FL 33452
(305) 335-3695
■ **Dimensions:**
338' left and right;
410' center
(same as Shea Stadium)
■ **Seating:** 7,500

■ **Built:** 1987
■ **Off-season use:**
St. Lucie Mets, Florida
State League (Class A);
Mets minor league Winter
Instructional League
■ **Practice site:** At the
stadium daily at 10:00 A.M.
■ **Game time:** 1:00 P.M.
■ **Most convenient airport:**
West Palm Beach.

St. Lucie County Sports Complex — the new Florida home of the New York Mets — will open for the 1988 Spring Training season. The brand-new facility will have dimensions identical to Shea Stadium. When completed, it will stand as a tribute to the speed of modern day construction: in the spring of 1987 there wasn't even a road to the stadium site. The Mets will play a full schedule of games in the stadium in Spring Training 1988.

Situated on 100 picturesque acres, surrounded by pine and palm trees and a large lake, the Mets' complex contains seven baseball diamonds. The main stadium has a roofdeck over the grandstand, which is fairly large by Spring Training standards. Bleachers extend down both lines, and there are good views from every seat.

The players' batting cages are just outside the main entrance and are accessible to fans. The clubhouse is under the grandstand, and if you haven't gotten an autograph off the box and bleacher railings, you should position yourself next to the batting tunnels on the north side of the stadium, for players emerge there.

## Getting to the Stadium

Take **Route 1** to Prima Vista Boulevard, west to Bay Shore Boulevard. From there, it is another two miles to the stadium, which will be on your right.

*Parking:* The stadium lot can provide parking for 2,500 cars.

## Tickets

New York Mets
P.O. Box 8808
Port St. Lucie, FL 33452
(305) 335-3695

The team's printed schedule is available in early January. All 6,500 reserved seats have been claimed for 1988. Very limited single-game seats can be ordered by mail and paid for by personal check, or they can be bought at the box office with cash. No phone orders or credit card orders will be accepted, but a phone inquiry is advised.

*Prices:* Grandstand $6; bleacher $4.

## Team Hotel

The Mets had not chosen their hotel when this book was produced.

## Players' Favorite Leisure Spots

Because 1988 will be the Mets' first year in the area, their favorite hangouts will be discovered after they arrive. But here are some suggestions: Mr. Laughs, Shuckers, and Banana Ma.

## Previous Spring Training Locations

The Mets' move to St. Lucie will be their first. From their first year in 1962 through the spring of 1987, the Mets played all of their exhibition home games in St. Petersburg, sharing with division rivals, the St. Louis Cardinals.

## Hottest Prospects

Let's set the facts straight. The Mets did *not* have a winning record in 1962, their first year in Grapefruit League competition. The rag-tag team of has-beens and never-to-be's had too many players who had left their best performances in the '50s and a few who had performed well in the '40s, notably Richie Ashburn, Gil Hodges, and Gene Woodling. Their 12–15 Florida record, however, gave them almost one-third as many victories as they gained during their entire first regular season.

They were led by the venerable one, Casey Stengel, who looked out over his squad in St. Petersburg and was heard to exclaim: "Can't anyone here play this game?" Apparently not, for the team lost its first regular-season game in the Polo Grounds and went on to lose 119 more, establishing a new Major League record for futility. But National League baseball was back in New York, and the fans loved them.

The best of the raw recruits that first year was 26-year-old Al Jackson. At 8–20, the rookie pitcher joined veteran Roger Craig in the 20-game-loser category. Rod Kanehl came off the bench to become a versatile regular, playing five positions, and 17-year-old bonus baby Ed Kranepool came up at the end of the year, his first of 18 with the Mets. He was hitting high-school pitching as the Mets worked out at their first spring camp.

As inept as the first-year Mets were, it must be remembered they were world champions seven years later, largely propelled by their youth movement.

Ron Hunt, a legitimate prospect given his .309 batting average at Austin, started at second base in 1963 and hit .272. The next year he raised his average to .303 and was named to the All-Star team, the first home-grown Met to be so honored. Hunt was a scrapper and set a Major League record for being hit by a pitch, one that stood until 1986 when Don Baylor painfully broke it.

The 1965 season produced two players who would figure significantly in better times, pitcher Tug McGraw and outfielder Ron Swoboda. With other teams, they might have stayed down for an additional year, but the Mets needed immediate help. McGraw went 2–7 while Swoboda managed to hit but .228. Still, they were paving the road to the top.

The 1966 season was a strange one in New York. It was the first time the Mets would be out of last place, and the first year since 1924 that the Yankees would end up there. Part of the credit for the Mets' rise went to Cleon Jones, who had been up for cups of coffee in 1963 and 1965. He came up for good in 1966, hitting a respectable .275. He followed that with a .297 average in 1968 and a rousing .340 in the championship year of 1969.

The Mets tried out eight rookie pitchers in 1967, but the only one good enough to stick was the franchise, Tom Seaver. Tom Terrific put together a 16–13 record and was named the Rookie of the Year by the Baseball Writers' Association. Two years later, he won the Cy Young Award with a record of 25–7. Also in 1967 slick-fielding rookie shortstop Bud Harrelson was ready to replace the aging Ed Bressoud, and his grit became an essential championship ingredient.

Another mound mainstay arrived in 1968. Jerry Koosman posted a brilliant 19–12 mark for the ninth-place Mets, and was named *The Sporting News*' top rookie pitcher in the NL. He finished second to Johnny Bench in the Rookie of the Year voting.

Nolan Ryan, a future Hall of Famer, also came up in 1968. Ryan had smoked at Greenville in 1966, posting a 15–2 record, but it took him two years to convince the Mets that he knew where the plate was. Ryan was 6–9 that first year. He won only six again in the championship year of 1969 but was immense in the third game of the NL playoff against the Braves, the game that effectively launched his extraordinary career. No fastballer has been more durable than Ryan; he holds the Major League all-time strikeout record, and was still a force in 1987.

Kranepool, McGraw, Swoboda, Jones, Seaver, Koosman, Ryan: it was extraordinary for a new team to develop so much talent so quickly. The storybook season of 1969 was the result. The Amazin' Mets jumped from ninth place to the world championship, a leap never before achieved and likely never to be matched.

Tim Foli arrived in the spring of 1970 as the most touted rookie in Mets' history. The 19-year-old had a good spring and was angry when he was sent down to the minors. When Wayne Garrett went into the army in 1971, it opened up a spot for Foli.

He and Ken Singleton, another fine-looking rookie in 1971, went to Montreal for Rusty Staub the following year as the Mets searched for a veteran star to blend with their youth. The trade, however, violated the Mets' belief in their farm system. Foli and, especially, Singleton starred for other teams into the '80s. The Mets with Staub eked out a pennant in 1973 but were not again a factor for more than decade, often ending up in the cellar.

In 1972 the Mets established the John J. Murphy Award, named after the Mets' General Manager during the 1968–69 seasons. The award is given each year to the top rookie in Spring Training. The first winner was John Milner, who led the team that year with 17 homers, the only Met in double figures. He topped them again in 1973, hitting 23. The other fine rookie in the 1972 camp was pitcher Jon Matlack. Brought up at the end of 1971 after going 11–7 at Tidewater, Matlack was 0–3 for the Mets. He was, however, one of the few bright spots for the team in 1972, posting a 15–10 record and winning Rookie of the Year honors. But the Mets' farm system had, for the most part, hit a dry spell.

Mike Vail was the leading prospect in the strike-shortened 1976 camp. Vail was a throw-in in a 1974 trade with the Cards; he was leading the International League in hitting and RBI when the Mets called him up in August 1975. He batted .302, hitting in 22 straight games to tie a league record for rookies. But Vail slumped to .217 in 1976 and was sold to Cleveland during Spring Training, 1978. Craig Swan, who for years had been "the Mets' pitcher of the future," finally arrived in 1976, posting a modest 6—9 record. Though he spent eight more seasons in New York, he was never the mound leader the Mets had hoped would replace Seaver, who was traded to Cincinnati in June 1977 for several prospects, a move that exasperated Mets fans.

New York native Lee Mazzilli was expected to add some speed to the lineup in 1977 and won the Murphy Award that spring. Mazzilli stole seven bases in a seven-inning game in his first year in the pros. He stole 22 for the Mets while hitting a solid .250. But the prize rookie was Steve Henderson, who couldn't find a spot in the Reds outfield and came to the Mets in the Tom Seaver trade. Henderson hit .297 and missed being Rookie of the Year by one vote.

Two infielders were voted the top spring rookies in 1979 and 1980, but neither Kelvin Chapman nor Mario Ramirez would do much for New York. The top prizes were three pitchers. Neil Allen went 6–10 with 8 saves in 1979, and Jeff Reardon was 8–7 with a fine 2.62 ERA the following year. Also in 1980 Mark Bomback went 10–8.

Two hot prospects in the 1981 camp were pitcher Tim Leary and outfielder Mookie Wilson. Leary had the better spring but never made it in New York despite his talent. But Mookie, International League Rookie of the Year in 1979, came off the bench in May to start the rest of the 1981 season, hitting .271. He made a number of all-rookie teams and was seventh in the voting for NL Rookie of the Year honors.

Darryl Strawberry, the most highly touted rookie since Foli, arrived in 1983. The number one player selected in the June 1980 draft, he won the Murphy Award but started off in Tidewater. Called up on May 4th, he went on to hit 26 home runs, a Mets rookie record, and ran away with the NL Rookie of the Year vote.

An equally impressive rookie pitcher appeared the next year in Dwight Gooden, *Baseball America*'s Minor League Player of the Year in 1983. Gooden didn't win the Murphy Award, which went to Yale star pitcher Ron Darling, but he shone during the regular season. His 276 strikeouts were a Major League rookie record, eclipsing Herb Score's mark, and his 11.39 K's per nine innings was also a rookie high. He missed being a unanimous choice for Rookie of the Year by one vote (which went to Philadelphia's Juan Samuel). Darling, meanwhile, had a fine season himself, going 12–9 and being named to *Baseball Digest*'s All-Rookie Team. He and Gooden would be mainstays of the staff in the coming years. The rookie drought was over.

Reliever Roger McDowell was the best of the crop in 1985. On the disabled list most of 1984, Roger was 8–6 with the Mets, and his 17 saves led all NL rookies. The Mets had a good one in 1987. Dave Magadan, who had four straight .330-plus years in the minors, came up at the end of 1986 to hit .444. A contact hitter with just one home run in his last three minor league seasons, Magadan was a former college Player of the Year.

With a farm system now the envy of most teams, the Mets are once again relying on their home-grown talent and are well positioned for the future.

## Top Rookies Each Spring

1962  Al Jackson, pitcher
1963  Al Moran, shortstop; Ron Hunt, second base
1964  Ron Locke, pitcher
1965  Ron Swoboda, outfield
1966  Cleon Jones, outfield; Bud Harrelson, shortstop

1967  Tom Seaver, pitcher
1968  Jerry Koosman, pitcher
1969  Rod Gaspar, outfield; Gary Gentry, pitcher
1970  Tim Foli, shortstop
1971  Tim Foli, shortstop
1972  John Milner, outfield; Jon Matlack, pitcher
1973  Harry Parker, pitcher
1974  Bob Apodaca, pitcher
1975  John Stearns, catcher
1976  Bruce Boisclair, outfield
1977  Lee Mazzilli, outfield; Steve Henderson, outfield
1978  Mike Bruhert, pitcher
1979  Kelvin Chapman, second base; Neil Allen, pitcher
1980  Mario Ramirez, shortstop; Jeff Reardon, pitcher
1981  Tim Leary, pitcher; Mookie Wilson, outfield
1982  Ron Gardenhire, shortstop; Charlie Puleo, pitcher
1983  Darryl Strawberry, outfield
1984  Ron Darling, pitcher; Dwight Gooden, pitcher
1985  Roger McDowell, pitcher
1986  Kevin Mitchell, outfield
1987  Dave Magadan, third base

## NL Rookies of the Year
1967  Tom Seaver, pitcher
1972  Jon Matlack, pitcher
1983  Darryl Strawberry, outfield
1984  Dwight Gooden, pitcher

## Prospects to Watch in 1988
The Mets once again have the most prospects in the minors of any Major League franchise, and there are six or more who could be number one in another organization.

**Kevin Elster**, *shortstop*. The smooth-fielding Elster is rated the top prospect in the International League.

**Randy Milligan**, *first base*. Milligan was rated right behind Elster and was named both the MVP and Rookie of the Year in the International League in 1987.

**Greg Jefferies**, *shortstop*. The Texas League All-Star was *Baseball America's* Minor League Player of the Year in 1986 and followed that with the Texas League MVP award in 1987, batting .367 at Jackson.

# NEW YORK YANKEES

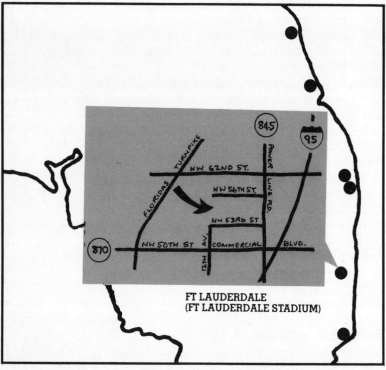

FT LAUDERDALE
(FT LAUDERDALE STADIUM)

■ **Current site:**
Fort Lauderdale Stadium
5301 Northwest 12th Avenue
Ft. Lauderdale, FL 33309
(305) 776-1921
■ **Dimensions:** 320′ left,
330′ right; 401′ center
■ **Seating:** 7,337
■ **Built:** 1962
■ **Off-season use:**
Ft. Lauderdale Yankees,

Florida State League
(Class A); some high
school games are also
played there
■ **Practice site:** at the
stadium daily at 10:30 A.M.
■ **Game times:** 1:30 P.M.
(day); 7:30 P.M.(night)
■ **Most convenient airport:**
Ft. Lauderdale.

The Yankees' city-owned winter home has less charm than the classic "House that Ruth built" in the Bronx; it is a functional and capacious spring site. The ballpark sits at the intersection of two back streets, a couple of blocks from the intersection of two main roads. Near game time, those two blocks can take quite a while to cover. The parking lots aren't paved, which is no problem if it isn't raining but quite a muddy nuisance if it is.

The stands are not distinctive; a symmetrical arc of permanent seats is extended by bleachers down both lines. There is cover for the reserved seats but not the boxes. The batting cages are not accessible to the fans. The players' entrance is in the right-field corner, and autographs can be obtained there and off the railings of the box seats and bleachers.

## Getting to the Stadium

Take **Interstate 95** to Commercial Boulevard West. Take that to Northwest 12th Avenue, and make a right. Go straight to the stadium.

*Parking:* The lot holds 3,000 cars.

## Tickets

> New York Yankees
> Fort Lauderdale Stadium
> 5301 Northwest 12th Avenue
> Ft. Lauderdale, FL 33309
> (305) 776-1921

The schedule is available in late November. Most boxes are already sold to previous subscribers, but some reserved seats are available. Season and single-game tickets may be purchased as soon as the schedule is made available. Payment for advance sales must be made by check. Sell-outs occurred on seven occasions in 1987.

*Prices:* Box $8.50; grandstand $7; bleachers $4.

## Team Hotel

> Ft. Lauderdale Marriott-Cypress Creek
> 6650 North Andrews Avenue
> Ft. Lauderdale, FL 33309
> (305) 771-0440

Three New York-area radio shows regularly broadcast from the hotel lobby. Art Rust, Jr. hosts a show on WABC, Dave Sims has one on WNBC, and Richard Neer and Rick Cerone – *not* the catcher – are on WNEW-AM.

## Players' Favorite Leisure Spots
The Yanks favor Gibby's, a steakhouse, Shooter's and Yesterday's, both located on the Intracoastal waterway, Joseph's, a family-oriented establishment, Stan's, and Lou Piniella's favorite place, Frankie's. For a little more excitement, the players enjoy jai-alai, the Hollywood dog track, and harness racing at Pompano Park.

## Previous Spring Training Locations
| | |
|---|---|
| 1903–04 | Atlanta, GA |
| 1905 | Montgomery, AL |
| 1906 | Birmingham, AL |
| 1907–08 | Atlanta, GA |
| 1909 | Macon, GA |
| 1910–11 | Athens, GA |
| 1912 | Atlanta, GA |
| 1913 | Hamilton, Bermuda |
| 1914 | Houston, TX |
| 1915 | Savannah, GA |
| 1916–18 | Macon, GA |
| 1919–20 | Jacksonville, FL |
| 1921 | Shreveport, LA |
| 1922–24 | New Orleans, LA |
| 1925–42 | St. Petersburg, FL |
| 1943 | Asbury Park, NJ |
| 1944–45 | Atlantic City, NJ |
| 1946–50 | St. Petersburg, FL |
| 1951 | Phoenix, AZ |
| 1952–61 | St. Petersburg, FL |
| 1962–present | Ft. Lauderdale, FL |

## Hottest Prospects
The Yankees are one of three teams in the Major Leagues — the Mets and Dodgers are the others — that present an award to the outstanding rookie each spring. It's a way of applauding fine performance during the Grapefruit League season, but it in no way assures a spot on the roster. Indeed, several of the award winners, such as Gordon Windhorn in 1959, never earned further recognition.

The Yankees' rookie prize is called the James P. Dawson Award, established in honor of the *New York Times* sportswriter who covered the Yankees during Spring Training in the '50s.

The writers vote to select the recipient. The first winner, in 1956, was Norm Siebern. Three subsequent winners went on to win Rookie of the Year honors: Tony Kubek in 1957, Tom Tresh in 1962, and Thurman Munson in 1970.

Tresh was in camp in 1960 when the Yankees, third-place finishers the year before, found themselves in the unaccustomed spot of not having to defend a title. But it wasn't Tresh, with his .243 average at Binghamton in 1959, whom the Yankees were counting on. It was Mickey Mantle and the new slugger, Roger Maris, acquired after his third Major League season from Kansas City in exchange for a quartet of Yanks: Hank Bauer, Don Larsen, Norm Siebern, and Marv Throneberry. And Maris didn't disappoint, hitting an even 100 home runs in his first two years in New York, the last breaking Babe Ruth's single-season record of 60, and winning two consecutive MVP awards.

Their big bats notwithstanding, the Yankees were looking for pitching help. In 1960, during Casey Stengel's last season at the helm, they thought John James would be the answer. *The Sporting News* tabbed him the top AL pitching prospect, and he went 5–1 that year. But he never won another game in the Majors. The next season, the Yankees turned to a big right-hander, Roland Sheldon, who had turned in a sparkling 15–1 record at Auburn in 1960. He didn't disappoint, going 11–5 to supplement Maris, Mantle, and a suddenly crack staff of Whitey Ford, Ralph Terry, and second-year hurler Bill Stafford as the Yanks moved back to the top with a World Series win over Cincinnati.

The spring of 1962 saw the addition of four sterling rookies to help New York to a repeat championship. With Kubek in the service, the Yankees brought in young shortstop Tom Tresh, the son of former Major League catcher Mike Tresh. He turned in some shining statistics that year — hitting 20 home runs, driving in 93, and starring in the World Series in his best season in the Majors — and was named AL Rookie of the Year.

Another rookie, one who was not expected to make the team in 1962, was Jim Bouton, who had gone 14–8 with Amarillo the year before. But Bouton went along as the last pitcher for an exhibition game against the Cardinals and, with the game tied in the tenth inning, was put in to finish up. By the fourteenth inning, he was still throwing hard. Catcher John Blanchard came out to instruct him. "Hey, Meat," he told Bouton, "just get the damn ball over and let 'em hit it. I got a golf date and Yogi's got dinner plans." "But John," Bouton replied, "I'm trying to make the team." "You're not going to make the club," Blanchard retorted. "You're only pitching 'cause we don't have anyone else."

Then Blanchard went behind the plate and started telling the Cardinal hitters what to expect. Nevertheless, Bouton won the game and went on to post the best pitching stats in camp that spring. Over the next three years, he won 47 games for the Bombers, including a glittering 21 with a 2.53 ERA the year after Blanchard's rebuke, before arm injuries curtailed his career.

An Amarillo teammate of Bouton, Joe Pepitone, would also make the team in 1962. Based on his solid .316 average in 1961, *The Sporting News* picked Pepitone over Tresh as the rookie to watch. Another fine rookie that year was Phil Linz, who would become Bouton's roommate and was a solid utility infielder the next few years.

For three consecutive years, the Dawson award went to a young outfielder: Arturo Lopez in 1965, Roy White in 1966, and the man tabbed as "the next Mickey Mantle," Bill Robinson, in 1967. Lopez would last just 38 games in the Majors, while Robinson spent just three of his 16 Major League years in pin-stripes, starring most notably for Pittsburgh in the late '70s. But White, coming off a fine 1965 season at Columbus, where he led the International League in hitting, would become a Yankee mainstay in left field for 14 seasons.

In 1968 the sportswriters showed why they were writing for a living rather than judging baseball talent: they bypassed Stan Bahnsen and selected Mike Ferraro as the recipient of the Dawson Award. Ferraro appeared briefly for the Yanks in 1966, hitting .179, and his average slipped even further in 1968. He went to the expansion Mariners in 1969. Bahnsen, who had been an All-American at Nebraska in 1965, appeared in four games for the Yanks in 1966 and had thrown two no-hitters in the minors, one a perfect game for Syracuse in 1967. He was ready for the big time in 1968, posting a 17–12 record for the struggling Yankees and winning the AL Rookie of the Year Award.

Another solid rookie in 1968 was Bobby Cox, who took the third-base job from Charlie Smith. The following year, the Dawson co-winner, Jerry Kenney, won an infield spot, and Cox was out of the Majors until he returned as a coach and manager in Atlanta and Toronto. He is now the Braves' general manager. Bobby Murcer also — and finally — arrived in 1969. He had been up briefly in 1965 and 1966 as a shortstop but couldn't crack the lineup. But for the next six years — a period of frustration in the Bronx — Murcer was the team leader.

The players picked the talent in 1970 when *Sport* magazine, in a poll of Major Leaguers, selected Thurman Munson as the player most likely to win Rookie of the Year honors. It was quite a recommendation for a catcher who had played fewer than 100 games in the minors, and Munson didn't disappoint. He hit .302 that year to win Rookie of the Year. Munson won the MVP award in 1976, becoming the only Yankee to win both. He died when his private plane crashed in the middle of the 1979 season.

Although the Dawson Award was not given in 1971, there were a few candidates available. George Zeber was in camp, as were Frank Baker and Ron Blomberg. Blomberg became the first player ever to go to bat as a DH, in 1973. Rusty Torres came up at the end of 1971 and hit .385 in nine games, giving hope to Yankee followers. Rusty might have been up a year earlier if not for a freak accident. Considered a phenom by the Yankees in 1970, he was asked to do a TV commercial with Johnny Bench, in which Torres would slide into home and Bench would tag him. On the twenty-first take, he tore ligaments in his knee.

The 1975 crop featured three rookies who would go on to star for other teams: outfielder Terry Whitfield, the 1973 Carolina League MVP, and pitchers Scott McGregor, the Yanks' top draft pick in 1972, and Tippy Martinez. The two pitchers went to Baltimore, while Whitfield was traded to San Francisco. But the Yankees got their top rookie of 1976 in a trade: Willie Randolph, who has owned the second-base job ever since, was acquired from Pittsburgh. A number of infielders, including Mickey Klutts, Damaso Garcia, and George Zeber, would come along, only to be traded away because of Randolph's lock on the keystone sack position.

Zeber was awarded the Dawson prize in 1977, as the writers selected him over a young lefty with an inflated Grapefruit League ERA. But Ron Guidry proved that his 1976 Syracuse record of 5–1 with an 0.68 ERA was no fluke. He started the season in the bullpen but moved quickly into the starting rotation and posted a 16–7 record, followed in 1978 by one of the finest years ever produced by a pitcher: 25–3 with a 1.74 ERA, which won him the Cy Young Award.

Mickey Klutts was a good-looking rookie in camp in 1977 and again in 1978. The co-MVP in the International League in 1976, he broke his hand in Spring Training in 1977 and was sent down. Up again, he couldn't crack the Yankees' line-up and was traded in June 1978. From 1978 through 1981 pitchers won the Dawson prize, although none of the four would make their mark with the team. Jim Beattie won in 1978, followed by Paul Mirabella, Mike Griffin, and Gene Nelson.

Rookies have had a hard time breaking into George Steinbrenner's line-up, as the owner who can't tolerate losing has traded for veteran stars and signed free agents. Even Don Mattingly had a long wait. Finally, after four .300-plus years in the minors, he seemed ready in 1983. The 1980 Southern League MVP, an All-Star in every league in which he played, the Yankees' minor league player of the year in 1981, Mattingly had "can't miss" stenciled across his chest. He was in the line-up on opening day in 1983 but was sent down to punish International League pitchers for two months when the Yankees moved Ken Griffey to first to make room for newcomer free agent Steve Kemp. That arrangement didn't last long, and Mattingly was back in late June, hitting .283 for the year. He lived up to his billing the next year, hitting .343 and driving in 110 runs. Mattingly's 1987 season was full of home run milestones. First he tied Dale Long's mark by hitting at least one homer in eight straight games. Then, on September 29, he hit his sixth grand slam of the year, breaking the single-season record of five held by the Cubs' Ernie Banks (1955) and the Orioles' Jim Gentile (1961).

No Yankee rookie since 1983 has made much of an impact on the team. Catcher Scott Bradley and pitcher Bob Tewksbury had fine springs in 1985 and 1986, respectively, but were never regulars, though Tewksbury made several starts before being traded to Pittsburgh. With Mattingly at first, it was a foregone conclusion that the 1987 Dawson winner, Orestes Destrade, would be back in Columbus before the season started.

### Annual James P. Dawson Award Winners
1960  John James, pitcher
1961  Roland Sheldon, pitcher
1962  Tom Tresh, shortstop
1963  Pedro Gonzalez, second base
1964  Pete Mikkelsen, pitcher
1965  Arturo Lopez, outfield
1966  Roy White, outfield
1967  Bill Robinson, outfield
1968  Mike Ferraro, third base
1969  Jerry Kenney, shortstop; Bill Burbach, pitcher
1970  John Ellis, catcher
1971  none

1972 Rusty Torres, outfield
1973 Otto Velez, outfield
1974 Tom Buskey, pitcher
1975 Tippy Martinez, pitcher
1976 Willie Randolph, second base
1977 George Zeber, second base
1978 Jim Beattie, pitcher
1979 Paul Mirabella, pitcher
1980 Mike Griffin, pitcher
1981 Gene Nelson, pitcher
1982 Andre Robertson, shortstop
1983 Don Mattingly, first base
1984 Jose Rijo pitcher
1985 Scott Bradley, catcher
1986 Bob Tewksbury, pitcher
1987 Orestes Destrade, first base

## AL Rookies of the Year
1962 Tom Tresh, shortstop
1968 Stan Bahnsen, pitcher
1970 Thurman Munson, catcher
1981 Dave Righetti

## Prospect to Watch in 1988
*Jay Buehner*, *outfield*. A classic home run hitter with power to all fields, Buehner was one of the top three sluggers in the International League in 1987. He is also a fine fielder and had possibly the best outfield arm in the League.

# CHAPTER 5

*Theme Park Group*

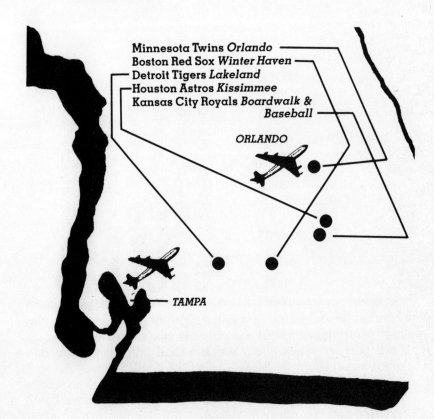

Minnesota Twins *Orlando*
Boston Red Sox *Winter Haven*
Detroit Tigers *Lakeland*
Houston Astros *Kissimmee*
Kansas City Royals *Boardwalk & Baseball*

*ORLANDO*

*TAMPA*

THE AREA SOUTH and west of Orlando on Interstate 4 is becoming Florida's alternative to Southern California as a family-oriented, formatted vacation destination. Sparked by SeaWorld and Disney World/Epcot Center, the area is now adding movie studios (Disney and Universal), complete with tours. Its newest big theme park is Boardwalk & Baseball. Orlando is well on its way to becoming an eastern and inland version of Los Angeles, *with* the amusement centers and freeways and *without* the ocean and mountains. Its international airport is convenient for all the Theme Park Group teams.

## THEME PARK DISTANCES

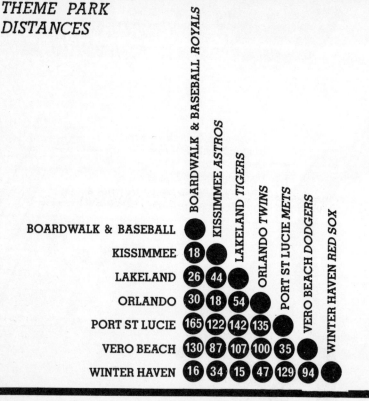

| | BOARDWALK & BASEBALL ROYALS | KISSIMMEE ASTROS | LAKELAND TIGERS | ORLANDO TWINS | PORT ST LUCIE METS | VERO BEACH DODGERS | WINTER HAVEN RED SOX |
|---|---|---|---|---|---|---|---|
| **BOARDWALK & BASEBALL** | ● | | | | | | |
| **KISSIMMEE** | 18 | ● | | | | | |
| **LAKELAND** | 26 | 44 | ● | | | | |
| **ORLANDO** | 30 | 18 | 54 | ● | | | |
| **PORT ST LUCIE** | 165 | 122 | 142 | 135 | ● | | |
| **VERO BEACH** | 130 | 87 | 107 | 100 | 35 | ● | |
| **WINTER HAVEN** | 16 | 34 | 15 | 47 | 129 | 94 | ● |

Judged only by the amount of Spring Training action, the area is a little thin. But neutral fans would pick this group if their party requires some less baseball-intensive, nonbeach amusement choices.

The Twins play in a charming little stadium in the middle of town, with Orlando's large football stadium (the Citrus Bowl) looming over the right-field fence.

The Astros' camp in Kissimmee is an ultramodern facility with ultramodern security sensibilities that make the players and the practice sessions less accessible to the fans than in most of the other spring facilities.

The Red Sox in Winter Haven and the Tigers in Lakeland — one to one and a half hours down the road from the heart of the Theme Park area near Disney World — represent the "old style" of Spring Training within this group: ballparks that have been there for a while, accessible practice fields, a feeling of tradition and history.

A fan who is willing to drive a little bit farther to broaden the baseball scope of a Theme Park Group visit can get to the nearest Gulf Coast teams (the Cards in St. Petersburg, for example) or to Dodgertown in Vero Beach on the East Coast in a couple of hours.

## THEME PARK AIRPLAY

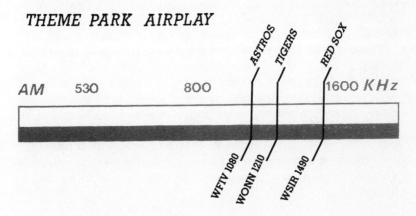

The Royals' just-constructed facility within Boardwalk & Baseball is similar to the Astros' base in Kissimmee — an environment that tends to insulate the fans from the charm of the Spring Training experience. But then again, there is a large baseball-oriented amusement park right there on the premises.

Boardwalk & Baseball, aside from some pretty standard amusement park features, has a variety of attractions for the baseball fan. Probably the most interesting is a 100-item exhibit called "A Taste of Cooperstown," a sampling of memorabilia provided by the National Baseball Hall of Fame, including uniforms and equipment used by a pantheon of stars: Ruth, Gehrig, Williams, Spahn, Aaron, up to present-day heroes like Yastrzemski, Seaver, Carlton, and Rose. Since Cooperstown itself is several hours' drive from the nearest

Major League City, it is useful that Spring Training visitors can avail themselves of this sample of material in the center of Major League action.

Boardwalk & Baseball also features a 27-minute film sponsored by Kodak called *The Eternal Game*, batting and pitching machines, special edition baseball cards created by Topps, and an opportunity to create a baseball card of yourself.

If you stay in any of the dozens of hotels and motels at the freeway interchanges near Disney World, you are within a fairly small triangle whose corners are defined by the Twins', Astros', and Royals' ballparks. These corners are all within a half-hour of each other, with the Tigers and Red Sox only a little farther away to the west. The theme-park action — Disney World, Epcot Center, Wet 'n' Wild, SeaWorld, and Malibu Grand Prix Racing — is practically outside the front door. Regular and easy bus service to all the theme parks from Orlando-area hotels makes it possible to split one rental car between fans and nonfans traveling together to this team group.

The trade-off that the fan makes basing in the Theme Park Group is losing the ocean. Although you can reach the Gulf Coast driving two hours west (and pass Busch Gardens on the way) or the Atlantic driving an hour or so east (and end up right near Cape Canaveral), most people don't go on vacation to drive 50–100 miles to the beach. The lure of the amusement parks — particularly Disney World and Boardwalk & Baseball — is the most enticing element, aside from interest in one of the Theme Park Group teams, beckoning a Spring Training visitor to this area.

## Batting Cages

Orlando: Boardwalk & Baseball, at the intersection of Interstate 4 and Highway 27, (800) 826-1929 (U.S.), (800) 367-2249 (Florida), (813) 424-2424 (Canada); baseball and softball cages.

Orlando: Malibu Castle Park, 5863 American Way, (305) 351-7093; five baseball cages, three softball cages, open 10 A.M. to 11 P.M. Sunday to Thursday, 10 A.M. to 11 P.M. Friday and Saturday.

Kissimmee: Kissimmee Driving Range (305) 847-6502, three baseball cages, open 2 to 8 P.M. seven days a week.

## Sunny-Day Alternatives

*Disney World/Epcot Center,* Lake Buena Vista: The ever-popular theme park and Experimental Prototype City of Tomorrow.

Walt Disney World Central Reservations, PO Box 40, Lake Buena Vista 32830. (305) 824-8000.

*Audubon House,* Maitland: Large aviary, gallery, gift shop. 1101 Audubon Way, Maitland. (305) 647-2615.

*Scenic Boat Ride,* Winter Park: Hour-long tour of Kraft Azalea Gardens, the Isle of Sicily, large estates on Lake Osceola, Winter Park. (305) 644-4056.

*Church Street Station,* Orlando: Hot-air balloon rides, restaurants, antique shops. 129 West Church Street, Orlando. (305) 422-2434.

*Airboat Rentals U-Drive,* Kissimmee: Tour the swamps in a rented boat or canoe. U.S. 192, six miles east of Interstate 4, Kissimmee. (305) 847-3672.

*Gatorland Zoo,* Kissimmee: World's largest alligator farm, with 4,000 gators and crocs; cypress swamp with boardwalk trail. U.S. 441, Kissimmee. (305) 857-3845.

*Cypress Gardens,* Winter Haven: Water-skiing shows, zoo, Florida's only ice-skating show. Three miles southeast of Winter Haven on County Road 540, in Cypress Gardens. (813) 324-2111.

## Rainy-Day Activities

*Morse Gallery of Art,* Winter Park: World's largest collection of Tiffany glass and jewelry. 133 East Welbourne Avenue, Winter Park. (305) 644-3638.

*Beal-Maltbie Shell Museum,* Winter Park: More than 2 million shells; samples of almost every known shell. Holt Avenue, Rollins College, Winter Park. (305) 646-2364.

*Orlando Science Center and John Young Planetarium,* Orlando: Fun, educational activities relating to computers, electricity, space travel; daily planetarium shows. Loch Haven Park, 810 East Rollins Street, Orlando. (305) 896-7151.

*Places of Learning,* Orlando: Free activities like a giant chessboard, a map of the U.S. that takes up an acre, and a large selection of children's books and games in the "Parent's Store." 6825 Academic Drive, Orlando. (305) 345-1038.

*Tupperware World Headquarters,* Kissimmee: Model kitchen with demonstration of ways to use Tupperware; Gallery of Historic Food Containers; free Tupperware sample at end of free tour. U.S. 441, Kissimmee. (305) 847-3111.

*Xanadu,* Kissimmee: 15-room "Home of the Future" with polyurethane construction, computer-selected meals, and a waterfall spa. At the intersection of U.S. 192 and S.R. 535, Kissimmee. (305) 396-1992.

***Medieval Times Dinner Tournament:*** Eleventh-century banquet, complete with jousting knights, serving wenches, delicious food, and no silverware. U.S. 192, Kissimmee. Toll-free nationwide: (800) 327-4024; toll-free in Florida: (800) 432-0768; in Kissimmee, call 396-1518.

## Day Trips

To the north: ***Silver Springs,*** near Ocala, is less than two hours away from Orlando. Glass-bottom boat tours of the world's largest limestone artesian spring. Jungle cruise, deer park, antique car collection. One mile east of Ocala on S.R. 40, just off Interstate 75, in Silver Springs. (904) 236-2121.

To the east: ***Kennedy Space Center*** at Cape Canaveral, with frequent tours, is an easy drive from Orlando (about an hour).

# BOSTON RED SOX

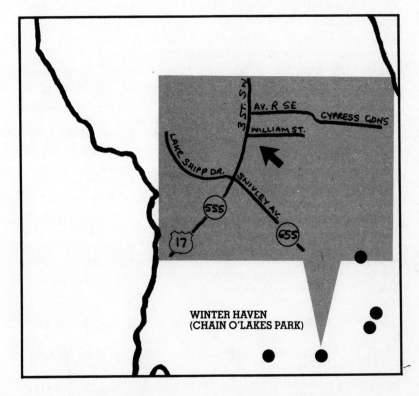

**WINTER HAVEN
(CHAIN O'LAKES PARK)**

■ **Current site:**
Chain O'Lakes Park,
Cypress Gardens
Boulevard,
Winter Haven, FL 33880.
(813) 293-3900
■ **Dimensions:** 340' left
and right; 420' center
■ **Seating:** 4,800

■ **Built:** 1966
■ **Off-season use:** Winter
Haven Red Sox, Florida
State League (Class A)
■ **Practice site:** At the
park daily at 10:30 A.M.
■ **Game time:** 1:05 P.M.
■ **Most convenient airport:**
Orlando or Tampa

Chain O'Lakes Park was built in 1966 and has been undergoing expansion and renovation during the last several years. A city-owned park leased by the Red Sox, it also hosts baseball fantasy camps, such as the one run by Denny Doyle, and has been the site of the Red Sox's entire minor league operation since 1970, when it was relocated from Ocala.

Located in Winter Haven, the park is a relatively long way from the hottest vacation spots in Florida: 30 to 45 minutes from Epcot and Boardwalk & Baseball, and at least that far from the Tampa-St. Pete area. Once you've found Winter Haven, you won't have much trouble locating Chain O'Lakes Park.

The path from the parking lot brings you first to the ticket office behind the third-base stands. The behind-home-plate entrance is up a hill. If you stay on the parking lot level around the hill, you'll come to a practice field where minor leaguers are often hard at work while the Major Leaguers take batting practice in the stadium. A regular feature of the Red Sox camp is the presence of Hall of Famer Ted Williams, who owns a hotel in Winter Haven and often drops by to work with the young hitters.

The batting cages are down the right-field line beyond the point where a fan can catch a good glimpse of them. Batting practice home runs are quite catchable, however, from behind the left-field fence, if you spend some time there before you enter the park. Autograph opportunities sometimes occur after the game when players may emerge from behind home plate. The players' parking is behind the right-field fence in an area fenced off from the fans.

Ten rows of wooden bleachers extend from the extreme left-field corner to about 50 feet beyond third base. The "permanent" seats, five rows of boxes and thirteen rows of seats behind them, wrap around the infield as far as the edge of the infield dirt down each line. From the middle of the baseline out, the last eight rows of seats are unbacked.

Oddly enough in such an intimate and informal park, there are obstructions. Telephone poles that serve as light standards are on the field in foul ground at the extreme outside corner of the box seats down each line. The poles interfere with the view into the outfield from the last two sections of boxes and the general admission seats behind them. Only a narrow band of seats from the edge of the screen to about 30 feet from the bases is totally unobstructed.

## Getting to the Stadium

Get off **Route 27** onto Cypress Gardens Boulevard (**Route 540**). Travel east on **Route 540** for six miles, and you can see the stadium.

*Parking:* The stadium parking lot has a capacity of 1,800 and is never full.

## Tickets

> Chain O'Lakes Park
> Cypress Gardens Boulevard
> Winter Haven, FL 33880
> (813) 293-3900

The team's schedule is available in November, and both season tickets and single-game tickets go on sale on January 15. The box office opens at the time of the team's first workout, February 23. Until then, tickets may be ordered by mail. Payment on all mail-order tickets must be made by personal check. Nine of the Red Sox home exhibitions were sold out in 1987.

*Prices:* Box $6; reserved $5; general admission $4; children $2.

## Team Hotel

> Holiday Inn
> U.S. 17
> Winter Haven, FL 33880
> (813) 294-4451

There are occasional live remote broadcasts from the lobby.

## Players' Favorite Leisure Spots

There are several Winter Haven restaurants, representing a variety of styles, frequented by the players. Christy's, Sundowner and Nostalgia are all semiformal. For Italian food, there is Mario's, a formal restaurant, and Tony's, which is family-oriented and less expensive. Other informal eateries are Gary's Harborside, which features seafood, and Harieston's, featuring Cajun cuisine. Rumours Lounge and Howard Johnson's are next to the Holiday Inn. The Pool Bar is in the Holiday Inn itself.

## Previous Spring Training Locations

| | |
|---|---|
| 1901 | Charlottesville, VA |
| 1902 | Augusta, GA |
| 1903–06 | Macon, GA |
| 1907–08 | Little Rock, AR |
| 1909–10 | Hot Springs, AR |

1911        Redondo Beach, CA
1912–18     Hot Springs, AR
1919        Tampa, FL
1920–23     Hot Springs, AR
1924        San Antonio, TX
1925–27     New Orleans, LA
1928–29     Bradenton, FL
1930–31     Pensacola, FL
1932        Savannah, GA
1933–42     Sarasota, FL
1943        Medford, MA
1944        Baltimore, MD
1945        Pleasantville, NJ
1946–58     Sarasota, FL
1959–65     Scottsdale, AZ
1966–present   Winter Haven, FL

## Hottest Prospects

In 1960 the Red Sox, under Pinky Higgins, were in the midst of their youth movement, a changing of the guard. Since the contending years of the late '40s, the Sox had not managed a finish higher than third. 1960 would be no different, nor would any of the succeeding years until 1967, when the Red Sox, coming off a ninth-place finish in 1966, would top the American League.

Although named the best-looking prospect in the 1960 camp, Carl Yastrzemski had to wait a year in the wings, since there was still a fellow named Williams finishing up a career in left field that spanned four decades. Yaz had another good spring in 1961 and assumed Williams's mantle. Don Schwall, the 6'6" hurler who had posted a 16–9 record at Minneapolis the previous year, also earned a promotion in 1961. Sent down until mid-May, Schwall came back to post a 15–7 record, by far his best Major League season, and was named AL Rookie of the Year. He was the only Red Sox player to appear in the second 1961 All-Star game, a 1–1 tie in Fenway Park.

The 1961 season produced two other promising rookie pitchers, Galen Cisco and Wilbur Wood, whose careers elsewhere moved in opposite directions. Cisco went south to suffer with the expansion Mets, losing 15 and 19 games in 1963 and 1964. Wood neither won nor saved a game in his first four seasons despite his fiendish left-handed knuckleball; he then garnered 164 victories the next 13 years, including four 20-win seasons in a row for the White Sox.

The 1962 season produced another 6'6" rookie pitcher who became a Boston legend. Dick Radatz only pitched a little more than four seasons for some weak Red Sox teams, but he fully earned his nickname: The Monster. The dominant relief pitcher of his era, he saved 100 games for the Sox — 35 percent of the team's victories from 1962 to 1965 — and averaged better than one strikeout per inning.

The spring of 1964 produced a remarkable 10 rookies who went north but only one would be memorable. Tony Conigliaro, who grew up just north of Boston, was an immediate star. The youngest player ever to hit 100 home runs, he had a swing tailor-made for Fenway Park, and his fame seemed assured. But Conigliaro's destiny was tragic instead. Hit in the face by a Jack Hamilton fastball in mid-1967, he missed the following year with blurred vision. He recovered valiantly the next two years, hitting a career-high 36 homers in 1970 to average more than 25 for his first six seasons. But he never fully overcame the injury and floundered thereafter. A greater tragedy awaited him after retirement: a massive stroke left him crippled and paralyzed, though not broken. His courageous efforts at rehabilitation in the loving care of his family have inspired Boston fans more than anything he ever did on the field.

The top prospect of 1965 was Rico Petrocelli, who would treat fans to 13 solid seasons at short and third. Joining him in Fenway was a lanky rookie pitcher, 6'5" Jim Lonborg, who made the jump after one year in the minors. Lonborg's career in Boston was to be meteoric. He won the Cy Young Award in 1967, after leading the Impossible Dream team into the World Series with 22 wins. He broke his leg skiing the following winter and never regained his form in Boston, though he enjoyed several productive years in Philadelphia.

The Red Sox had a bumper crop of rookies in 1966. Joe Foy was named in a *Sport* magazine poll as most likely to win Rookie of the Year. Foy was the 1965 International League MVP and Rookie of the Year and was *The Sporting News'* Minor League Player of the Year. Given that build-up, his merely competent three years in Boston could only be disappointing to the demanding Fenway faithful. The Bosox also had the 1965 Eastern League's MVP, George Scott. He blasted 27 rookie homers to earn his nickname: The Boomer. Reggie Smith debuted as a starter at second base in the championship year of 1967 but soon backpedaled to center field, where he stayed seven years. And Sparky Lyle also arrived for the Impossible Dream, recording the first of his 238 career saves. Lyle was traded to the Yankees straight up for Danny Cater during Spring Training in 1972, a deal that horrified Sox fans who remembered the loss of Babe Ruth 52 years earlier.

In 1969 rookie outfielders Billy Conigliaro (Tony's brother) and Joe Lahoud were supposed to compete for the one remaining outfield job, but both did so well that starter Jose Tartabull was sent to the minors before opening day. Mike Nagy was the surprise of 1970, making the jump to the Red Sox after just 39 games in the pros. He fashioned a 12–2 record for the best winning percentage in baseball and was runner-up for Rookie of the Year. Like Schwall's, his first year was by far his best. Military service limited his appearances the next season and cut his record to 6–5, and he won only two games thereafter.

Doug Griffin was easily the best Bosox rookie in 1971. Handed the second-base job, he hit .307 in the spring and .244 during the regular season while performing brilliantly in the field. The following year the Red Sox showcased a true prize. After hitting just .212 in the Grapefruit League, Carlton Fisk hit .293 during the season and led the league in triples. Despite leading the AL in errors by a catcher (15), he won the Gold Glove. Fisk was the first unanimous choice for AL Rookie of the Year.

The spring of 1974 was a rosy one for the Red Sox. Rick Burleson shone: he hit .300 and took over the shortstop job in mid-May, batting .284 during the season to be named the Red Sox top rookie. Juan Beniquez hit .348 in spring camp, and .267 during the year while filling in capably in the outfield. But 1974 paled beside 1975.

No two rookie teammates have ever broken in with more resounding performances than Fred Lynn and Jim Rice. The fact that 1975 was an exciting, pennant-winning year made their debuts even more special. Lynn had not even been in camp in 1974, but he came up at the end of that year to give Fenway fans a taste of things to come. He hit .419 in 15 games and fielded like the All-Star he would soon be. The next year, he was the first player to win both Rookie of the Year and the MVP. Fred hit 21 homers and a rookie-record 47 doubles, while knocking in 105 runs. He also had a .331 average. The other stick of rookie dynamite was Jim Rice, who had prepared for the Majors with consecutive International League triple crowns, in 1973 and 1974. A DH for half the year before moving into left field, Rice hit .309 with 102 RBI and 22 home runs. A broken wrist in

September kept him out of the playoff series in which the Sox dethroned the Oakland A's, winners of the three previous World Series. He was sorely missed in the dramatic seven-game Series loss to Cincinnati.

Strong-hitting Butch Hobson and Pitcher Don Aase were the top prospects in 1976. Over the winter, Aase threw two no-hitters in the Florida Instructional League. In his first spring game, he got Rod Carew to hit into a triple play, but he would have to wait until 1977 to break into the Majors. His excellent 6–2 rookie season made him valuable trade bait, and he was dealt to the Angels for second baseman Jerry Remy. With its short left-field wall, Fenway Park has been inhospitable to most lefthanded pitchers. Indeed, the Red Sox have developed precious few who have lasted in Boston. Many more needed a change of scene to reach their potential, as exhibited by John Tudor and Bobby Ojeda. The top rookies in 1979 and 1981, they now star for St. Louis and the New York Mets as they never could for the Sox.

Two players developed by the Sox farm system are currently dominating the American League, one at the plate and one on the mound. Wade Boggs had five .300-plus seasons in the minors, the best being his last one at Pawtucket when he led the International League in hitting with a .335 average, before the Red Sox finally deemed him ready in 1982. He improved on this in the Majors. Taking over for Carney Lansford when the third baseman was injured, he never left the lineup, moving to first when Lansford returned. His .349 average was the highest ever by an American League rookie (in at least 100 games) and he finished third in the Rookie of the Year voting, behind Kent Hrbek and Cal Ripken. Lansford was traded to Oakland for Tony Armas after the 1982 season, and Boggs has been a fixture at third ever since — and a terror at the plate, leading the league in hitting four of the last five years. His .350+ lifetime average is now fourth in Major League history.

Two years after Boggs debuted, Roger Clemens was a non-roster invitee to Spring Training. Clemens had won the final game in the 1983 College World Series and then went 7–2 in two stops in the minors, posting ERAs of 1.24 and 1.38. He started the 1984 season in Pawtucket and then came north to post a 9–4 record for Boston. He won the 1986 and 1987 Cy Young Awards and will, barring injury, long be one of the league's dominant pitchers.

The Red Sox' 1987 camp may have provided the building blocks for years to come. The most notable rookie contributors were Ellis Burks, the fleet centerfielder, and outfielder/DH Mike Greenwell, whose .300+ average and clutch hitting drew raves. DH Sam Horn, catcher John Marzano, and outfielder Todd Benzinger rounded out a quintet of prize rookies, all of whom were starters by the end of the summer.

## Top Rookies Each Spring

| 1960 | Carl Yastrzemski, outfield |
|------|----------------------------|
| 1961 | Carl Yastrzemski, outfield |
| 1962 | Dalton Jones, second base |
| 1963 | Dalton Jones, second base |
| 1964 | Rico Petrocelli, shortstop |
| 1965 | Rico Petrocelli, shortstop |
| 1966 | Joe Foy, third base |
| 1967 | Reggie Smith, second base/outfield |
| 1968 | Joe Lahoud, outfield |
| 1969 | Billy Conigliaro, outfield |
| 1970 | Luis Alvarado, shortstop; Ken Brett, pitcher |
| 1971 | Doug Griffin, second base |
| 1972 | Carlton Fisk, catcher |
| 1973 | Mario Guerrero, shortstop |
| 1974 | Rick Burleson, shortstop; Juan Beniquez, outfield |
| 1975 | Don Aase, pitcher |
| 1976 | Don Aase, pitcher |
| 1977 | Bob Stanley, pitcher |
| 1978 | Bobby Sprowl, pitcher; Ted Cox, third base |
| 1979 | John Tudor, pitcher |
| 1980 | Dave Stapleton, second base |
| 1981 | Bob Ojeda, pitcher |
| 1982 | Wade Boggs, third base; Bruce Hurst, pitcher |
| 1983 | Mike Brown, pitcher |
| 1984 | Roger Clemens, pitcher; Al Nipper, pitcher |
| 1985 | Steve Lyons, third base |
| 1986 | Wes Gardner, pitcher |
| 1987 | Ellis Burks, outfield |

## AL Rookies of the Year

| 1961 | Don Schwall, pitcher |
|------|----------------------|
| 1972 | Carlton Fisk, catcher |
| 1975 | Fred Lynn, outfield |

## Prospects to Watch in 1988

**John Leister,** *pitcher.* While most of the Pawtucket team in the International League moved north to the Red Sox in mid-season, a few fine prospects were left. The most outstanding was former Stanford righthander Leister. He had a brief and unsuccessful trial with the Red Sox early in the season but recovered well when sent back down and was 11–4 through August.

**Jody Reed,** *shortstop.* He batted close to .300 all year at Pawtucket and hit well above that when brought up to the Red Sox at the end of the year. Reed will strongly challenge incumbent Spike Owen for the starting shortstop job in 1988.

# DETROIT TIGERS

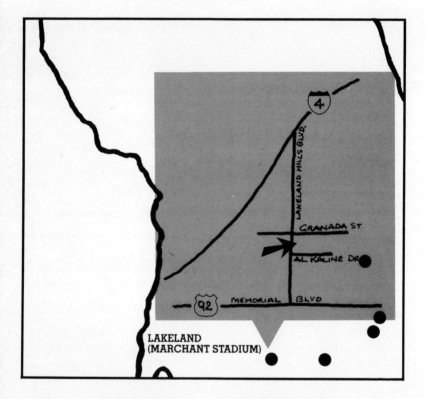

LAKELAND HILLS BLVD.

GRANADA ST

AL KALINE DR.

MEMORIAL BLVD

LAKELAND
(MARCHANT STADIUM)

■ **Current site:**
Joker Marchant Stadium
Lakeland Hills Boulevard
Lakeland, FL 33801
(813) 682-1401
■ **Dimensions:** 340' left
and right; 420' center
■ **Seating:** 4,200
■ **Built:** 1966

■ **Off-season use:**
Lakeland Tigers, Florida
State League (Class A)
■ **Practice site:** At the
stadium daily at 10:00 A.M.
■ **Game times:** 1:30 P.M.
(day), 7:30 P.M. (night)
■ **Most convenient airport:**
Orlando or Tampa

The Tigers have trained continuously at Lakeland since 1934, except for the World War II years. Joker Marchant Stadium was built in 1966 by the city of Lakeland and was named after the city's long-time director of Parks and Recreation.

In many ways, a visit to Joker Marchant Stadium is the quintessential Spring Training experience. The Tigers are rooted in Lakeland; and the town, not on the coasts and not in the Disney World orbit, revolves around the Tigers while they are there.

The stadium is being remodeled for 1988, to include left-field bleachers. Reserved seats are among the most difficult to obtain in Spring Training, but don't let that scare you off. There are plenty of general-admission and standing-room tickets, and if you get there early, you can get a pretty decent seat.

The Tigers tend to attract their legendary veterans to Spring Training; fans often get to see the likes of Al Kaline and Bill Freehan in uniform again around the cage in Lakeland. Autographs can be garnered along the front railing of the boxes and bleachers, before and after the games. In addition, players are accessible near the Tigers' clubhouse down the left-field line and around the nearby batting cages.

### Getting to the Stadium
Take **Interstate 4** east and exit at **Memorial Boulevard.** Follow **600-A**, which is also U.S. 92, east for three and a half miles to Lakeland Hills Boulevard. Then go north to the stadium driveway, which is named Al Kaline Drive.

Or take **I-4** west; take the second **Route 33** exit to 600-A and continue as above.

*Parking:* The lot has a capacity of 1,500, but parking in the area is virtually limitless. There are twelve acres of parking on runways of an old Air Force base nearby.

### Tickets
> Detroit Tigers
> Joker Marchant Stadium
> Lakeland Hills Boulevard
> Lakeland, FL 33801
> (813) 682-1401

Printed schedules for the exhibition season are available in October. Even then, however, there are no available box seats. Bleachers and general-admission seats are available on a first-come, first-served basis. Single-game seats go on sale March 1. All purchases must be made at the box office. No mail or phone

orders are accepted. Seven games were sell-outs in 1987.
   *Prices:* General admission $4; bleachers $2.50.

## Team Hotel
   Holiday Inn Central
   910 East Memorial Boulevard
   Lakeland, FL 33801
   (813) 682-0101

## Players' Favorite Leisure Spots
There is only one main drag in Lakeland, South Florida
Boulevard, with every fast-food restaurant imaginable, as well
as Foxfire, a restaurant and club. Also located here are Howard
Johnson's, Bennigan's, Hooter's, and Sweetwater's.

## Previous Spring Training Locations
| | |
|---|---|
| 1901 | Detroit, MI |
| 1902 | Ypsilanti, MI |
| 1903–04 | Shreveport, LA |
| 1905–07 | Augusta, GA |
| 1908 | Hot Springs, AZ |
| 1909–10 | San Antonio, TX |
| 1911–12 | Monroe, LA |
| 1913–15 | Gulfport, MS |
| 1916–18 | Waxahachie, TX |
| 1919–20 | Macon, GA |
| 1921 | San Antonio, TX |
| 1922–26 | Augusta, GA |
| 1927–28 | San Antonio, TX |
| 1929 | Phoenix, AZ |
| 1930 | Tampa, FL |
| 1931 | Sacramento, CA |
| 1932 | Palo Alto, CA |
| 1933 | San Antonio, TX |
| 1934–42 | Lakeland, FL |
| 1943–45 | Evansville, IN |
| 1946–present | Lakeland, FL |

## Hottest Prospects
The Tigers had finished no higher than fourth place in the regular season since 1950, and 1960 would be no different. They
finished sixth. But they acquired untried first-baseman Norm
Cash from Cleveland for Steve Demeter just after Spring

Training, a steal if ever there was one. Demeter got five at bats for Cleveland without a hit, his last turn in the Majors. Cash was an immediate star, hitting .286 his first year in Detroit, then a league-leading .361 with 41 homers and 132 RBI, pacing the 1961 Tigers to a club-tying 101 victories. That would have won the Triple Crown and MVP in many other years, but Cash happened to run up against Roger Maris's record-setting 61 homers and 142 RBI, which helped keep the Yankees eight games up on the Tigers. Cash's brilliant season — one of the finest ever produced — is often overlooked as a result.

Third-baseman Steve Boros was touted by *The Sporting News* as the best of the Tigers' 1960 spring prospects, but he spent the year in Denver, finishing the year hitting .317 and leading the Pacific Coast League in RBI. One of his teammates at Denver was Jake Wood. Both were in the starting infield for Detroit in 1961.

*The Sporting News* picked Dick Egan as the Tigers' brightest prospect in the 1963 camp, overlooking the man who would be their catcher for fourteen years. Bill Freehan hit .283 at Denver in 1961 and took over the catcher's job at Detroit in 1963, with a fielding percentage of .995, a rifle arm, and a powerful bat. Freehan would soon be catching two of the league's finest pitchers, who joined him on the roster in 1963. Mickey Lolich had impressed the previous spring; he went 5–9 his first year up but won 18 the next and was on his way. Denny McLain took a season longer to develop, but the wait was worth it as he won 108 games from 1965–69, including 31 in 1968 (for the MVP) and 24 in 1969, copping the Cy Young Award each year.

Based on Willie Horton's .326 average with the Tigers at the end of the 1963 season, he looked to be 1964's best prospect. But Horton slumped and was sent down to Syracuse for more seasoning. He was back to stay in 1965, hitting 29 homers and knocking in 104 runs in one of the best years of his long career. His 1964 teammate, Jim Northrup, came up with Horton in 1965, but he, too, found Major League pitching a puzzle and ended his first year hitting .205. "The Silver Fox," as he was known, soon got his bearings, and he, Horton, and Freehan were leaders of the 1968 championship team. Mickey Stanley, promoted for good in 1966, patrolled center field.

Rookies the next few years had a hard time making the Tigers' powerful squad. Les Cain was a spring sensation on the mound in 1970 but was still demoted for further seasoning, though he returned to win 12 games. In the regular season, Elliot Maddox had a fine year and was voted the Tigers' Rookie of the Year. He was rewarded by being traded along with Denny McLain, who was by then out of favor, to the Washington Senators for two players who would perform brilliantly in their stead: pitcher Joe Coleman and third-baseman Aurelio Rodriguez.

The 1974 Tiger rookie award went to Ron LeFlore, who made the jump to the Majors in less than two seasons after being paroled from Southern Michigan prison. At 26, LeFlore was an old rookie. He had not played baseball in high school and made an impression on scouts while playing for the prison team. LeFlore started the 1974 season with Lakeland. There, he hit .339, with 79 runs scored in 93 games, and was brought up to the Tigers when Mickey Stanley broke his hand. Centerfield was his, and blazing speed made him an added threat at the plate.

Tom Veryzer was one of the most heralded rookies in years when he came to camp in 1975. The Tigers' number one pick in the June 1971 draft, Veryzer was an MVP in his first year in pro ball and an All-Star the next two. He had brief stints with the Tigers in 1973 and 1974 and would stick in 1975, though he never hit as well as expected. The best of the young pitchers, Vern Ruhle, went 11–12 and shared the best rookie label.

Who can forget 1976, the Year of the Bird? The Tigers didn't even have Mark Fidrych on their spring roster though the most colorful character to hit the Majors since Dizzy Dean impressed enough to make the team. Manager Ralph Houk kept him on the bench for five weeks because he didn't think Fidrych was ready. The brilliant rookie soon changed that opinion. He would talk to the ball, talk to his teammates after a good play, smooth the mound with his hands, and was so refreshingly eccentric that the whole country cheered his success. Fidrych posted a 19–9 record to easily win Rookie of the Year honors. But the following year, tendonitis cut short his marvelous career and he won just 10 more games for the Tigers. Sadly for baseball fans, the Bird was gone from the Majors five years after he started, confused and despondent that the game he loved so much could have betrayed him.

The number one pick in the nation in the January 1976 draft was Steve Kemp, who had a "can't miss" label in the spring of 1977 after his .386 finish for Evansville. He was in the starting lineup in his rookie year and had some excellent years for the

Tigers before being traded to the White Sox for Chet Lemon after the 1981 season. But the surprise of the spring and regular season was, like Fidrych, a nonroster pitcher. Dave Rozema, 12–4 at Montgomery, had a glittering 15–7 record for the Bengals and was named the AL's top rookie pitcher. It was, by far, his best of eight seasons in Detroit.

The 1978 season's rookie crop could arguably be called the best in decades for the Tigers, and perhaps for any team. Leading the group was smooth-fielding second-baseman Lou Whittaker, up from Montgomery, who hit .285 and won the American League's Rookie of the Year award. At shortstop was his partner from Montgomery, Alan Trammell, who hit .268 for the Tigers and made the AL All-Rookie team. They have remained the league's top keystone combination and going into 1987 had the same lifetime batting average of .281. Evansville's contribution was the AL's top catcher, Lance Parrish, who struggled his first year with the Tigers, hitting .219. But he hit his stride the following season, raising his average to .276, and was the AL's All-Star catcher several seasons before opting for free-agency in 1987.

All eyes were on Kirk Gibson in the spring of 1980. Picked by *Sports Illustrated* as the year's best prospect, and possessing that rare combination of blazing speed and real power, he began by living up to his billing. He was leading the Tigers with 9 homers when he injured his wrist on June 7 and never returned to action. Gibson has proved almost as fragile as he is talented. When he got hurt again two years later, 1982's top prospect, Glenn Wilson, filled in capably. Wilson was traded to Philadelphia during Spring Training 1984 for relief pitcher Willie Hernandez, who would key the Tigers' unbelievable 35–5 start that year en route to a divisional run-away and eventual World Series victory.

Howard Johnson arrived in 1982, though he wouldn't start at third for two years, and then only sporadically. He was traded to the Mets and in 1987 set the National League record for home runs by a switch hitter.

Pitcher Eric King, obtained by the Tigers in an October 1985 trade with San Francisco, was the best-looking rookie of the 1986 crop, his 11 wins the most by a Tiger rookie since Rozema's 15 in 1977. Also included in that trade was a young catcher who would make Detroit fans, at least in 1987, forget Lance Parrish's free agent defection. Matt Nokes surprised many people by hitting close to .300 and with power, and by having as fine a season as any catcher in baseball.

## Top Rookies Each Spring

1960    Steve Boros, third base; Dick McAuliffe, second base
1961    Steve Boros, third base; Jake Wood, second base
1962    Mickey Lolich, pitcher
1963    Dick Egan, pitcher
1964    Willie Horton, outfield
1965    Jim Northrup, outfield
1966    Mickey Stanley, outfield
1967    Pat Dobson, pitcher; Jim Price, catcher
1968    Tom Matchick, shortstop
1969    Mike Kilkenny, pitcher
1970    Les Cain, pitcher; Elliot Maddox, outfield
1971    Mike Adams, outfield
1972    Chuck Seelback, pitcher
1973    Dick Sharon, outfield
1974    Ron Cash; Ron LeFlore, outfield
1975    Tom Veryzer, shortstop; Vern Ruhle, pitcher
1976    Dave Rozema, pitcher
1977    Steve Kemp, outfield
1978    Lou Whitaker, second base; Alan Trammell, shortstop
1979    Lynn Jones, outfield
1980    none
1981    Kirk Gibson, outfield
1982    Rick Leach, first base
1983    Dave Gumpert, pitcher
1984    Barbaro Garbey, third base
1985    Nelson Simmons, outfield
1986    Eric King, pitcher
1987    Steve Searcy, pitcher

## AL Rookie of the Year

1976    Mark Fidrych, pitcher

## Prospects to Watch in 1988

**Tim Tolman,** *outfield.* Tolman started 1987 at Toledo and steadily improved his average over the year. He was hitting .324 when the Tigers called him up in August.

**Rey Palacios,** *catcher.* He was the International League's All-Star catcher at Toledo and could well stick as a backup to Matt Nokes.

# HOUSTON ASTROS

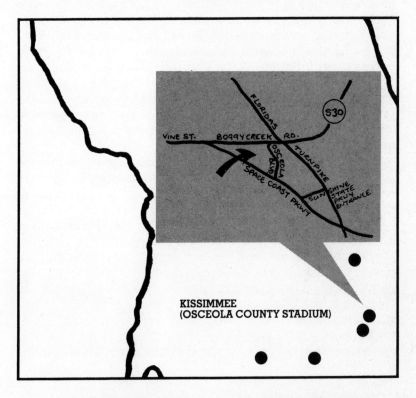

KISSIMMEE
(OSCEOLA COUNTY STADIUM)

■ **Current site:**
Osceola County Stadium
1000 Osceola Boulevard
Kissimmee, FL 32743
(305) 933-5400
■ **Dimensions:**
330' left and right;
410' center
■ **Seating:** 5,100
■ **Built:** 1984
■ **Off-season use:**
Osceola Astros, Florida

State League (Class A);
the Senior Division of the
Little League World Series
and local high school and
Little League games are
also played there.
■ **Practice site:** At the
stadium daily at 10:00 A.M.
■ **Game times:** 1:35 P.M.
(day) 7:35 P.M. (night)
■ **Most convenient airport:**
Orlando

Ground was broken for Osceola County Stadium in the summer of 1984. It opened in the spring of 1985, its $5.5 million construction cost paid by tourist taxes through the county's Tourist Development Council. The complex includes four practice fields and the main stadium, as well as executive offices and media facilities.

Like many of the newer ones, the Astros' facility is very well designed and contains great sightlines and convenient parking. But it was designed with a modern sense of "security", which makes it less intimate and less fun than the older settings.

You wend your way through a vast parking lot to a spot outside the stadium. Practice diamonds ring the facility, and the public has access to them when a game is not on in the main stadium. Otherwise, cyclone fences prevent the unauthorized from strolling past a batting cage.

Stands wrap the infield to a point about 50 feet beyond the edge of the dirt. There are five rows of boxes and 14 rows of reserves. Sometimes, the last two sections of reserves are sold as general admission.

Players are fairly accessible to fans as they come into the park through a gate in the left-field corner, and the friendlier players on both teams will give autographs before and after the games off the railing of the stands.

### Getting to the Stadium
Take **Interstate 4** to **441**, south through downtown Kissimmee to the ballpark.

*Parking:* The parking lot is vast and is adjacent to the stadium.

### Tickets
> Osceola County Stadium
> P.O. Box 2229
> Kissimmee, FL 32742
> Hotline during Spring Training: (305) 933-2520
> Year-round phone: (305) 933-5400

The pre-season schedule is available in early January. Season and single-game tickets go on sale at the same time. Season tickets may be ordered by phone only, using Visa or Master-Card. Single-game tickets may be purchased at the box-office, which opens shortly before the first workout, or by phone, using Visa or MasterCard.

*Prices:* Box $6; reserved $5; general admission $4.

## Team Hotel
Fantasy World Club Villas
2935 Hart Avenue
Kissimmee, FL 32741
(305) 396-1808
There is no actual lobby; activities include barbecues run by the Orbiters' fan club.

## Players' Favorite Leisure Spots
The players often visit the Fantasy World Villas, as well as area restaurants, including Olive Garden, an Italian restaurant; Casa Gallardo, which features Spanish cuisine; Murphy's, which serves seafood and steaks; and the Kissimmee Steak Company, located next to the ballpark.

## Previous Spring Training Locations
1962–63  Apache Junction, AZ
1964–84  Cocoa Beach, FL
1985–present  Kissimmee, FL

## Hottest Prospects
Eyes must have been flashing in anticipation at the end of Houston's first Spring Training in 1962. The Colt .45s, as they were then called, went 17–11 in the Grapefruit League. This was the best first spring ever for an expansion team, and Houston finished the regular season ahead of both the expansion Mets and the Chicago Cubs, albeit way under .500.

Houston had invested heavily in young talent, signing 120 players in 1962 alone (compared with the Cardinals' 14). Twenty rookies played for Houston that first year, and while none will make it to the Hall of Fame, there were some solid players. Dave Giusti was the best of the first-year pitchers, although he was demoted to the minors in 1963 after elbow surgery. He led the Pacific Coast League in shutouts and came back up in 1964. Rookie Merritt Ranew was his batterymate in Houston's first year.

Even then, Houston was strong behind the plate. In 1963 Ranew lost his job to rookie John Bateman. One year later, the team's top prospect, Jerry Grote, leapfrogged over Bateman and was named by *The Sporting News* as the Colt .45s' top rookie in camp.

After two years in the minors, interrupted by brief stints with Houston, Joe Morgan was ready in 1965. Based on his .323, all-everything year in 1964 with San Antonio, he was picked by the players in a *Sport* magazine poll as the best candidate for Rookie of the Year. The 5'7" Morgan had a fine season and was named by *The Sporting News* as the NL's top rookie, though he was nosed out by Jim Lefebvre in the writers' official balloting. Young pitcher Larry Dierker, signed in 1964 in a bidding war with 17 clubs, was kept on the Astros squad in 1965 and responded with a 7–8 season, on his way to becoming one of the staff aces.

Morgan's Texas League teammate, Sonny Jackson, was the best-looking rookie in 1966. Jackson played two years in Houston before going to Atlanta in a trade for Denis Menke and Denny Lemaster.

Doug Rader must have been wondering what he had to do to make the club in the spring of 1967. After hitting a home run and a double and making a great game-ending play, he was told he was going down to Oklahoma City. He came up in mid-year, hit .333 for the Astros and claimed third base for the next eight seasons. With a fine baseball mind, Rader has been both a coach and a manager since retiring as a player.

After losing seasons in the minors, Houston didn't expect a great deal out of Tom Griffin in 1969. But the hard thrower was the outstanding spring rookie, struck out 200 during an 11–10 season, and was named *The Sporting News'* top NL rookie pitcher. As often seems to be the case, especially with pitchers, Griffin's rookie season was arguably his best, though he had a 14-year career in the Majors.

The 1970 season featured two great young hitters in camp. Slugger John Mayberry stayed with the Astros, but young, smooth-fielding Cesar Cedeno was sent down for more experience. Hitting .373 at Oklahoma City he was quickly brought back up. The Astros gave up too early on Mayberry, trading him to Kansas City, where he promptly belted 25 homers, on the way to 255 in his lengthy career. But Houston recognized Cedeno's combination of speed and power. He patrolled center field for many years and, with fellow outfielder Bob Watson, who also became a regular in 1970, formed a murderous one-two punch in the middle of the order.

Six-foot-eight flame-thrower J.R. Richard was clearly the prospect to watch in 1972. He struck out 202 batters in 172 innings in AAA ball in 1971 and was brought up in September to pitch against the Giants. He fanned 15, tying Karl Spooner's debut record set in 1954 for Brooklyn. Brought along slowly, Richard went just 1–0 with the Astros in 1972 and then a shoulder

**separation** slowed his progress in 1973 and 1974. But from 1975 through the first half of 1980, Richard racked up Hall of Fame stats, twice leading the league in strikeouts with his intimidating speed.

Richard had complained during the 1980 season, however, that he didn't feel right, though the team doctors could find nothing wrong. Finally, within days of striking out three in the 1980 All-Star game, he had a stroke while warming up and collapsed on the mound. He bravely rehabilitated himself and attempted a comeback in the minors, but he was never the same. One can only imagine Richard on the current Astros staff, joining all-time strikeout leader Nolan Ryan and Mike Scott in what would have been the most imposing trio of arms in baseball history.

Greg Gross, after a .323 year in Denver in 1973, broke into the starting lineup in 1974, giving the Astros an ideal leadoff hitter. He hit .324 for the year and was named *The Sporting News'* Rookie of the Year. The next year, Rob Andrews took over at second base, as had his brother Mike in Boston eight years earlier.

Jeff Leonard, the "player to be named later" when the Astros sent Joe Ferguson to the Dodgers, was faced with the task of beating out a crop of good outfielders in 1979. The year before, he had an impressive season at Albuquerque: .365, 93 RBI, and 33 stolen bases. He met the challenge, forcing Cedeno to first base, and hit a solid .290 for Houston in his first full year in the Majors, though displaying none of the power he would unveil as a Giant three years later.

Another impressive outfielder, Danny Heep, showed up in camp in 1980 sporting a .327 average at Columbus. Yet he could never break into the regular lineup, and after three years in Houston, Heep went to the Mets for hard-throwing Mike Scott, who had yet to develop the split-fingered fastball that has made him a big winner.

Alan Knicely, with two .300-plus seasons at Tucson, was the prize newcomer in camp in 1982. Bill Doran, a .302 hitter at Tucson in 1982, came up at the end of the season and virtually took the second-base job away from Phil Garner.

Arguably the best Astros rookie in the past few years has been first-baseman Glenn Davis. The only true slugger on a light-hitting team, he has led the team in homers the last two years.

Charlie Kerfeld, with a 4–2 record under his ample belt after being called up at the end of 1985, was counted on for bullpen help, although his spring ERA was 4.50. He did well in 1986 but reported to camp overweight in 1987 and was sent down after a poor start.

## Top Rookies Each Spring

| | |
|---|---|
| 1962 | Dave Giusti, pitcher |
| 1963 | John Bateman, catcher |
| 1964 | Jerry Grote, catcher |
| 1965 | Joe Morgan, second base |
| 1966 | Sonny Jackson, shortstop |
| 1967 | Doug Rader, third base |
| 1968 | Hector Torres, shortstop |
| 1969 | Tom Griffin, pitcher |
| 1970 | John Mayberry, first base; Cesar Cedeno, outfield |
| 1971 | Roger Metzger, shortstop |
| 1972 | J.R. Richard, pitcher |
| 1973 | J.R. Richard, pitcher |
| 1974 | Greg Gross, outfield; Cliff Johnson, catcher |
| 1975 | Rob Andrews, second base |
| 1976 | Mark Lemongello, pitcher |
| 1977 | Floyd Bannister, pitcher |
| 1978 | Joe Cannon, outfield |
| 1979 | Jeff Leonard, outfield |
| 1980 | Danny Heep, outfield |
| 1981 | Gary Rajsich, outfield |
| 1982 | Alan Knicely, catcher |
| 1983 | Bill Doran, second base |
| 1984 | Jeff Heathcock, pitcher |
| 1985 | Glenn Davis, first base |
| 1986 | Charlie Kerfeld, pitcher |
| 1987 | Chuck Jackson, third base; Ty Gainey, outfield |

## Prospect to Watch in 1988

**Jeff Heathcock,** *pitcher.* Drafted in June 1980, Heathcock was 9–0 with Daytona Beach in 1981. Called up at the end of the '83 and '85 seasons, he went 5–2 overall. Called up again at the end of 1987, he was 3–1 in his first four decisions.

# KANSAS CITY ROYALS

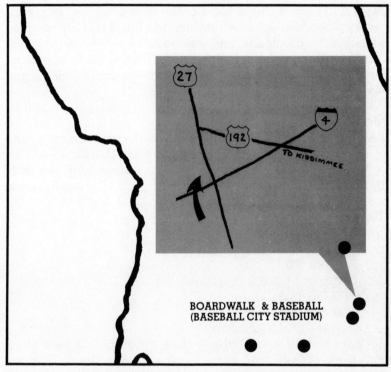

BOARDWALK & BASEBALL
(BASEBALL CITY STADIUM)

■ **Current site:**
The Stadium at
Boardwalk & Baseball
Boardwalk & Baseball
Intersection Interstate 4
and Highway 27
Orlando, FL 32802.
(800) 826-1939 (U.S.);
(800) 367-2249 (Florida);
(813) 424-2424 (Canada)
■ **Dimensions:** 330' left
and right; 410' center
(same as Royals Stadium)

■ **Seating:** 6,500
plus standing room
■ **Built:** 1987
■ **Off-season use:**
Baseball City Royals,
Florida State League
(Class A)
■ **Practice site:** At the
stadium daily at 10:30 A.M.
■ **Game times:** 1:30 P.M.
(day), 7:00 P.M. (night)
■ **Most convenient airport:**
Orlando

The Royals' new 6,500-seat stadium in Boardwalk & Baseball, the first theme park dedicated to baseball, will be inaugurated for the 1988 Spring Training season and has dimensions identical to those of Royals Stadium. The park organizers built the stadium with the goal of having a baseball game played in it every day of the year; they bought the Royals' Florida League farm club to start filling some of the slots after the Grapefruit season. In addition to the stadium, the Baseball City complex includes five diamonds, and is situated on what used to be the dump for Circus World. Following the lead of the Dodgers, the Royals have brought together their major and minor league operations in one location.

### Getting to the Stadium

Boardwalk & Baseball is 25 minutes southwest of Orlando, one hour northeast of Tampa, at **Interstate 4** and **U.S. 27.**

*Parking:* There are now 5,000 paved spaces, with two additional lots due by spring and plenty of grass lots near the park.

### Tickets

Kansas City Royals
Boardwalk & Baseball, Inc.
P.O. Box 800
Orlando, FL 32802
(800) 826-1939 (U.S.)
(800) 367-2249 (Florida)
(813) 424-2424 (Canada)

The schedule is available in late November. Tickets go on sale December 24, 1987, by mail at the above address. They can be purchased at the stadium ticket window starting March 4, 1988, when the Spring Training games begin. Cash, checks, and credit cards are accepted. Tickets for ballgames can be purchased as part of an admission ticket to Boardwalk & Baseball, or separately.

### Team Hotel

Stoffer Orlando Resort at SeaWorld
6677 Sea Harbor Drive,
Orlando, FL 32821
(305) 351-5555

Players who have been with the Royals more than three years can have their own accommodation.

## Players' Favorite Leisure Spots
Since 1988 is the Royals' first year in the area, they will soon discover their favorite spots.

## Previous Spring Training Locations
The Royals have trained in Ft. Myers, Florida since they entered the American League in 1969.

## Hottest Prospects
Like other expansion teams before and since, the first spring roster for the Kansas City Royals in 1969 was made up of aging veterans and untried rookies. The best of the new crop appeared to be speedy outfielder Pat Kelly, obtained from the Twins. He had appeared briefly, if unimpressively, for Minnesota, but he blossomed as a Royal, hitting .264 in 112 games and finishing fourth in the rookie voting by *The Sporting News*. Kelly, however, soon moved on to the White Sox.

The Rookie of the Year in the AL in 1969 was another Royal outfielder. Lou Piniella had played in his first Major League game in Baltimore at the end of 1964 and didn't reach the Majors again until the tail end of the 1968 season, in Cleveland. He joined the Royals in early April of 1969 and hit a home run in his first spring at-bat for them. He hit well through the year, finishing the season with a team-high batting average of .282, and beat out Mike Nagy for the Baseball Writers of America rookie award. Another promising rookie, first-baseman Mike Fiore, picked up from the Baltimore organization, hit .274 for the Royals in 1969 but was traded to the Red Sox during the 1970 season and was a part-timer thereafter.

Amos Otis was the prize newcomer in 1970. His .327 average in 1969 at Tidewater prompted the Royals to trade Joe Foy to the Mets for Otis's services, a trade the Mets wish they'd never made. Otis starred in center field in Kansas City the better part of 14 seasons, combining power, speed and great defensive abilities.

Two prospects in the 1971 camp were Ken Huebner, a .307 hitter at Elmira, and Bob Garibaldi, 15–10 at Phoenix. Monty Montgomery, after going 10–11 in the minors in 1971 and finishing the season at K.C. at 3–0, with a 2.14 ERA, was a pitcher to watch in 1972. All of them raised hopes, but none prospered in the Majors.

The 1973 camp sported two fine rookies fresh from the Omaha farm team: pitcher Steve Busby and outfielder Jim Wohlford, who had hit .291 while making the All-Star team. Busby had come up long enough in 1971 to post a 3–1 record with an ERA of 1.58. He won 16 games his first year, 22 the next, and might have won the Cy Young Award had not Catfish Hunter posted 25 wins. Busby's promising career was cut short by arm problems in 1976.

Also in camp in 1973 was a nonroster third-baseman destined to be one of the great hitters of his era. Sent to San Jose, where he hit .274 before coming up to K.C. in September, George Brett took over the third-base job for the next season and relinquished it only in 1987 when he moved to first to make room for Kevin Seitzer. Brett was, in his prime, the finest hitter in the game.

The 1975 rookies featured a pair of teammates from Omaha: Dennis Leonard, sporting a 12–13 record, and outfielder Tom Poquette. who had hit .305. Leonard would be the prize. He posted 15 wins his first year and three 20-win seasons in the next five years. A serious knee injury caused him to miss all of 1984 and 1985, but he returned the following year in dramatic fashion, pitching a shutout his first game. Fans everywhere rooted him on, but the time away had depleted his skills, and he retired at the end of the year. The 1976 camp featured two pitchers, Mark Littell and Bob McClure, and slugger Frank Ortenzio, who had hit 117 homers in seven minor league seasons but never made it in the Majors.

The 1978 camp opened with the appearance of one of the decade's most highly touted rookies, outfielder Clint Hurdle. Hurdle had had a brilliant 1977 season at Omaha, winning both the MVP and Rookie of the Year honors, and was the *Sports Illustrated* 1978 pre-season pick as Rookie of the Year. He had an unspectacular but solid year hitting .264 and was sent down briefly in early 1979 after losing his job to another 1978 phenom, speedster Willie Wilson. Their careers then moved in opposite directions. Hurdle could never duplicate his minor league greatness and eventually ended up in the Mets organization. His willingness to learn a tough new position — catcher — to improve his chances endeared him to fans and management, but with Gary Carter behind the plate, his chances were slim. Wilson blossomed in 1979, the first of four straight .300-plus seasons, and he also led the league in stolen bases.

The Royals had high hopes for the 1979 top prospect, Luis Silverio. Brought up at the end of 1978, he had hit a surprising .545 in 8 games for the Royals. But in Spring Training in 1979, Silverio injured his leg sliding into a base against Japan's Sebik Lions ballclub and was out for the season. He never was able to make it back to the Majors, and his 11 at-bats produced the highest Royals' season and lifetime batting averages.

Their prospects the next few years didn't pan out. Bill Paschall had been 14–9 at Omaha in 1979 and 7–8 in 1980, but he never won a game in the Majors. Tim Ireland, up from Omaha, where he hit .297 in 1980, caught the coaches' eyes when he successfully pulled the hidden ball trick in a spring game against the Reds. He lasted briefly in 1981. The Royals had high expectations in 1984 for Butch Davis, who had hit .344 after being promoted at the end of 1983. He could manage only a paltry .147 in 1984 before going back down to Omaha.

But the drought ended with the emergence in the 1984 camp of a 19-year-old pitcher with excellent credentials from the previous year. Bret Saberhagen had been 16–7 with two farm clubs and showed enough stuff in the spring to stick, the youngest player to make the Royals roster. He didn't disappoint during the season, going 10–11 and pitching superbly in the League Championship Series. The next year, Saberhagen won 20 games and moved ahead of Babe Ruth as the fifth youngest pitcher ever to accomplish that feat.

Although most of the media attention was focused on Bo Jackson in the spring of 1987, many knowledgable baseball people said that third-baseman Kevin Seitzer was the best-looking Royals prospect in years. He finished fourth in batting in each of his four minor league seasons and hit .323 in 28 games for the Royals at the end of 1986. The experts were right. Jackson's strikeouts and his decision to play both football and baseball overshadowed his offensive contributions. Seitzer pushed George Brett to first base, and the rookie hit spectacularly all season, challenging for the batting title.

## Top Rookies Each Spring

1969   Pat Kelly, outfield
1970   Luis Alcarez, second base
1971   Ken Huebner; Ron Garibaldi, pitcher
1972   Monty Montgomery, pitcher
1973   Steve Busby, pitcher
1974   Ruppert Jones, outfield
1975   Dennis Leonard, pitcher
1976   Mark Littell, pitcher
1977   Joe Zdeb, outfield; John Wathan, catcher
1978   Clint Hurdle, outfield
1979   Bill Paschall, pitcher

| 1980 | Bill Paschall, pitcher |
|------|------------------------|
| 1981 | Tim Ireland, first base |
| 1982 | Onix Concepcion, shortstop |
| 1983 | Danny Jackson, pitcher |
| 1984 | Butch Davis, outfield;  Bret Saberhagen, pitcher |
| 1985 | John Morris, outfield;  Buddy Biancalana, shortstop |
| 1986 | Tony Ferreira, pitcher |
| 1987 | Kevin Seitzer, third base |

## AL Rookie of the Year

| 1969 | Lou Piniella, outfield |
|------|------------------------|

## Prospect to Watch in 1988

**Gary Thurman,** *outfield.* The righthanded-hitting Thurman batted .294 at Omaha and is expected to get a shot at an outfield spot with the Royals in 1988.

# MINNESOTA TWINS

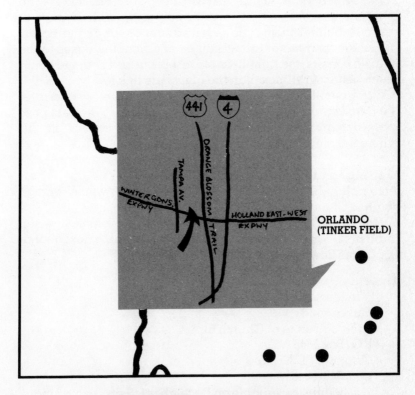

■ **Current site:**
Tinker Field
Tampa Avenue at
Church Street
Orlando, FL 32855
(305) 849-6346
■ **Dimensions:** 332' left
and right; 412' center
■ **Seating:** 5,500
■ **Built:** 1912,

modernized in 1963
■ **Off-season use:**
Orlando Twins,
Southern League
(Class AA)
■ **Practice site:** At the
stadium daily at 10:00 A.M.
■ **Game time:** 1:30 P.M.
■ **Most convenient airport:**
Orlando

Tinker Field was named for shortstop Joe Tinker (as in Tinker-to-Evers-to-Chance), who lived in Orlando. The original ballpark was a typical wooden grandstand, which was built in 1912. The present stadium was first used in 1963, with fans sitting on the bare concrete where seats were to be installed.

Tinker is a charming old urban stadium in the midst of a very modern urban sprawl. It sits in the lee of the much larger Citrus Bowl, which rises visibly above the right-field fence. The permanent stands, eight rows of box seats with 15 rows of reserves behind them, don't even extend as far as the bases. Bleachers for general admission extend from the bases to the outfield corners: the right-field bleachers are elevated, providing much better sightlines than the bleachers in left.

Players will occasionally give autographs before and after the game off the bleacher and box seat railings. The best post-game autograph opportunities are behind the third base stands, where the players emerge after the game.

## Getting to the Stadium
Take Holland East-West Expressway to Tampa Avenue, and go south to Church Street.

*Parking:* The Tinker Field lot holds 1,000 vehicles. When that's not enough, additional parking is available next door at the Citrus Bowl.

## Tickets
Minnesota Twins
Tinker Field
Tampa Avenue at Church Street
P.O. Box 5645
Orlando, FL 32855
(305) 849-6346

The schedule is available on December 1. Season and single-game tickets can be ordered beginning in early December. Payment must be made by check or money order. Six games were sold out in 1987. Note: 3,000 general admission seats are sold on the day of the game only.

*Prices:* Box $6; reserve $5; general admission $3.

## Team Hotel
Court of Flags
5715 Major Boulevard
Orlando, FL 32819
(305) 351-3340

Few big-leaguers actually stay at the hotel, and there are no fan-oriented activities.

## Players' Favorite Leisure Spots
The restaurants most frequented by the Twins are Villa Rosa and Villanova, both Italian, and Friday's, a steakhouse. In addition, the players often attend the dog races at the San Lando Kennel Club.

## Previous Spring Training Locations
*Washington Senators 1901–60*
*Minnesota Twins 1961–present*

| | |
|---|---|
| 1901 | Phebus, VA |
| 1902–04 | Washington, DC |
| 1905 | Hampton, VA |
| 1906 | Charlottesville, VA |
| 1907–09 | Galveston, TX |
| 1910 | Norfolk, VA |
| 1911 | Atlanta, GA |
| 1912–16 | Charlottesville, VA |
| 1917 | Atlanta, GA |
| 1918–19 | Augusta, GA |
| 1920–29 | Tampa, FL |
| 1930–35 | Biloxi, MS |
| 1936–42 | Orlando, FL |
| 1943–45 | College Park, MD |
| 1946–present | Orlando, FL |

## Hottest Prospects
It has been said over the years that one could field an All-Star team of players the Twins let go for various reasons, and many of them were developed in the team's farm system. Cal Griffith's Washington Senators set up residence in the Twin Cities for the 1961 season, and sprinkled among the aging veterans and Harmon Killebrew's thunderous bat was a remarkable number of good-looking rookies. The ripest of the crop was young Ziolo Versalles, who had been up briefly with the Senators in 1959 and '60 but finally seemed ready to take over the shortstop job. He responded by hitting .280, which turned out to be his career best, even higher than his MVP year of 1965.

Teaming with Versalles at second base in 1962 was a prize rookie named Bernie Allen. Allen had been a star quarterback at Purdue, signed with Minnesota, and played only 80 games in the minors. He was so impressive in Spring Training that he won the starting job, and he remained at second five years before being traded to the Washington club that was formed on Griffith's departure. Another infielder who shone in 1962 was third-baseman Rich Rollins. Up for 13 games in 1961, Rollins hit .294 and improved that to .298 for 1962. Not only did Rollins start at third base in the 1962 All-Star game, a rare feat for a rookie, he also had more votes than any other AL player, including Mickey Mantle.

*The Sporting News* named Jim Roland the AL's best pitching prospect in the spring of 1963, but he spent most of the season on the disabled list while compiling a 4–1 record. Jimmie Hall, a seven-year minor-league veteran, made the team as a late-inning defensive replacement for Harmon Killebrew. Interestingly, he didn't start a game until early June and he still hit 33 homers. His home run total declined every year thereafter in Minnesota.

By 1964, the Twins couldn't keep Tony Oliva out of the starting lineup. The minors' top hitter in 1961 with a .410 average, he was up briefly in 1962 and 1963 and hit over .400 in each trial. Showing it was no fluke, he hit a league-leading .323 in his first full season, the first rookie to win the batting crown, and repeated as batting champ again the following year. Of course, Oliva was the AL Rookie of the Year as well as the Twins' MVP.

Though only a rookie, Dave Boswell was counted on in 1965 despite his Major League debut. Brought up in late 1964, his first game was against the Red Sox. His first pitch was hit for a homer by Felix Mantilla, his second pitch was ripped for a double by Tony Conigliaro, and Carl Yastrzemski did the same to his third pitch. When Dick Stuart, the next batter, came to the plate, Boswell yelled in, "You're not a first ball hitter too?" Boswell went 2–0 in 1964 and 6–5 in 1965, finally winning big with 20 in 1969.

The Twins were blessed again in 1967 with another Rookie of the Year when Rod Carew arrived after three seasons in the minors. Finishing sixth in the league in hitting, Rod was the AL All-Star second-baseman his first year. He was the AL's leading hitter seven times, with a high of .388 in 1977.

Bob Darwin was technically not a rookie in 1972, being two days over the limit, but he was virtually a newcomer. Darwin spent seven years in the minors as a pitcher, coming up for short stints with both the L.A. Dodgers and Angels. With a Major League ERA over 10, he wisely abandoned pitching for the outfield and tore up Spring Training with the Twins, hitting .333 with 19 RBI. He continued his hot hitting during the regular season, leading the Twins with 80 RBI. The following year saw the emergence of relief specialist Bill (Soup) Campbell. One of the best in the game, he won 30 games and saved another 51 in 1976 and '77 for Minnesota and Boston, successfully closing 44 percent of his teams' victories.

In 1975 the Twins featured Lyman Bostock, a .333 hitter the previous year at Tacoma. Bostock started the 1975 season in the minors, but after pasting PCL pitching to the tune of .391, he returned to the Majors. Like Campbell the year before, he opted for free agency when Griffith refused to increase his salary, taking his .336 batting average to the Angels after the 1977 season. He played most of one year with the Angels before being killed in a tragic shooting, which snuffed out a promising career.

In the spring of 1976, *Sports Illustrated* named the Twins' young catcher, Butch Wynegar, the phenom of the year, which is even more impressive considering that Wynegar was not even on the Twins' spring roster. Wynegar responded by hitting .260 and fielding capably behind the plate. *The Sporting News* picked him as the rookie Player of the Year, although the Writers' Association rookie accolades understandably went to Detroit pitcher Mark Fidrych.

Gary Ward was the best of a trio of young hitters in 1981, including Dave Engle and Mark Funderburk. Ward hit .282 in Toledo in 1980, before coming up to the Twins and hitting .463 in three games. His big bat unlimbered a year later, producing 28 home runs for the last-place Twins.

1982 and 1984 featured a pair of minor league MVPs as the top prospects in the Twins' camp. Kent Hrbek was the MVP at Viselia in 1981, hitting .379, with 29 homers and 111 RBI. Brought up in August 1981, he hit a home run in his first game to beat the Yanks. Tim Teufel was the International League's MVP in 1983 with 27 home runs and an even 100 RBI and took over John Castino's job at second base.

What will always be referred to as "the strange case of Jim Eisenreich" began in the spring of 1982, when the young outfielder was tabbed one of the purest hitters to come along in years. A good hitter in the spring, Jim was afflicted with Tourette's syndrome, an illness that caused him to shake uncontrollably, especially in the outfield. Fans did not understand his illness and ragged him mercilessly for his behavior, which forced him to quit baseball in 1984 after three partial seasons. He sought treatment and with medication was able to control the symptoms enough to play semipro baseball in Minnesota. Gradually and heroically, he worked his way back to the Majors. Picked up by Kansas City in 1987, he was hitting .383 at Memphis when he was promoted to the Royals' roster. The Twins' compensation for his rights was just $1.

The 1987 top rookies were pitcher Steve Gasser, rated the number one prospect in the Midwest League, and first-baseman Gene Larkin. Larkin started the spring in the minors but was quickly brought back by the Twins, becoming the first Columbia graduate to play in the Majors since Lou Gehrig.

## Top Rookies Each Spring

| | |
|---|---|
| 1961 | Zoilo Versalles, shortstop |
| 1962 | Rich Rollins, third base |
| 1963 | Jim Roland, pitcher |
| 1964 | Tony Oliva, outfield |
| 1965 | Dave Boswell, pitcher |
| 1966 | Pete Cimino, pitcher |
| 1967 | Rod Carew, second base |
| 1968 | Rick Renick, shortstop |
| 1969 | Chuck Manuel, outfield |
| 1970 | Danny Thompson, second base |
| 1971 | Steve Barber, pitcher |
| 1972 | Steve Brye, outfield;  Bob Darwin, outfield |
| 1973 | Bill Campbell, pitcher;  Glenn Borgmann, catcher |
| 1974 | Craig Kusick, first base |
| 1975 | Lyman Bostock, outfield |
| 1976 | Butch Wynegar, catcher |
| 1977 | Randy Bass, outfield |
| 1978 | Hosken Powell, outfield |
| 1979 | Danny Goodwin, first base/DH |
| 1980 | Rick Sofield, outfield |
| 1981 | Gary Ward, outfield |
| 1982 | Jim Eisenreich, outfield;  Kent Hrbek, first base |
| 1983 | Jeff Reed, catcher |
| 1984 | Tim Teufel, second base |
| 1985 | Jeff Reed, catcher |
| 1986 | Steve Lombardozzi, second base |
| 1987 | Gene Larkin, first base |

## AL Rookies of the Year
| | |
|---|---|
| 1964 | Tony Oliva, outfield |

1967    Rod Carew, second base
1979    John Castino, second base
        (co-Rookie of the Year with Alfredo Griffin, Toronto)

## Prospect to Watch in 1988

**Jeff Bettinger,** *pitcher.* The righthanded Bettinger was 11–8 through mid-August for Portland, the team with the worst second-half record in the Pacific Coast League. He was called up to the Twins on September 1.

# CHAPTER 6

*Gulf Coast Group*

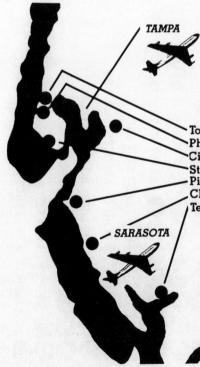

TAMPA

Toronto Blue Jays *Dunedin*
Philadelphia Phillies *Clearwater*
Cincinnati Reds *Plant City*
St. Louis Cardinals *St. Petersburg*
Pittsburgh Pirates *Bradenton*
Chicago White Sox *Sarasota*
Texas Rangers *Port Charlotte*

SARASOTA

THIS GROUP IS the most baseball-rich of the Spring Training team clusters. At the hub is the Cardinals' beautiful Al Lang Stadium in St. Petersburg, where thousands of boats moored in the marina outside the left-field fence provide the most beautiful backdrop available to the Spring Training spectator. The Phillies, in Clearwater, are less than a half-hour up the peninsula from downtown St. Petersburg. Dunedin, the Blue Jays' site, is the next town up the road. Across the bay and less than an hour away, the Reds train in their new facility in Plant City.

The drive across the southern causeways from the Cards' facility to where the Pirates train in Bradenton (a half-hour from St. Petersburg) and the White Sox train in Sarasota (a half-hour beyond Bradenton) is among the most beautiful in Spring Training-dom and is even worth taking as a side-trip. Both the Pirates and White Sox will spend Spring Training 1988 in their ancient ballparks, relics that almost scream out: "baseball history made here." The Sox will have a new facility in Sarasota to replace Payne Park in 1989.

## GULF COAST DISTANCES

| | BRADENTON PIRATES | CLEARWATER PHILLIES | DUNEDIN BLUE JAYS | LAKELAND TIGERS | PLANT CITY REDS | PORT CHARLOTTE RANGERS | ST PETERSBURG CARDINALS | SARASOTA WHITE SOX | WINTER HAVEN RED SOX | BOARDWALK & BASEBALL ROYALS |
|---|---|---|---|---|---|---|---|---|---|---|
| **BRADENTON** | ● | | | | | | | | | |
| **CLEARWATER** | 42 | ● | | | | | | | | |
| **DUNEDIN** | 47 | 5 | ● | | | | | | | |
| **LAKELAND** | 66 | 54 | 59 | ● | | | | | | |
| **PLANT CITY** | 43 | 44 | 49 | 7 | ● | | | | | |
| **PORT CHARLOTTE** | 63 | 105 | 110 | 129 | 122 | ● | | | | |
| **ST PETERSBURG** | 26 | 19 | 24 | 53 | 46 | 89 | ● | | | |
| **SARASOTA** | 13 | 55 | 60 | 79 | 72 | 50 | 39 | ● | | |
| **WINTER HAVEN** | 76 | 69 | 74 | 15 | 22 | 139 | 68 | 89 | ● | |
| **BOARDWALK & BASEBALL** | 92 | 80 | 85 | 26 | 33 | 155 | 79 | 105 | 16 | ● |

Forty more minutes down the coast from Sarasota, in Port Charlotte, is the Texas Rangers' brand-new facility, a training complex that pops up in the middle of a generally undeveloped part of the Gulf Coast.

The Gulf Coast beaches rival those across the state on the Atlantic, although they tend to be less developed and a little less accessible to much of the action. But with so many baseball teams, who has time for the beach? The old cities of Sarasota and Bradenton stand in marked contrast to rapidly developing Tampa and St. Petersburg and are themselves valid tourist attractions.

Where best to base yourself in this group depends on a lot of personal considerations, as the options are varied.

If you'd like to visit some of the theme parks or the Theme Park Group teams, putting yourself in Tampa makes the most sense. If you like the beach, the outer stretch from Clearwater Beach to St. Petersburg Beach puts you very close to three teams (the Phils, Cards, and Blue Jays) and right on the Gulf of Mexico in the middle of a popular college-vacation zone. The drawback is the potential for travel delays as you cross the causeways back to civilization. If you have no particular interest except to be in the center of the action, downtown St. Petersburg near Al Lang Stadium would be appropriate. And if you would like a little Old World charm as part of your vacation, Sarasota is probably the best place to stay.

## Batting Cages

Bradenton: Pirates' Cove, 5410 14th Street West, (813) 755-4608; six baseball cages, three softball cages.

Tampa: Malibu Grand Prix, 14320 North Nebraska, (813) 977-6273; seven baseball cages, two softball cages, open 11 A.M. to 11 P.M. Monday to Thursday, 11 A.M. to 12 midnight Friday, 10 A.M. to 12 midnight Saturday, 10 A.M. to 11 A.M. Sunday.

Clearwater: Storm's Golf to Baseball, 2495 Gulf to Bay Boulevard (813) 797-5431, baseball only, open 9 A.M. to 10 P.M., seven days.

## Sunny-Day Alternatives

*Spongeorama,* Tarpon Springs: Exhibit center at the heart of the Sponge Docks, a National Historic Landmark with displays and boutiques. 510 Dodecanese Boulevard, Tarpon Springs. (813) 937-4111.

*Jose Gasparilla,* Tampa: World's only fully rigged pirate ship. Anchored off Bayshore Boulevard, home of the world's longest continuous sidewalk (6½ miles).

*Busch Gardens,* Tampa: African safari with more than 3,000 animals, monorail, skyride, brewery tours — with sample. 3000 Busch Boulevard (2 miles east of I-275, 2 miles west of I-75), Tampa. (813) 971-8282.

*Fort DeSoto Park,* St. Petersburg: 900 acres of swimming beaches, picnic areas and white herons; fort built in 1898. On five islands directly south of St. Petersburg Beach, accessible only by toll bridge. (813) 462-3347.

*Derby Lane,* St. Petersburg: Greyhound races. 10400 block of North Gandy Boulevard. (813) 576-1361.

## Rainy-Day Activities

*Museum of Science and Industry,* Tampa: Hands-on exhibits of Florida's industries and natural phenomena. 4801 East Fowler Avenue, Tampa. (813) 985-5531.

*Dunedin Scottish,* Dunedin: Store and mail-order business for just about everything Scottish — sporrans, tartans, ginger beer, marmalade . . . 1401 Main Street, Dunedin. (813) 734-7606.

*Salvador Dali Museum,* St. Petersburg: A short walk from Al Lang Field, one of the world's most fascinating one-artist shows. 1000 Third Street South, St. Petersburg. (813) 823-3767.

*Ringling Museum,* Sarasota: Circus museum; art museum with fine Baroque collection; circus impresario John Ringling's home. 3 miles north of downtown Sarasota on U.S. 41. (813) 355-5101.

## Rainy-Day Activities

*Museum of Science and Industry,* Tampa: Hands-on exhibits of Florida's industries and natural phenomena. 4801 East Fowler Avenue, Tampa. (813) 985-5531.

*Dunedin Scottish,* Dunedin: Store and mail-order business for just about everything Scottish — sporrans, tartans, ginger beer, marmalade . . . 1401 Main Street, Dunedin. (813) 734-7606.

*Salvador Dali Museum,* St. Petersburg: A short walk from Al Lang Field, one of the world's most fascinating one-artist shows. 1000 Third Street South, St. Petersburg. (813) 823-3767.

*Ringling Museum,* Sarasota: Circus museum; art museum with fine Baroque collection; circus impresario John Ringling's home. 3 miles north of downtown Sarasota on U.S. 41. (813) 355-5101.

# GULF COAST AIRPLAY

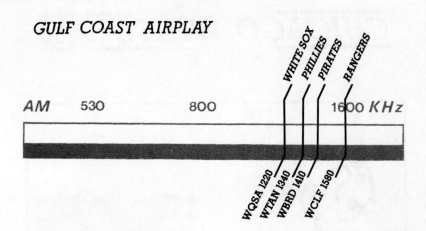

## Day Trips

To the north: ***Weeki Wachee Springs,*** Weeki Wachee. Live "mer-maids", tropical gardens, wildlife. Junction of U.S. 19 and S.R. 50, Weeki Wachee. (904) 596-2062.

***Homosassa Springs Nature World,*** Homosassa Springs. Man-atee refuge, Gator Lagoon, petting zoo. U.S. 19, Homosassa Springs. (904) 628-2311.

To the east: ***Boardwalk & Baseball*** is about an hour away, ***Disney World and Epcot Center*** about 2 hours. See Theme Park Group listings.

# CHICAGO WHITE SOX

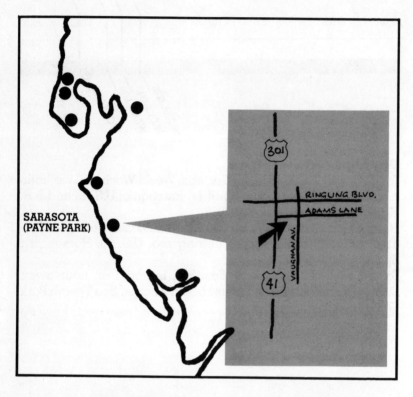

■ **Current site:**
Payne Park
2052 Adams Lane
(off Washington Street)
Sarasota, FL 34237
(813) 953-3388
■ **Dimensions:** 340' left
and right; 400' center
■ **Seating:** 5,000 plus
standing room
■ **Built:** 1961
■ **Off-season use:**
Sarasota White Sox, Gulf

Coast League (Rookie);
high school tournament
games also played there;
other teams in the Gulf
Coast League play there
at night as it is the
only park in the league
with lights.
■ **Practice site:** At the
stadium daily at 10:00 A.M.
■ **Game time:** 1:00 P.M.
■ **Most convenient airport:**
Sarasota or Tampa

The White Sox have trained since 1960 at Payne Park, named after Christy Payne, an oilman who was a partner of John D. Rockefeller and who donated 60 acres, including the park site, to Sarasota.

The spring of 1988 is scheduled to be the last for this historic old park. Despite the worst parking shortage in either the Grapefruit or Cactus Leagues, it is well worth a visit. Payne Park is situated in the center of a charming old Gulf City, and the parking problem is due to the fact that the stadium was built before many people started driving to games. And it looks the part. Rumor has it that the Sarasota police refrain from ticketing illegally parked cars during White Sox games, but this has not been officially confirmed.

There is the usual arc of stands, extended only to first and third base. There are only two to five rows of box seats and fourteen to fifteen rows of reserves, which are under a roof overhang. Down the left-field line from the infield dirt to the corner of the outfield are fifteen rows of bleachers. A telephone pole in foul territory creates a slight obstruction from some of the bleacher seats.

Autographs can be garnered off the front railing of the boxes and bleachers. The batting cages are at the practice facility, Smith Field (see below). There is a special closeness between players and fans at Payne Park: the players walk from the clubhouse to the stadium through fans collected down the right field line, an even better chance for an autograph.

## Getting to the Stadium
From the south: Take **Interstate 75** to Bee Ridge Boulevard, west to Sarasota. Then take **Highway 41,** the Tamiami Trail, until **301** splits off from it, and continue north. Payne Park is on the right, at the corner of Washington Street and Ringling Boulevard.

From the north: Take **I-75** to the University Parkway exit, and go west for about six miles to **301** South, which leads to the ballpark.

To get to the practice site, Smith Field, take the same route as to the ballpark. Smith is a mile and a half east of Payne, at 12th and Tuttle.

*Parking:* There is no parking at the stadium itself, but there are several lots within four blocks, and there is apparently an informal understanding with the city not to ticket on-street parkers on game days.

## Tickets
Chicago White Sox
Payne Park
P.O. Box 1702
Sarasota, FL 33578
(813) 953-3388

Printed schedules are available in late November. Last season's season-ticket holders have the first right of refusal and will be contacted by the Sarasota Sports Committee to see if they wish to retain their seats. Season tickets may be ordered between December 20 and January 26. Payment must be made by check. On January 26, single-game tickets go on sale. All advance sales must be paid for by check. Three times in 1987 the White Sox sold out Payne Park.

*Prices*: Box $6; reserved $5; general admission $4; children $3.

## Team Hotel
Sarasota Days Inn
4900 North Tamiami Trail
Sarasota, FL 33580
(813) 355-9721

Very few of the Major League players stay at the hotel, and there are no scheduled activities for fans. Most players stay at condos at Siesta Key or Lido Beach.

## Players' Favorite Leisure Spots
Sarasota is a fairly quiet town. You will most likely find the players hanging out in the restaurants and clubs on St. Armand's Circle.

## Previous Spring Training Locations
| | |
|---|---|
| 1901–02 | Excelsior Springs, MO |
| 1903 | Mobile, AL |
| 1904 | Marlin Springs, TX |
| 1905–06 | New Orleans, LA |
| 1907 | Mexico City, Mexico |
| 1908 | Los Angeles, CA |
| 1909–10 | San Francisco, CA |
| 1911 | Mineral Wells, TX |
| 1912 | Waco, TX |
| 1913–15 | Paso Robles, CA |
| 1916–19 | Mineral Wells, TX |
| 1920 | Waco, TX |

| 1921 | Waxahachie, TX |
| 1922–23 | Seguin, TX |
| 1924 | Winter Haven, FL |
| 1925–28 | Shreveport, LA |
| 1929 | Dallas, TX |
| 1930–32 | San Antonio, TX |
| 1933–42 | Pasadena, CA |
| 1943–44 | French Lick, IN |
| 1945 | Terre Haute, IN |
| 1946–50 | Pasadena, CA |
| 1951 | Pasadena/Palm Springs, CA |
| 1952 | Pasadena/El Centro, CA |
| 1953 | El Centro, CA |
| 1954–59 | Tampa, FL |
| 1960–present | Sarasota, FL |

## Hottest Prospects

The White Sox came to Sarasota for the first time in 1960, having deserted Tampa as a Spring Training site. The Sox had a veteran team, one that had captured the pennant the year before, only to lose to the Dodgers in the Series, and the only team besides Cleveland to interrupt the Yankees' string of pennant winners from 1947 through 1964.

With a veteran team, there was little room for Joe Hicks, picked by *The Sporting News* as the best prospect in camp. Hicks hit just .191 before being shipped to the Senators, who passed him on to the Mets. The Sox had a better rookie the next year in Floyd Robinson, who had spent 1954 through 1960 at San Diego in the Pacific Coast League. Robinson hit .310 and .312 his first two seasons at Comiskey Park, pushing incumbent Al Smith from right to third base.

In 1963 *The Sporting News* gave its rookie player and pitcher awards to a pair of White Sox gems, Pete Ward and Gary Peters. Ward had a .328 AAA average the year before and had come to the Sox in the trade that sent Luis Aparicio to Baltimore. Ward hit a rousing .295 for the Pale Hose and finished second in the Rookie of the Year vote. Peters had made brief appearances for the Sox four years running before he finally stayed in 1963, compiling a glittering 19–8 record with a 2.33 ERA. He was named the AL Rookie of the Year and followed that with 20 wins the next year. Another rookie pitcher, Dave DeBusschere, 10–1 at Savannah the year before, had less success with the Sox, posting a 3–4 mark before turning to professional basketball and starring with the Knicks.

In 1964 *The Sporting News* named Don Buford the best-looking prospect in the AL spring camps. He had led the American Association in just about everything the previous year and hit a solid .262 as a starter at second base for the Sox. His speed and occasional power were greatly valued; at the end of 1967 he was dealt to the Orioles as the White Sox reacquired Luis Aparicio.

Tommie Agee, acquired from Cleveland as part of a three-way deal, hardly looked like a hot prospect in the spring of 1966. At Indianapolis in 1965 he had 8 home runs and a .226 batting average in 106 games. But in 1966 he hit .273 for the Sox, while leading the team in homers with 22. Slumping the next season, he was traded to the Mets for Tommy Davis and three others and played a major role for the Miracle Mets in 1969.

Duane Josephson was the All-Star catcher in two minor leagues before becoming a Sox regular in 1967 and '68. Carlos May, coming off a .354 season with Appleton, was the top prospect for the Sox in 1968. While he hit only .179 in 17 games for the Pale Hose that year, he hit .281 the next and was named by *The Sporting News* as the top rookie player in the AL. The big pitching prospect in 1969 was Dennis O'Toole, younger brother of Cincy's Jim O'Toole. Dennis would be up and down with the Sox for five years, without winning, losing, or saving a game, never meeting the requirements that would cause him to lose his rookie status.

Bucky Dent, best remembered as a Yankee for his home run that beat the Red Sox in the 1978 playoff, opened at second base for the White Sox in 1974, after a brief trial the previous year. The Sox touted Chet Lemon in the spring of 1976: an infielder his previous three years in the minors, Lemon made the switch to center field and won the starting job in camp. He went on to make the Topps All-Rookie Team in 1976 and was second to Dwight Evans with a .992 fielding percentage. Lemon had six outstanding years with the White Sox before going to Detroit after the 1981 season for Steve Kemp.

The diminutive Harry Chappas caught the fancy of management and fans in 1979. Chappas, at 5'3", was the shortest player in the Majors since 3'7" Eddie Gaedel in 1951 and got a great deal of attention as a result. His three years in Chicago were spent in a utility role. During that time, the Sox's current star, right-fielder Harold Baines, emerged. After three seasons in the minors, the 21-year-old Baines arrived in 1980 and was a regular from the start. He had originally been "scouted" in Little League by Sox owner Bill Veeck, when both of them lived on Maryland's Eastern Shore.

Like Mike Colbern in the spring of 1979, the 1981 prospect Ricky Seilheimer was tagged "the White Sox catcher of the future." In March of that year, however, the Sox signed free-agent Carlton Fisk, relegating any catching prospect to the bench. Colbern and Seilheimer were not heard from again. But LaMarr Hoyt and Richard Dotson were. The two right-handers were minor league acquisitions in 1977, Hoyt coming from the Yankees for Dent. They had been up briefly in 1979 and stuck the next year, posting 9–3 and 12–10 records. Three years later they won 24 and 22, respectively, with Hoyt copping the Cy Young Award as the White Sox won the AL West.

Best friends Ron Kittle and Greg Walker were considered top prospects in 1982. Kittle had hit 40 homers the previous year in the minors, but the Sox sent him out to the Pacific Coast League for more seasoning. And what a seasoning he had! Fifty home runs, 144 RBI, a .344 average, and the MVP award. He showed it was no fluke by cranking out 35 homers, two short of the rookie record then held by Al Rosen, and being named to the All-Star team in 1983, when he was also named the AL Rookie of the Year. Walker took a little longer to develop but was ensconced at first base by 1984, a fine hitter and equally skilled fielder.

The Sox were blessed again in 1985 with Ozzie Guillen, the third Venezuelan shortstop for the Pale Hose. The other two were named Carrasquel and Aparicio. Up from the Pacific Coast League, where he hit .296, Ozzie made only 12 errors to set a Sox record at shortstop. He walked just 12 times but hit .273 to be named the Rookie of the Year in the American League.

## Top Rookies Each Spring

1960    Joe Hicks, outfield
1961    Floyd Robinson, outfield
1962    Joel Horlen, pitcher
1963    Pete Ward, third base; Gary Peters, pitcher
1964    Don Buford, second base
1965    Ken Berry, outfield
1966    Tommie Agee, outfield
1967    Duane Josephson, catcher

| 1968 | Carlos May, outfield |
|------|----------------------|
| 1969 | Carlos May, outfield |
| 1970 | Rich McKinney, third base |
| 1971 | Lee Richard, shortstop |
| 1972 | Jorge Orta, second base |
| 1973 | Jerry Hairston, outfield |
| 1974 | Bucky Dent, shortstop; Brian Downing, catcher |
| 1975 | Nyles Nyman, outfield |
| 1976 | Chet Lemon, outfield |
| 1977 | Ken Kravec, pitcher |
| 1978 | Thad Bosley, outfield |
| 1979 | Wayne Nordhagen, outfield; Harry Chappas, shortstop |
| 1980 | Harold Baines, outfield |
| 1981 | Ricky Seilheimer, catcher |
| 1982 | Ron Kittle, outfield |
| 1983 | Ron Kittle, outfield |
| 1984 | Joel Skinner, catcher |
| 1985 | Ozzie Guillen, shortstop |
| 1986 | Russ Morman, first base |
| 1987 | Ron Karkovice, catcher |

## AL Rookies of the Year

| 1963 | Gary Peters, pitcher |
|------|----------------------|
| 1966 | Tommie Agee, outfield |
| 1983 | Ron Kittle, outfield |
| 1985 | Ozzie Guillen, shortstop |

## Prospects to Watch in 1988

**Jack McDowall,** *pitcher.* The righthander is the best in a thin crop of prospects. He is expected to move into the starting rotation for the Pale Hose in 1988.

**Randall Rollin,** *designated hitter.* Playing for Birmingham (AAA), he was the only White Sox farm hand above Class A to make an All-Star team.

# CINCINNATI REDS

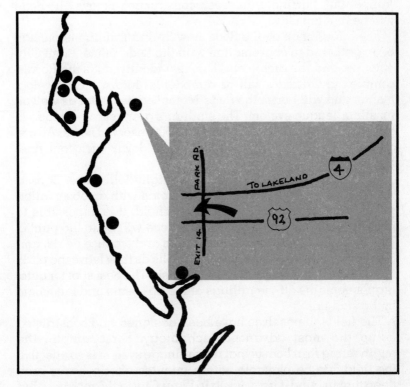

PARK RD.

EXIT 14.

TO LAKELAND

4

92

■ **Current site:** Reds'
Spring Training Complex
Park Road
Plant City, FL 33566
■ **Dimensions:**
550' left and right;
400' center
■ **Seating:** 6,500

■ **Built:** 1988
■ **Off-season use:** Unclear
at time of publication
■ **Practice site:** At the
stadium daily at 10:00 A.M.
■ **Game time:** 1:00 P.M.
■ **Most convenient airport:**
Tampa

As this book was about to go to press, the authors confirmed that the Reds' longstanding plan to move to their new Spring Training headquarters in Plant City looked as though it would become a reality. The complex is located 22 miles east of Tampa. The stadium and adjoining facilities have not yet been built, though the construction is now underway, and should be completed in time for Spring Training games in March 1988. It is possible the facility will not be completed on schedule, in which case the Reds would likely return to Al Lopez Field in Tampa. But, barring unforeseen construction delays, the Reds will be in Plant City.

The information on the Reds' new Spring Training home has been gathered in conversation with the Reds' office, Plant City officials, and the architects. The new facility, as is the Royals' complex in Orlando, will be a model for future such developments, and will house the Reds' Major League roster as well as its minor league system. The stadium's grandstand extends to the bases, with 1,500 box seats and 3,500 reserved seats. All are covered. There are 750 bleacher seats down each foul line, beyond which are the bullpens.

Two batting cages are outside the right-field fence. Beyond them is a cloverleaf of four practice fields with an observation tower in the middle and a practice infield. It is impossible to judge at this point how accessible these will be to the public. The clubhouse is between the stadium and practice fields, and players may be available for autographs as they leave the park, though you'll find this out when you visit. The best spot for autographs remains off the railings of the box seats and bleachers in the stadium.

The fields themselves have been designed and constructed using the most advanced technology. For example, the engineering firm boasts that the drainage system is so effective the field can be playable within minutes after a heavy rain. Keep that in mind if it's pouring in Plant City in the morning, but clears just before game time.

## Getting to the Stadium
Take **Interstate 4** to the **Park Road** exit, which is 22 miles east of Tampa and 7 miles west of Lakeland. Go south on Park Road for 2½ miles, through two sets of traffic lights. The stadium is on your right.

*Parking:* A large grass lot holds 1,700 cars.

## Tickets

As of this writing, the new Reds' complex does not have telephones installed, though they will be in by next spring. The printed schedule of Spring Training games should be available by December 15. Season and single-game tickets may be ordered by mail beginning January 1. Payment may be in the form of a check or money order, and ought to be placed using the Spring Training Ticket Order Form. This may be obtained by writing to:

> Cincinnati Reds
> 100 Riverfront Stadium
> Cincinnati, OH 45202
> (513) 421-4510

*Prices:* Ticket prices for the new stadium have not yet been determined. As a guide, prices at Al Lopez Field were $6.00 for box seats and $4.00 for general admission.

## Team Hotel

> Holiday Inn
> 2011 North Wheeler Street
> Plant City, FL 33566
> (813) 752-3141

## Players' Favorite Leisure Spots

It is difficult to know whether the Reds' players will gravitate back to their favorite emporia in the Tampa area, will find new places in Plant City, or will frequent the Tigers' choices in Lakeland. Probably a combination.

## Previous Spring Training Locations

| | |
|---|---|
| 1901–02 | Cincinnati, OH |
| 1903 | Augusta, GA |
| 1904 | Dallas, TX |
| 1905 | Jacksonville, FL |
| 1906 | San Antonio, TX |
| 1907 | Marlin Springs, TX |
| 1908 | St. Augustine, TX |
| 1909 | Atlanta, GA |
| 1910–11 | Hot Springs, AR |
| 1912 | Columbus, GA |
| 1913 | Mobile, AL |
| 1914–15 | Alexandria, LA |
| 1916–17 | Shreveport, LA |
| 1918 | Montgomery, AL |

| 1919 | Waxahachie, TX |
| 1920 | Miami, FL |
| 1921 | Cisco, TX |
| 1922 | Mineral Wells, TX |
| 1923–30 | Orlando, FL |
| 1931–42 | Tampa, FL |
| 1943–45 | Bloomington, IN |
| 1946–87 | Tampa, FL |
| 1988 | Plant City, FL |

## Hottest Prospects

The Reds in the 1960s arguably had the finest crop of rookies of any Major League club in that decade. Many of them would win Rookie of the Year honors from either the Baseball Writers or *The Sporting News*. They formed the engine of the Big Red Machine, which won division or league titles six times in the 1970s and consecutive World Series titles in 1975 and 1976. Most of those vital cogs were honed in the Cincinnati farm system, although one, Joe Morgan, was the Rookie of the Year while with Houston.

The 1960 season marked the Cuban invasion of the Reds' Spring Training camp, with prospects Rogelio Alvarez, Joe Azcue, Tony Gonzalez, and Leo Cardenas, to be *The Sporting News'* top NL rookie, in camp. Another Hispanic rookie was Venezuelan Elio Chacon. Only Cardenas would stay with the Reds, their shortstop through most of the '60s. Hardthrowing Jim Maloney also arrived in the spring of 1960. He took three years to develop, then won 23 games in 1963 and was a mainstay of the staff for much of the decade.

Three good-looking rookies in the 1962 camp were Cookie Rojas, Tommy Harper, and Sammy Ellis. Ellis was 10–3 at Columbia in 1961 and went on to post a 12–6 mark in the Pacific Coast League in 1962. He was named *The Sporting News'* top NL prospect in 1964 and didn't disappoint, going 10–3 that year and 22–10 the next before fading.

There was only one rookie prospect in 1963, but he was a gem. Up from Macon, where he had hit .330, Pete Rose won Rookie of the Year honors, the first of his many awards. His Macon infield teammate, Tommy Helms, was in camp in 1964 but had to wait until 1966 to make the Reds roster. And, like Rose, he was named the NL Rookie of the Year, playing mostly at third base, though he moved to second the next year when Rose shifted to the outfield. The Reds in 1964 also boasted Billy McCool, who would be the loop's top rookie pitcher with a 6–5 record; Chico Ruiz; and the top prospect in their system, Mel Queen, whose father, Mel, had been a pitcher with the Giants and the Pirates in the '40s and '50s. Queen was an outfielder in 1964 but never learned to hit Major League pitching. His .179 career average no doubt prompted his switch to the mound, where had one outstanding season with 14 wins in 1967.

The spring of 1965 saw the arrival of Tony Perez, who had been the Pacific Coast League RBI leader in 1963, with 107, and had been up briefly the next year. Two young sluggers were also in camp: Lee May, with 25 homers and 110 RBI at Macon, eventually pushed Perez to third base; Art Shamsky arrived after 43 homers in two minor league seasons. After two years of seasoning, May went on to hit .265 in 1967 and be named *The Sporting News'* Rookie of the Year.

The best rookie in 1968 was a young catcher who played in 26 regular-season games for the Reds at the end of 1967. With a "can't miss" label, Johnny Bench went on to be named Rookie of the Year and is a sure Hall of Fame candidate for his stellar play over the next 15 years. He holds the Major League record for homers by a catcher with 389. Almost overlooked in 1968 was another rookie whose reputation as a leader and clutch hitter would be made in Kansas City: Hal McRae.

Two high-school All-Americans were the top prospects in the 1969 camp: Bernie Carbo, who had been picked ahead of Bench in the 1965 draft, and shortstop Darrell Chaney. Carbo came up to stay in 1970, and was named *The Sporting News'* Rookie of the Year.

The 1970 spring saw two rookie shortstops, Frank Duffy and Dave Concepcion, fighting Woody Woodward for the job. Concepcion won the battle, split the job in 1970, and has been there ever since. Two fine looking rookie pitchers also made the team that year. Wayne Simpson's first season, at 14–3, suggested greatness to come; but the powerful righthander could never duplicate it. Don Gullett, however, was a sustained success. Only a year earlier, Gullett had been pitching for Lynn (Ky.) High School. At 19, he was a starter/reliever, but left the bullpen in 1971 and went 16–6. Despite arm problems, he was a consistent winner; his .686 percentage is one of the all-time best, though he was 34 games short of the 300 he needed to have played in to make the official list.

In 1971 Ross Grimsley arrived as the Reds' "sure thing," but he started the year at Indianapolis. He was 6–0 in the minors when the Reds brought him back up, and he won 10 games that year for Cincinnati. In May 1971 the Reds fortuitously traded Duffy to the Giants for a young slugger who had not yet matured, but who would prove a steal. George Foster didn't start until 1974; he soon discovered his power and in 1977 became the first player since Willie Mays in 1965 to hit 50 or more home runs. Though nobody has done it since, George Bell, Mark McGwire and Andre Dawson came very close in 1987.

The spring of 1973 marked the arrival of Ed Armbrister, Ken Griffey, and Dan Driessen, all of whom would start the year at Indianapolis. Armbrister's claim to fame in the Majors came in the 1975 World Series, when he appeared to interfere with Red Sox catcher Carlton Fisk's throw to second base; replays showed he had, in fact, impeded Fisk's throw, though the call was never made. Driessen came up quickly in 1973, hitting .301 in 102 games. Like Perez, he was equally comfortable at third and first. Griffey hit .384 for the Reds the last six weeks of the 1973 season and has been a .300 hitter ever since in Cincinnati, New York, and Atlanta.

The top rookie in 1975 was Doug Flynn, who had been signed in 1972 after impressing the Reds in an open tryout. He hit a solid .268 while filling in off the bench but was shipped to the Mets in 1977 as one of a quartet of players for Tom Seaver. Two young pitchers in 1976, Santo Alcala and Pat Zachry, went on to post 11–4 and 14–7 records respectively. Zachry's win total was the most by a rookie that year. Alcala faded fast, but Zachry was another component in the Seaver trade a year later.

The 1977 season was finally Ray Knight's year. He had been in camp the previous three springs, and this year pounded Grapefruit League pitching at a .385 clip. During the season he hit .261 in limited action, and became the Reds' starting third baseman in 1979. Married to professional golfer Nancy Lopez, Knight has played for four teams the last seven years. Junior Kennedy, a 10-year minor league veteran, made the most of Spring Training, hitting .357 to win a spot as a backup infielder and 28-year-old rookie, hitting .255 for the season.

Cincinnati native Ron Oester was impressive enough after a late-season trial in 1979 that the Reds allowed free agent Joe Morgan to slip away to Houston in 1980. Oester hit .277 in 100 games that year and, though he hasn't made fans forget Morgan, has nonetheless been a consistent infielder since. Charlie Liebrandt stuck and posted a 10–9 record, though the clever lefty has enjoyed his best years in Kansas City. Mario Soto finally developed, also winning 10 games; nobody denies he has one of baseball's best arms, though injuries and attitude have prevented his being a consistent star.

In 1983 Gary Redus arrived with impressive AAA credentials: a .333 batting average, 54 stolen bases, and 93 RBI. He hit just .247 in his first full season, though he led the by-then weakened Reds with 17 homers.

Two of the top prospects in 1984 and 1985 were pitchers. John Franco quickly established himself as a bullpen stopper, appearing in 195 games in his first three years. The next year, lefty Tom Browning won 20 regular-season games, the most by a National League rookie since Harvey Haddix won 20 in 1953. Browning was awarded the Rookie of the Year award.

Eric Davis was handed the center-field job in Spring Training of 1985, but a disappointing spring earned him a trip to Denver. He hit 15 homers and stole 35 bases in 65 games there before being recalled. His brilliant performance since then has made him the Reds' franchise player of the '80s. Kal Daniels came up part-way through the 1986 season to bat .320; he followed that by leading the team in hitting in 1987 and looks to be an outfield partner of Davis's for many years to come.

## Top Rookies Each Spring
1960 Leo Cardenas, shortstop
1961 Ken Hunt, pitcher
1962 Sammy Ellis, pitcher
1963 Pete Rose, second base
1964 Sammy Ellis, pitcher
1965 Art Shamsky, outfield
1966 Tommy Helms, third base
1967 Gary Nolan, pitcher
1968 Johnny Bench, catcher
1969 Darrell Chaney, shortstop
1970 Don Gullet, pitcher; Bernie Carbo, outfield
1971 Ross Grimsley, pitcher
1972 Ed Sprague, pitcher
1973 Dan Driessen, third base
1974 Tom Carroll, pitcher
1975 Doug Flynn, second base; Pat Darcy, pitcher
1976 Pat Zachry, pitcher
1977 Ray Knight, third base
1978 Junior Kennedy, second base

1979  Jay Howell, pitcher
1980  Ron Oester, second base
1981  Bruce Berenyi, pitcher
1982  Paul Householder, outfield
1983  Gary Redus, outfield
1984  John Franco, pitcher
1985  Tom Browning, pitcher; Eric Davis, outfield
1986  Kal Daniels, outfield
1987  Pat Pacillo, pitcher

## NL Rookies of the Year
1963  Pete Rose, second base
1966  Tommy Helms, third base
1968  Johnny Bench, catcher
1976  Pat Zachry, pitcher
      (co-Rookie of the Year with Butch Metzger, San Diego)
1985  Tom Browning, pitcher

## Prospect to Watch in 1988
*Rob Lopez*, pitcher.  Lopez had an oustanding year for a mediocre
Vermont AA team and was voted the Eastern League's best
pitcher in 1987.

# PHILADELPHIA PHILLIES

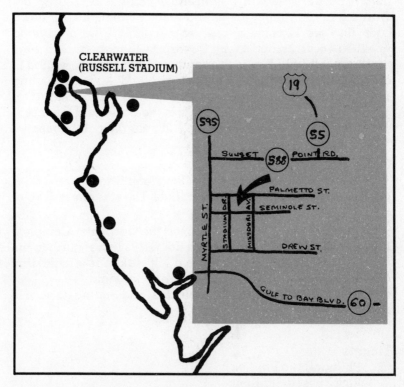

CLEARWATER
(RUSSELL STADIUM)

19
595
55
SUNSET 588 POINT RD.
PALMETTO ST.
MYRTLE ST.
STADIUM DR.
MISSOURI AV.
SEMINOLE ST.
DREW ST.
GULF TO BAY BLVD. 60

■ **Current site:**
Jack Russell Stadium
800 Phillies Drive
Clearwater, FL 33515
(813) 441-8638
■ **Dimensions:** 340' left
and right; 400' center
■ **Seating:** 5,347
■ **Built:** 1955

■ **Off-season use:**
Clearwater Phillies,
Florida State League
(Class A)
■ **Practice site:** At the
stadium daily at 10:00 A.M.
■ **Game time:** 1:05 P.M.
■ **Most convenient airport:**
Tampa

Jack Russell Stadium was built in 1955. Prior to that year, since their arrival in Clearwater from Miami in 1947, the Phillies had used a smaller ballpark located where the parking lot beyond the left-field foul line now stands. Russell, a former Major League pitcher, settled in Clearwater after his retirement and later became city commissioner. The city owns the facility.

Jack Russell Stadium is superbly maintained. The color and quality of the grass, condition of the running track around the field, and the stands are noticeably better than the Spring Training norm. Arcing the infield to the edge of the dirt down each line are 12 rows of box seats with 11 rows of covered reserved seats behind them. There are 12 rows of bleachers down the left-field line to the corner, without any elevation to assist the sightlines. Down the right-field line are batting cages and a workout area near the Phillie clubhouse. Autographs can be had off the front row of the boxes and bleachers and after the game as the players exit near their clubhouse.

### Getting to the Stadium
Take **Route 60** west, fork right on **Cleveland Street,** take a right on **Greenwood** and a right on **Seminole.** The stadium will be in view.

To get to the practice field, named the Carpenter Complex, take **Route 60** to **19,** *not* Alternate Route 19. Travel north to the first light, Drew Street, and make a left. Take Drew to the first light, Coachman Road. The fields are on the right.

*Parking:* The lot holds 1,000 vehicles, and finding a space is never a problem.

### Tickets
Philadelphia Phillies
Jack Russell Stadium
800 Phillies Drive
Clearwater, FL 33515
(813) 442-8496

The team schedule is available starting January 1. Season tickets and single-game tickets go on sale on February 15. All payment for advance sales must be made by personal check. Tickets cannot be ordered by phone. The Phils sold out three times in 1987.

*Prices:* Box $5; grandstand $4; bleachers $3; children $1. Prices subject to change.

## Team Hotel
Quality Inn
120 U.S. Highway 19 North
Clearwater, FL 33575
(813) 799-1116
Very few players actually stay here. Many of them have apartments or rent condominiums each year. Nobody from the front office stays here, and there are no activities at the hotel.

## Players' Favorite Leisure Spots
There are many restaurants in the area, including Tio Pepe, which serves Mexican food, Bob Heilman's Beachcomber on the beach, and the Showboat Dinner Theater. Also, there is the dog track, Derby Lane, in St. Petersburg, which players from many teams frequent.

## Previous Spring Training Locations
| | |
|---|---|
| 1901 | Philadelphia, PA |
| 1902 | Washington, NC |
| 1903 | Richmond, VA |
| 1904 | Savannah, GA |
| 1905 | Augusta, GA |
| 1906–08 | Savannah, GA |
| 1909–10 | Southern Pines, NC |
| 1911 | Birmingham, AL |
| 1912 | Hot Springs, AR |
| 1913 | Southern Pines, NC |
| 1914 | Wilmington, NC |
| 1915–18 | St. Petersburg, FL |
| 1919 | Charlotte, NC |
| 1920 | Birmingham, AL |
| 1921 | Gainesville, FL |
| 1922–24 | Leesburg, FL |
| 1925–27 | Bradenton, FL |
| 1928–37 | Winter Haven, FL |
| 1938 | Biloxi, MS |
| 1939 | New Braunfels, TX |
| 1940–42 | Miami Beach, FL |
| 1943 | Hershey, PA |
| 1944–45 | Wilmington, DE |
| 1946 | Miami Beach, FL |
| 1947–present | Clearwater, FL |

## Hottest Prospects

The 1959 International League champion Buffalo Bisons produced a number of prospects for the 1960 Phillies, including shortstop Bobby Wine and pitchers Art Mahaffey, who would lose 19 in 1961 and turn around to win the same number the next year, and Dallas Green, most recently the Cubs' General Manager. But the Phils remained in the cellar, where they had been in 1958 and 1959, and made it four in a row in 1961.

Mahaffey's 19 victories led the Phils back over the .500 mark in 1962, supported by rookie Jack Hamilton's nine wins. The top rookie of the fine 1963 spring crop played only 10 games with the Phils that year; but Richie Allen came back in 1964 to anchor at third base, hit the first of his 351 career homers, and, with a .318 average, win Rookie of the Year honors. Ray Culp made the club and had a fine year in 1963, winning 14 and recognition as *The Sporting News'* top NL rookie pitcher. Marcelino Lopez also had an impressive spring in 1963 but after four games was sent down. He came back two years later to win the AL's top rookie pitcher award with the California Angels.

Meantime, Hamilton was traded in December 1963 to Detroit with Don Demeter for pitcher Jim Bunning, who would, with Allen, lead the Phillies to almost-certain victory in 1964, only to see the pennant slip away in the team's ill-timed collapse.

A top Phillie prospect in the spring of 1967 was Steve Arlin, who attended camp while on vacation from Ohio State Dental School. The Phils financed his dental school bills for three more years, but in the end determined he would not help them. Their judgment appears correct: Arlin wound up in San Diego and lost 19 in 1971 and 21 the following year.

The Phils' farm teams were winning — none finished lower than second in 1968 — and in 1970 they bore fruit: 12 rookies, the most in the Majors, made the Phillies' roster. They included Greg Luzinski, who would finally start in 1972, and two Pacific Coast League All-Stars: keystoners Larry Bowa and Denny Doyle. Bowa moved right into the starting shortstop's spot, bumping one of 1969's top rookies, Don Money, to third. Bowa would hold shortstop for the rest of the decade, flanked at second for several years by Doyle. He led the NL in fielding five times during the '70s. Doyle moved on to the Angels, then to the Red Sox midway in their 1975 pennant race, and ended his career in Boston.

The top prospect in 1973 was third-baseman Mike Schmidt, who was injured in the spring and started the season on the disabled list. He had hit the first of his more than 500 career home runs in a brief trial the year before, and the Phils handed him the third-base job. He barely hit his weight the first year, weighing in at .196, but greatness was around the corner. Schmidt went to .282 in 1974 with 116 RBI, and led the circuit in homers, something he would do six more times in the next decade. Another leading rookie in 1973 entered the starting line-up, commencing a career as durable as Schmidt's would be. Bob Boone, son of former Major League infielder Ray Boone, hit a respectable .261 and showed the great arm that would make him one of the finest defensive catchers of his era playing for the Phils and Angels.

The Phils had high hopes for young pitcher Tom Underwood in 1975, and he came through, at least at home. Underwood was 12–2 at Veteran's Stadium but just 2–11 on the road. Despite his 27–20 career record with the Phils, he was traded in mid-1977 to the Cardinals for Bake McBride. That year the Phils' rookie crop featured hopefuls Keith Moreland, shortstop Todd Cruz, and pitchers Kevin Saucier and Randy Lerch. Only Lerch would make the team, something he would have done the year previous but for the addition of veteran Jim Kaat. Lerch went 10–6 in 1977 despite a horrendous ERA over five. Warren Brusstar's ERA was half that, and he was 7–2 after being recalled, his best Major League season.

Marty Bystrom came up at the end of 1980 and glistened: he started six games, won five of them (with no losses), and promised even more with a 1.50 ERA. He could never repeat that early success. Throughout that year, Lonnie Smith showed that his six impressive minor league seasons were no fluke. His .330 average at Oklahoma City in 1979 finally convinced the Phils to give him a shot, and he topped it, hitting .339 and stealing 33 bases in his first season. He followed that with a .324 average the next year, but by then the Phils had lost faith in Boone behind the plate. Coveting Cleveland's young star Bo Diaz, they involved Smith in a three-way trade with the Indians and Cardinals, and he ended up in St. Louis.

Rookie Juan Samuel hit just .216 in the spring of 1984, but his .277 average at the end of the 1983 campaign assured him a starting job. The faith was justified as he broke the Phillies' 78-year-old team stolen base record with 72 and was named *The Sporting News*' rookie player of the year. He finished second to Dwight Gooden in the Baseball Writers' official rookie vote and has been a Phils fixture ever since.

The top prospect in 1987 was pitcher Marvin Freeman, who won 13 games at Reading in double-A and won twice in the Majors at the end of the 1986 season. His great arm was sometimes sabotaged by control problems, but his promise was obvious.

## Top Rookies Each Spring
1960   Frank Herrera
1961   Clarence Coleman
1962   Ted Savage, outfield
1963   Richie Allen, third base
1964   Richie Allen, third base
1965   Dave Bennett, pitcher
1966   none
1967   Steve Arlin, pitcher
1968   Don Money, shortstop
1969   Larry Hisle, outfield
1970   Denny Doyle, second base
1971   Roger Freed, outfield
1972   Greg Luzinski, outfield
1973   Bob Boone, catcher
1974   Jerry Martin, outfield
1975   Tom Underwood, pitcher
1976   none
1977   Randy Lerch, pitcher
1978   Kevin Saucier, pitcher
1979   Jose Martinez, pitcher
1980   Scott Munninghoff, pitcher
1981   Marty Bystrom, pitcher
1982   Len Matuszek first base
1983   Tony Ghelfi, pitcher
1984   Juan Samuel, second base
1985   John Russell, catcher
1986   Fred Toliver, pitcher
1987   Marvin Freeman, pitcher

## NL Rookie of the Year
1964   Richie Allen, third base

## Prospects to Watch in 1988
*Keith Hughes*, *outfield*. Acquired from the Yankees, he was dealt away and then retrieved, and is rated highly.

**Ken Jackson**, *shortstop.*  He hit close to .300 all year for AA Reading, and his fielding skills are certainly of Major League calibre.

# PITTSBURGH PIRATES

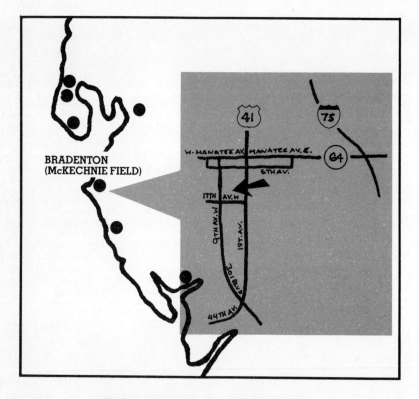

BRADENTON
(McKECHNIE FIELD)

■ **Current site:**
McKechnie Field
17th Avenue and
9th Street West
Bradenton, FL 33505
(813) 748-4610
■ **Dimensions:** 370' left
and right; 410' center
■ **Seating:** 5,000

■ **Built:** 1953
■ **Off-season use:**
Pirate rookie and
instructional camps
■ **Practice site:** At the
field daily at 10:00 A.M.
■ **Game time:** 1:00 P.M.
■ **Most convenient airport:**
Sarasota or Tampa

McKechnie Field, a city-owned stadium, was built in the early '50s, although it looks much older. It has also been used by the Boston and Milwaukee Braves. The practice complex is now called Pirate City. Bill McKechnie, a ballplayer, coach, and manager for whom the stadium is named, retired to Bradenton, where he died in 1965. During his career, he managed the St. Louis Cardinals, the Boston Braves, and the Pirates, including the Bucs' World Championship team in 1925.

When Sarasota's Payne Park passes from the scene after the 1988 Spring Training season, McKechnie Field will be the last true replica of another era. This is a ballpark where it is very easy to summon up the image of Babe Ruth at bat or Al Simmons running across the outfield.

When you walk up to the stadium you pass an old Greyhound station behind home plate. Right next to it is Bill & Bev's Dugout, a hangout for coffee and breakfast that looks like it served Ruth and has done no interior decorating since.

McKechnie Field's charm is enhanced by old wooden seats (watch out for splinters) and a free-standing clubhouse down the left-field line. Spring Training oldtimers remember when the clubhouse area was not fenced off as it is now, but it is still easy to catch ballplayers going in and out before and after the games. An easy-to-reach spot at the railing of the left-field bleachers is a good place to get some autographs before and after a game.

The batting cages down the right-field line permit a bird's-eye view for fans watching a player working on his stroke. Occasionally, a ball will make its way under the protective netting and a fan can grab it. You can also expect foul pop-ups to land in the concession and food area behind home plate.

## Getting to the Stadium

From **Interstate 4**, get onto **Route 301 North.** Take that through Bradenton into **Manatee Avenue**, and take Manatee all the way to the ballpark.

*Parking:* The stadium lot is small, but there are plenty of other lots within walking distance.

## Tickets

Pittsburgh Pirates
McKechnie Field
17th Avenue and 9th Street West
Bradenton, FL 33505
(813) 748-4610

The team makes its Spring Training schedule available in early December. Season tickets may be purchased by mail from January 15 through February 1. Any checks received before January 15 will be sent back. But, rest assured, season tickets will be available, so there is no need to send your money early. Single-game tickets may be ordered by mail — and paid for by check — beginning February 8. The Pirates sold out one game in 1987.

*Prices:* Box $5; reserved $4; general admission $3; children $1.

## Team Hotel

There is no team hotel. Players and executives who do not stay in condominiums are at

Pirate City
1701 Roberto Clemente Memorial Drive
Bradenton, FL 33508
(813) 747-3031

Pirate City is not open to the public, and there are no fan-oriented activities provided there.

## Players' Favorite Leisure Spots

The players like to go to Holmes Beach, Bradenton Beach, and the Bradenton Mall. They also frequent Chili's and Bennigan's. Near their condominiums is a seafood place called Trader Jack's, where they often go to eat.

## Previous Spring Training Locations

| | |
|---|---|
| 1901–16 | Hot Springs, AR |
| 1917 | Columbus, AR |
| 1918 | Jacksonville, FL |
| 1919 | Birmingham, AL |
| 1920–23 | Hot Springs, AR |
| 1924–34 | Paso Robles, CA |
| 1935 | San Bernardino, CA |
| 1936 | San Antonio, TX |
| 1937–42 | San Bernardino, CA |
| 1943–45 | Muncie, IN |
| 1946 | San Bernardino, CA |
| 1947 | Miami Beach, FL |
| 1948 | Hollywood, CA |
| 1949–52 | San Bernardino, CA |
| 1953 | Havana, Cuba |
| 1954 | Fort Pierce, FL |
| 1955–68 | Fort Myers, FL |
| 1969–present | Bradenton, FL |

## Hottest Prospects

1960 would be a storybook year for the veteran Pirates, culminated by Bill Mazeroski's dramatic home run that defeated the Yankees in the World Series. Rookies couldn't crack the Bucs' line-up, though management had spring hopes for the pitcher tabbed by *The Sporting News* as the best-looking prospect in 1960. Jim Umbricht came off a 14–8 minor league mark the previous year but managed only one win with the pennant winners and was left unprotected in 1962, to be picked up by the Houston Colt .45s. Joe Gibbon fared better. The top spring performer in 1961 won 13 games that year and, though he never won more than 10 again, developed into a useful relief pitcher and lasted 13 seasons in the Majors.

Another pitcher, imposing 6'6" Bob Veale, impressed in camp in 1962 but was sent down after going 2–2. He would be back to produce one of the best winning percentages in the league through the mid-'60s with 67 victories from 1964–1967. Free-swinging first-baseman Donn Clendenon made the squad in 1962 and was a Pirate regular through 1968. He was not protected that winter, as the Pirates anticipated the arrival of Al Oliver the next spring. Clendenon was picked by the expansion Montreal Expos, who quickly traded him to Houston for Rusty Staub. But Clendenon refused to report to the Astros and sat out the first half of the year before the Mets picked him up as insurance during their first pennant year, 1969. Clendenon played an important role for The Amazin' Mets, hitting three home runs during the World Series victory over Baltimore.

*The Sporting News* tabbed Bob Bailey, coming off a .299 season at Columbus, as the top Bucs' prospect in 1963. His bat didn't materialize as expected, and he and young shortstop Gene Michael were dealt to Los Angeles in December 1966 for the Dodgers' brilliant but aging shortstop Maury Wills. But one of Bailey's 1962 Columbus teammates was destined to play the next 20 years in Pittsburgh and be one of the most celebrated players in Pirates history. Willie Stargell came up as an outfielder, occasionally relieving Clendenon at first. His first 11 homers came in 1963, unleashing the torrent to come, topped by 48 in 1971 and 44 two years later. "Pops," as he came to be known, suffered the lot of many sluggers and struck out often, ending his career second on the all-time list, behind Reggie Jackson.

The leading 1966 prospect was pitcher Steve Blass. He had been with the Bucs in 1964, displaying flashes of brilliance, and had spent the interim year at Columbus, winning thirteen times. He started slowly for the Pirates, then enjoyed some splendid years from 1968–72, winning 34 and losing only 16 the last two of those years, with an ERA well under 3.00. Unaccountably, he suffered mysterious control problems in 1973; his ERA ballooned over 9.00 as he couldn't find the plate, and he was forced to retire the following year.

Bob Robertson was a leading candidate in 1967 but would not find room at first base until 1970, after Clendenon's departure and Oliver's move to the outfield. Oliver outshined Robertson in the minors in 1967, hitting .315 at Columbus, and earning a faster promotion to the Majors. His 1969 rookie teammate was third-baseman Richie Hebner, whose .301 average was his highest as a regular in a long career. Hebner avoided winter ball, preferring to dig graves instead, surely one of the game's most eccentric off-season activities.

Catcher Milt May, outfielder Gene Clines, and second-baseman Rennie Stennett were all rookies in camp in 1971, and all played some that year. Stennett in particular was impressive, hitting .353 and claiming second base for a number of years to come. Hard-hitting Richie Zisk came up at the very end of 1971 but, unable to break into the outfield corps of Clemente, Stargell, and Oliver, had to wait until 1973. Clemente's tragic death the winter before offered Zisk the chance, and he spent the next 11 years producing the finest record of any Major Leaguer whose name begins with the alphabet's last letter.

Infielder Ken Macha faced much the same problem as Zisk in 1975. He came to camp having hit .345 with 100 RBI the previous season in the Eastern League but could not displace Hebner at third or the sure-handed Frank Taverash, who had taken over at short the previous year. Two Eastern League teammates of Macha's were considered good Pirates' prospects: Craig Reynolds, the Pirates' number one pick in the 1971 draft, and a young infielder they would quickly trade. Willie Randolph was packaged with two others for the Yankees' big righthander Doc Medich. Randolph has been the Yanks' second-baseman ever since and seems to improve with age.

Other prospects in 1975 included two former high school basketball players connected to future NBA rivals: pitchers John Candelaria, 6'7", and Jim Marshall, an inch shorter. "The Candy Man" had been New York City's second best all-time high school rebounder, behind Lew Alcindor. His Pittsburgh career grew more stormy with time, despite his stellar record, and he eventually moved to Anaheim with the Angels. Marshall was a high school teammate of the Celtics' Dave Cowens, but the connection didn't help him in the Majors.

The 1977 camp featured two outfielders, fleet Omar Moreno and powerful Tony Armas. Moreno hit .315 in the International League, and his ability to run down fly balls earned him the job in center and allowed the Bucs to trade Zisk to the White Sox for reliever Terry Forster. Moreno holds the Pirates' team mark for stolen bases with 96 in 1980. Armas never had a chance in Pittsburgh. At the end of Spring Training in 1977, he was sent to Oakland in a trade with Medich, for Phil Garner and Tommy Helms. Good for Armas: he, Dwayne Murphy, and Rickey Henderson formed the best outfield of the early '80s.

Don Robinson had unimpressive credentials to recommend him in 1978, with a 7–6 record at Shreveport the previous year. But he pitched his way onto the squad with a 1.69 spring ERA and followed that with the best of his Major League seasons: 14–6, and *The Sporting News* award as the NL's top rookie pitcher, the first Pirate rookie to win any kind of award. Robinson would win games with his bat as well as his arm: he has been used on occasion as a pinch-hitter, and his lifetime batting average would make many batters proud.

One wonders what happened to first-baseman Dorian Boyland, another top Columbus prospect in camp in 1979. Touted as potentially another Harmon Killebrew, Boyland was demoted before the season started; he had garnered his only two Major League hits and his only game in the field at the end of 1978. Demotion also faced catcher Tony Pena in 1980, though the reasons were much less obvious. Pena had hit .329 at Portland and .429 in eight games with the big club the year previous, and he continued that pace in Spring Training, hitting .324. Ed Ott was then the Bucs' capable catcher, and Steve Nicosia, spring 1979's top rookie, waited in the wings, so Pena had to bide his time despite his obvious talent. By 1982 he was the Pirate starter and would soon be recognized as one of the finest catchers in either League.

Everybody's favorite rookie in the 1981 camp, for sentimental and professional reasons, was second-baseman Vance Law, son of the star Pirate pitcher in the '50s and '60s, Vernon Law. Vance had posted solid AAA seasons of .310 and .295 but found the jump to the Majors a difficult transition and was dealt during Spring Training the next year to the White Sox in a minor transaction. Two years later he moved to Montreal where he has both started and been a utility infielder.

The top prospect in 1982 was second-bagger Johnny Ray, for whom the Pirates had swapped veteran Phil Garner to the Astros midway through the 1981 season. Ray quickly established himself as one of the league's best. His "top rookie" successors have been less successful. Joe Orsulak had a solid first year in 1984 and hit .300 the next, before slumping a bit in 1986. Mike Bielecki struggled after leading the Pacific Coast League in strikeouts while posting a 19–3 record in 1984; he came of age a bit in 1987, offering future hopes. The same could be said of Sid Bream, whose statistics have gradually improved each season.

Indeed, the Pirates are now heavily reliant on their youth, perhaps inspired by Sid Thrift, the youngest General Manager in the game. Their three legitimate stars, Pena, Ray, and pitcher Rick Reuschel, were traded away during the 1987 season in return for a flock of new talent. And the youth movement seems to be working: the Pirates were among the hottest teams in the Majors in August and September last year and finished greatly improved over the season before.

## Top Rookies Each Spring
1960  Jim Umbricht, pitcher
1961  Joe Gibbon, pitcher
1962  Donn Clendenon, first base
1963  Bob Bailey, third base
1964  Gene Alley, shortstop
1965  none
1966  Steve Blass, pitcher
1967  Bob Robertson, first base
1968  Al Oliver, outfield
1969  Richie Hebner, third base
1970  Angel Mangual, outfield
1971  Gene Clines, outfield
1972  Richie Zisk, outfield
1973  Fernando Gonzalez, third base
1974  Doug Bair, pitcher
1975  Ken Macha, third base
1976  Craig Reynolds, shortstop
1977  Omar Moreno, outfield
1978  Don Robinson, pitcher
1979  Steve Nicosia, catcher
1980  Tony Pena, catcher
1981  Vance Law, second base
1982  Johnny Ray, second base

1983   Brian Harper, outfield
1984   Joe Orsulak, outfield
1985   Mike Bielecki, pitcher
1986   Sid Bream, first base
1987   Bob Patterson, pitcher

## Prospects to Watch in 1988

*Vincente Palacios*, pitcher.  The top pitcher in 1987 for Vancouver in the Pacific Coast League, he had a 13–5 record and led the league in strikeouts and ERA.

*Mackey Sasser*, catcher.  Acquired from the Giants, Sasser was the Pacific Coast League All-Star catcher and is given a chance to start with the Bucs in 1988.

# ST. LOUIS CARDINALS

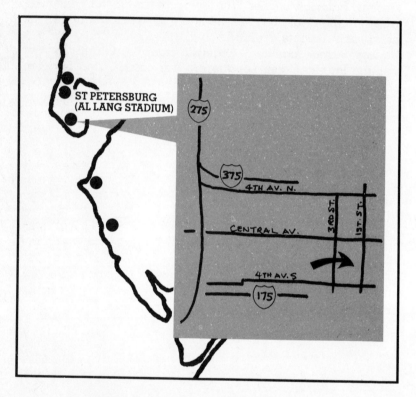

ST PETERSBURG
(AL LANG STADIUM)

275

375

4TH AV. N.

3RD ST.

1ST ST.

CENTRAL AV.

4TH AV. S

175

■ **Current site:**
Al Lang Stadium
180 2nd Avenue S.E.
St. Petersburg, FL 33701
(813) 896-4641
■ **Dimensions:**
330' left and right;
404' center
■ **Seating:** 7,229
■ **Built:** 1976

■ **Off-season use:**
St. Petersburg Cardinals,
Florida State League
(Class A)
■ **Practice site:** At the
stadium daily at 10:00 A.M.
■ **Game times:** 1:00 P.M.
(day), 7:30 P.M. (night)
■ **Most convenient airport:**
Tampa

Al Lang Stadium — named for the father of Florida spring baseball — is among the best Spring Training sites and this season, for the first time in many years, will be home to only one team, as the Mets have moved to Port St. Lucie. Al Lang combines great sightlines from all the permanent seats (which ring the field to the bases) and the picturesque charm provided by literally thousands of sailboats and yachts moored in Tampa Bay, just outside the left-field fence. But beware the bleacher seats in left field; not only is their lack of elevation a hindrance to seeing the ballgame, but you also miss the beautiful backdrop of the sailboats in the bay.

The permanent stands have eight rows of boxes, five rows of reserves, and 16 rows of general admission. Every seat is great.

In addition to the ballgame, Al Lang fans are entertained by a singing hot dog vendor (you can't miss him, particularly in the home 7th when he leads the crowd in "Take Me Out to the Ballgame") who calls his wares "tube steaks."

The extensive parking lot behind the left-field fence gives assurance that parking is never a problem; it also provides a great spot to wait for batting practice home runs before a ballgame.

The one drawback for the Spring Training fan at Al Lang is that it is among the more difficult places to secure autographs. The elevation of the permanent stands that provides the great sightlines makes it harder to catch the ballplayers walking by before and after a game. And the fact that parking facilities ring the park makes it difficult to predict exactly where to find exiting ballplayers after the game.

## Getting to the Stadium

Take **Interstate 275** to exit 9. The stadium will be just to your left at the bottom of the long exit ramp. The minor league practice facility, named Payson Field after the original Mets' owner, Joan Payson, is six miles west of Al Lang Stadium, at 7901 30th Avenue North.

*Parking:* There is plenty of parking nearby, in lots or on the street. The lots of the Bayfront Center and Hilton Hotel are both close.

## Tickets

St. Louis Cardinals
180 2nd Avenue S.E.
St. Petersburg, FL 33701

Early March: (813) 894-4773
Prior to Spring Training: call the St. Louis office at
(314) 421-3060.

The schedule is available on January 1. Season and single-game tickets may be purchased by personal check through the mail. Any orders received before January 1 will be returned. The Cards sold out three times in 1987.

*Prices:* Boxes $6; grandstand $4.50; bleachers $2.50.

## Team Hotel

St. Petersburg Hilton & Towers
333 1st Street South
St. Petersburg, FL 33701
(813) 894-5000

## Players' Favorite Leisure Spots

The players frequent three establishments in particular: 10 Beach Drive, Pepin's, and El Cap.

## Previous Spring Training Locations

| | |
|---|---|
| 1901–02 | St. Louis, MO |
| 1903 | Dallas, TX |
| 1904 | Houston, TX |
| 1905 | Marlin Springs, TX |
| 1906–08 | Houston, TX |
| 1909–10 | Little Rock, AR |
| 1911 | West Baden IN |
| 1912 | Jackson, MS |
| 1913 | Columbis, GA |
| 1914 | St. Augustine, FL |
| 1915–17 | Hot Wells, TX |
| 1918 | San Antonio, TX |
| 1919 | St. Louis, MO |
| 1920 | Brownsville, TX |
| 1921–22 | Orange, TX |
| 1923–24 | Bradenton, FL |
| 1925 | Stockton, CA |
| 1926 | San Antonio, TX |
| 1927–29 | Avon Park, FL |
| 1930–36 | Bradenton, FL |
| 1937 | Daytona Beach, FL |
| 1938–42 | St. Petersburg, FL |
| 1943–45 | Cairo, IL |
| 1946–present | St. Petersburg, FL |

## Hottest Prospects

The Cards came to Spring Training in 1960 having finished the previous year in seventh place, only the second time since 1916 they had finished that low. Stan Musial was starting his third decade with the team, his brilliant career on the wane. Everyone was looking for a better effort, and the team complied, finishing first in the Grapefruit League and third during the regular season.

A trade at the end of May that year brought a young Dominican second baseman to St. Louis who would be a solid fixture there for 11 more seasons. Julian Javier was picked up from Pittsburgh in exchange for a pitcher with a world-class nickname, "Vinegar Bend" Mizell. The 1960 season was also the first of 18 for lefty Ray Sadecki. His useful rookie mark of 9–9 was compiled after he returned from Rochester. Sadecki would win 20 games for the Redbirds in their 1964 World Championship year. Unfortunately, the rookie picked by *The Sporting News* as most likely to help the Cards in 1960 fizzled. Charlie James had hit .300 just once in four years in the minors and hit only .180 in 50 games as the Cardinals quickly realized he was not the answer.

In 1962 the Cards unveiled another good pitcher, Ray Washburn, who had led the International League in wins and ERA in 1961. He won 12 games his first year, fought off a shoulder injury the next and became one of the mainstays of the Cards' staff through the '60s. Dal Maxvill's .229 batting average at Charleston in 1961 didn't warrant him a promotion; as the season started he was sent to Tulsa for hitting instruction and responded with a .348 average, prompting his quick return to the Majors. Despite the instruction, Maxvill was always a light hitter; however, the Cards soon came to value his slick glove, and he and Javier were a splendid keystone combination until both were traded in 1972.

Jim Harris, the leading rookie candidate in 1963, never made it to the Majors, and the club put its money on Ed Spiezio, hoping he would be another infielder of the future. He wasn't in St. Louis but had a couple of useful seasons for the expansion San Diego Padres in 1969-70.

The leading rookie pitchers in 1966 and 1967 had meteoric careers. Larry Jaster won three complete games at the end of 1965, started the next year at Tulsa, and came up to notch an 11–5 record, followed by 9–7. He would win barely half as many the next four years and was quickly out of baseball. A Tulsa teammate of Jaster's, Dick Hughes, had a brief trial in

1966 and then posted a brilliant 16–6 rookie mark with a 2.68 ERA in 1967, good enough to have him named the NL's top rookie pitcher by *The Sporting News.* Tendonitis in Hughes's right shoulder cut his record to 2–2 the following year, his last in the Majors.

Big Mike Torrez was counted on in 1968 but never blossomed in St. Louis and was traded to the young Montreal team midway through the 1971 season. Though a consistent winner thereafter, Torrez found himself traded on five other occasions the next 12 years. Ted Simmons fared much better in St. Louis. Up for cups of coffee at the end of 1968 and 1969, Simmons stuck in 1970 and was the Redbirds' catcher through the decade, five times hitting over .300, before being part of the second massive Cardinals trade in four days in December 1980. Simmons went to Milwaukee with Pete Vuckovich and Rollie Fingers (whom the Cards had acquired four days before from San Diego) for several promising batters and pitchers.

The Cards had a couple of smooth-fielding rookies in camp in 1973. Ken Reitz, called by ex-Card Mike Shannon "probably the best fielder at third the team has ever had" became a starter alongside shortstop Mike Tyson. Reitz has, no doubt, the most symmetrical trading record in Major League history. Dealt to the Giants on December 8, 1975, he returned to the Cardinals December 10, 1976. Four years later, on December 9, 1980, he moved on to the Cubs. Tyson, too, ended up with the Cubs, after an admirable infield career with the Cards. Also closely watched in 1973 were Hector and Cirilio Cruz, brothers of Cardinal regular Jose Cruz. Headline writers were already warming up phrases like "Cards Cruz Control," but this would not be a replay of the Alou brothers in San Francisco: Hector started one year, 1976, but hit only .228 and faded. Cirilio never made it to the Majors.

Bake McBride was given the center-field job on the first day of Spring Training 1974, and he didn't disappoint, posting a .309 average with 30 stolen bases his first full year. He was passed over by *The Sporting News,* whose editors chose the Astros' Greg Gross as NL Rookie of the Year; but the Baseball Writers felt differently, and he was the first Cardinal to win official Rookie of the Year honors since Wally Moon and Bill Virdon won back-to-back awards in 1954–55.

The Cards traded Joe Torre at the end of the 1974 season to make room for their "can't miss" rookie of 1975, Keith Hernandez. He earned the reputation by leading the American Association in hitting at .351 in 1974. Hernandez started slowly, returning to Tulsa for the second half of 1975; but by 1976 he was solidly ensconced as the Cardinals' first baseman. Traded to the Mets in mid-1983, he remains one of the best in the game.

Ken Oberkfell and Tommy Herr arrived soon after Hernandez to create the infield that would carry the Cards to the top in 1982. Oberkfell's steady bat and glove anchored third base, while Herr patrolled the other side of the infield at second. Herr was the best Spring Training rookie in 1978, hitting a healthy .391 to lead the club, but wouldn't stick until Tyson was traded and Oberkfell moved to third the latter half of 1980. That Spring Training, slugging first-baseman Leon Durham was switched to the outfield, as he had no chance of playing ahead of Hernandez. He and Reitz were soon traded to the Cubs for relief pitcher extraordinaire, Bruce Sutter. The other leading prospect in 1980, Terry Kennedy, who had been *The Sporting News'* College Player of the Year at Florida State and hit .590 in his first stop in pro ball, was dealt the day before Durham to San Diego, in the Cardinals' trading frenzy at the end of the year.

Coming off a 13–9 record in the minors the previous year, Dave LaPoint was counted on to deliver in 1982, and he did. Alternating between the rotation and the bullpen, LaPoint posted a solid 9–3 record and pitched well in the Series. The surprise of the year was Willie McGee. Stolen from the Yankees' organization for pitcher Bob Sykes over the winter, he spent most of the spring in the minor league camp. McGee came up in May to replace the injured David Green and hit a solid .296, placing third in the Rookie of the Year voting. He has been the Cards' sterling center-fielder ever since.

Andy Van Slyke had broken his elbow in Spring Training 1981 but two years later brought his promising minor league record to St. Petersburg. He started the season back in the minors, but got his chance because of an injury to third-baseman Mike Ramsey and improved every season thereafter. Dealt to the Pirates for Tony Pena in the spring of 1987, he became the team leader. Danny Cox and Terry Pendleton both made their initial Major League contributions in 1984, and both have blossomed in the intervening years.

Everyone watched Vince Coleman in the spring of 1985. He had set a new American Association record in 1984 with 101 stolen bases, and it was just a matter of time before he terrorized the National League. He started the year in Louisville but was quickly brought up in April to replace Tito Landrum and never stopped running, establishing three Major League rookie records: stolen bases (110), times caught stealing (25), and fewest times hitting into a double play (3). A freak injury to Coleman during the World Series that year may have cost the Cardinals the title: a tarp rolled over his ankle damaging his foot, and he missed most of the seven game debacle won by Kansas City. Coleman was only the fourth player in history to be the unanimous choice for Rookie of the Year.

Todd Worrell came up at the end of 1985 and showed why he would win the Rookie of the Year award the next season, when the fireballing righthander saved 36 games. The top spring rookie in 1986, however, was another pitcher, Greg Mathews, who started the year in Louisville but returned to win 11 times, the most by a Cardinal rookie since Reggie Cleveland's 12 in 1971. Joe Magrane was *The Sporting News'* pick to be the top rookie in 1987, off his 9–6 record and 1.82 ERA at Louisville in 1986. He was a solid addition to the Cardinal's staff, prompting the September headline "Cards Deal Cubs Magrane Headache," and pitched a crucial shut-out against the Expos in the Cards' pennant drive.

## Top Rookies Each Spring

1960   Charlie James, outfield
1961   Bob Miller, pitcher
1962   Ray Washburn, pitcher
1963   Jim Harris
1964   Ed Spiezio, third base
1965   Ed Spiezio, third base
1966   Larry Jaster, pitcher
1967   Dick Hughes, pitcher
1968   Mike Torrez, pitcher
1969   Joe Hague, first base
1970   Ted Simmons, catcher
1971   Reggie Cleveland, pitcher
1972   Jim Bibby, pitcher
1973   Mike Tyson, shortstop; Ken Reitz, third base
1974   Bake McBride, outfield
1975   Keith Hernandez, first base
1976   Garry Templeton, shortstop
1977   Buddy Schultz, pitcher
1978   Tom Herr, second base
1979   John Fulgham, pitcher
1980   Leon Durham, first base; Terry Kennedy, catcher

1981   Andy Rincon, pitcher
1982   Willie McGee, outfield; Dave LaPoint, pitcher
1983   Andy Van Slyke, outfield
1984   Danny Cox, pitcher; Terry Pendleton, third base
1985   Vince Coleman, outfield
1986   Greg Mathews, pitcher
1987   Joe Magrane, pitcher

## NL Rookies of the Year
1974   Bake McBride, outfield
1985   Vince Coleman, outfield
1986   Todd Worrell, pitcher

## Prospect to Watch in 1988
*Lance Johnson, outfield*. All-everything in the American Association in 1987, at Louisville, the speedy Johnson is touted a "can't miss" prospect by Baseball America. He was voted the league's outstanding prospect by rival managers and was named both the American Association MVP and Rookie of the Year in 1987.

# TEXAS RANGERS

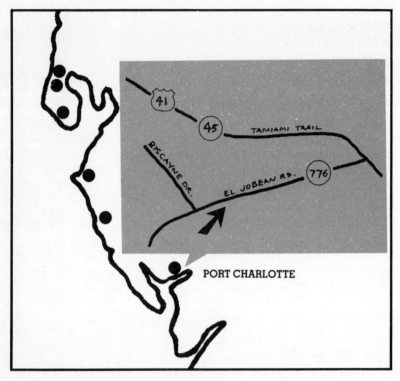

PORT CHARLOTTE

■ **Current site:**
Charlotte County Stadium
2300 El Jobean Road
Port Charlotte, FL 33949
(813) 625-9500
■ **Dimensions:** 340' left
and right; 410' center
■ **Seating:** 5,335
■ **Built:** 1985
■ **Off-season use:**

Port Charlotte Rangers,
Florida State League
(Class A); Gulf Coast
Rangers, Gulf Coast
League (Rookie)
■ **Practice site:** At the
stadium daily at 9:00 A.M.
■ **Game time:** 1:30 P.M.
■ **Most convenient airport:**
Sarasota or Tampa

Gulf Coast Group

Charlotte County Stadium opened in 1986, a full-fledged training facility that, for the first time, brings together all players in the Rangers' system. It contains five full practice fields and the stadium itself among its 82 acres. Indoor and outdoor batting cages and the clubhouse and office facilities round out the complex.

A modern stadium with great sight lines, Charlotte County has a field in superior condition. Six rows of box seats are backed up by 16 rows of reserves to the edge of the dirt down both lines.

Slightly off the beaten track, south of Sarasota, the park doesn't have the charm of some of the older locations. One can get autographs readily enough off the front row of the boxes, something Rangers' fans enjoy to the utmost. Perhaps because the team is somewhat isolated, a Rangers ticket is among the hardest to obtain in Florida.

## Getting to the Stadium

Take **Exit 32** off **Route 75** to **Route 41** (Tamiami Trail). Go left for two miles, then right on **State Road 776** (El Jobean Road) for one mile to the stadium.

*Parking:* There is plenty of parking. However, the lot gets muddy when it rains.

## Tickets

Texas Rangers
P.O. Box 3609
Port Charlotte, FL 33949
(813) 624–2211 (ticket office)
(813) 625–9500 (administrative office)

The printed schedule is available on December 1. Season tickets can be ordered by mail and paid for by personal check, beginning in December. Orders are filled on a first-come first-served basis. Any orders received before December 1 will be held. Single-game tickets may also be ordered by mail beginning in December. An additional $2 must be included per order for handling fee. The Rangers sold out 12 times in 1987.

*Prices:* Field box $6; reserved $5; grandstand $4.

## Team Hotel

Island Harbor Resorts
Placida Road
Cape Haze, FL 32946
(813) 697–4800

## Players' Favorite Leisure Spots

For excitement, the Rangers make the 30-minute drive to the dog track in Ft. Myers. Favorite restaurants include Oscar's Restaurant and the "Inn Between," near the hotel, which serves burgers and submarine sandwiches.

## Previous Spring Training Locations

*Washington Senators (1961–71)\**
*Texas Rangers (1972–present)*
1961–85   Pompano Beach, FL
1986–present   Port Charlotte, FL

*\*Note: The Senators in 1961 replaced the team that had moved to Minnesota that winter.*

## Hottest Prospects

The Washington Senators team that moved to Texas in the winter of 1971 switched divisions, moving logically into the West as Milwaukee came back East. The Senators had finished next to last in the East, ahead of only Cleveland, but they found the pickings even worse in the West, finishing dead last, some 20½ games behind the California Angels.

Hall of Famer Ted Williams had managed the team the previous three years and must have felt right at home among holdover veterans like Denny McLain, Don Mincher, and Frank Howard, all of them on the wane. There were a few good, young players to be found. Toby Harrah, in his second year as a starter, hit a solid .259; Dick Bosman had been a consistent winner on the mound in Washington; and two infield prospects were up from Denver, Jim Mason and Tom Ragland. Neither of them delivered a capable bat, though Mason would play nine years with his glove as a utility man.

The Rangers had some quality rookies in 1973. Pitcher Steve Foucault had been 7–0 at Burlington the previous year and responded with the lowest spring ERA, 2.25. Fellow moundsman Rick Waits had been 8–8 with Pittsfield but could never quite make it with the Rangers and was traded in 1975 to the Indians for veteran Gaylord Perry. One overlooked infielder whose talents were never showcased in Texas was Bill Madlock. He played 21 games at the end of 1973 and, despite hitting a splendid .351, was traded to the Cubs for another veteran star hurler, Ferguson Jenkins. The trade benefited both teams at the start: Jenkins won 25 games his first season in Texas and led the Rangers out of the cellar and over .500 in 1974. Madlock hit .313, .354, and .339 his three years with the Cubs, the latter two leading the league. Both were then traded, to the Red Sox and Giants respectively, for lesser players.

The 1974 camp opened with high hopes. Billy Martin had succeeded Whitey Herzog at the end of 1973, and the Rangers had David Clyde, one of the most celebrated high school pitchers in U.S. history. He had graduated the previous June, and the Rangers, ignoring the advice of many, sent him right to the mound as a starter. His 4–8 record under intense pressure offered hope he would improve; but his record fell to 3–9 in 1974 and he went to the minors, where he should probably have gone to begin with. He never achieved the results expected of him, though he did resurface for two years in Cleveland, and is a classic example of a player brought along too quickly.

Two nonroster players in the 1974 camp weren't expected to stick but ended up playing important roles. Mike Hargrove had been picked 571st in the draft, but hit .312 in the Florida Instructional League, attracting Martin's attention and gaining an invitation to camp. Hargrove found AL pitching almost as simple to solve as what he had faced in the minors. He finished the year at .323, second to Rod Carew, and was everyone's Rookie of the Year. Rifle-armed catcher Jim Sundberg also was a surprise. Like Hargrove, he had been spotted by Martin in the Instructional League, and with only Dick Billings in front of him, the catcher's job was soon his.

Tom Robson, up from Spokane, was the best of the newcomers in 1975. Listed as an outfielder, he had been a DH in the Pacific Coast League where he had won the MVP award by hitting .322, smashing 41 homers, and knocking in 131 runs. Strangely, he played only 23 games with the Rangers over two years and never did hit a homer in the Majors.

Elliot "Bump" Wills was the hot prospect in 1977, coming to camp with glittering stats from Sacramento: a .323 average and 90 RBI, despite his position high in the order. Maury's son was handed the starting job in Spring Training by Manager Frank Lucchesi, the fourth Rangers' manager since the move to Texas five years before. This so enraged incumbent second-baseman Len Randle that he punched out Lucchesi. Randle was quickly traded to the Mets and then moved five more times in less than two years. For his troubles, Lucchesi was fired part-way into the season, and three other men, Eddie Stanky, Connie Ryan, and eventually Billy Hunter guided the Rangers to an excellent 94 wins in an obviously turbulent season. Hunter survived another year before Pat Corrales took over in 1979, and Don Zimmer in 1981. All in all, the Rangers experienced nine managers in their first Texas decade, six in the last five years.

Len Barker, coming off a 4–1 record in 1977 after he was brought up from Tucson, looked like a definite starter for Texas in 1978. He won only one game in 1978 and was traded away as soon as the season ended, with Bobby Bonds, to Cleveland for pitcher Jim Kern and infielder Larvell Blanks. He won 19 games for the Indians two years later. Steve Comer was brilliant in his initial 1978 season, going 11–5 with a 2.30 ERA. He upped his wins to 17 the next year but would win only 16 more the next five years. At the end of the 1978 season, the Rangers sent four youngsters and Juan Beniquez to the Yankees for Sparky Lyle and an equivalent number of unproven players. Buried in the deal was a player the Rangers would hate to lose: Dave Righetti, for some years the ace reliever in the Yanks bullpen, holds the Major League record for saves in a season with 46.

Pat Putnam finally became a starter at first base in 1979 after trials the preceding two years. A year later, speedy Larue Washington earned his chance with 93 stolen bases and 146 RBI in two minor league seasons but was traded at the end of Spring Training 1980 to Montreal for the aging Rusty Staub. The Rangers thereby perpetuated the habit of signing stars past their prime who could deliver only short-term benefit. Staub hit .300 in his only Texas season; Washington, however, never made it back to the Majors.

The eyes of Texas were on one of the 1981 prospects, University of Texas graduate Jerry Gleaton, who had been 13–1 his last year in college and was the Rangers' first pick in the June, 1979 draft. After five games in the minors, he, like Clyde before him, was rushed to the big club. The Rangers hadn't learned their lesson: Gleason pitched in only 10 games with Texas without a win. He was traded to Seattle after the 1980 season for, among others, pitcher Rick Honeycutt. The other 1980 prospect was Bobby Johnson, nephew of Cub great Ernie Banks; he didn't have his uncle's bat and spent only parts of the next three seasons with the Rangers.

Texas had the AA batting champions in camp in 1982 (Mike Richardt, .354) and 1985 (Tom Dunbar, .337), but neither of them would make much of an impression in the Majors. Lanky pitcher Mike Smithson, acquired from the Red Sox, did well at Denver and was a bright hope in 1983; he did win 10 games but was dealt after the season to Minnesota for disaffected outfielder Gary Ward. Tom Henke did little in Texas in 1984 despite the promise shown in previous years: he saved only two games and his ERA of 6.35 convinced the Rangers to let him go to Toronto in the January, 1985 compensation pool. Clearly Texas misjudged his ability, as he has been the Blue Jay's stopper ever since, one of the league's most imposing relievers.

Finally, in 1986, the Rangers benefited from a rookie trade. Pete Incaviglia, the College Player of the Year in 1985, was originally signed by Montreal but was traded soon after to the Rangers for pitcher Bob Sebra. Incaviglia came to Spring Training in 1986 with extraordinary statistics. He had set NCAA single-season records in 1985 for home runs (48), RBI (143), total bases (285), and slugging percentage (an astounding 1.140) as he led Oklahoma State to the College World Series three straight years. He became only the third current Major Leaguer to make the jump from college ball directly to the Majors (Bob Horner and Dave Winfield were the others). And a successful jump it was, as Incaviglia slugged 30 homers his rookie year despite a vision problem that wasn't diagnosed until midseason.

The top prospect in 1987, Jerry Browne, also became a Ranger starter, suggesting that, perhaps, the team's rookie woes are over.

## Top Rookies Each Spring

1972  Jim Mason, shortstop
1973  Steve Foucault, pitcher
1974  Mike Hargrove, first base
1975  Tom Robson, first base
1976  Steve Barr, pitcher
1977  Bump Wills, second base
1978  Len Barker, pitcher
1979  Steve Comer, pitcher
1980  Larry McCall, pitcher
1981  Jerry Gleaton, pitcher
1982  Mike Richardt, second base
1983  Mike Smithson, pitcher
1984  Tom Henke, pitcher; Curtis Wilkerson, shortstop
1985  Tom Dunbar, outfield
1986  Pete Incaviglia, outfield
1987  Jerry Browne, second base

## AL Rookie of the Year
1974    Mike Hargrove, first base

## Prospect to Watch in 1988
*Keith Creel,* pitcher. After a mediocre start at Oklahoma City in 1987, Creel developed a sinkerball and started winning. He could help the Rangers in 1988.

# TORONTO BLUE JAYS

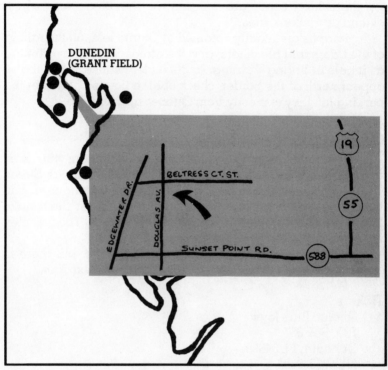

- **Current site:**
  Grant Field
  311 Douglas Avenue
  Dunedin, FL 34698
  (813) 733-9302
- **Dimensions:** 330' left,
  315' right; 390' center
- **Seating:** 3,417
- **Built:** 1930
- **Off-season use:**
  Dunedin Blue Jays,
  Florida State League
  (Class A); local high
  school games are also
  played there.
- **Practice site:** At the
  stadium daily at 10:00 A.M.
- **Game time:** 1:30 P.M.
- **Most convenient airport:**
  Tampa

Most of the Spring Training facilities are normally occupied by teams in the low minors and look small with Major League games in them, but they all look huge in comparison to the Blue Jays' facility. Grant Field is, in fact, a local high school facility.

The "permanent" seating, so often a misnomer in Spring Training parks, where a box seat might be a removable folding chair, is the smallest of any of the spring parks. The boxes and reserved seats extend only part-way to the bases. Most of the not-quite-3,500 seats are actually in the bleachers, which extend down both lines.

Autographs are readily obtained at Grant Field, off the railing of the boxes and bleachers, and the atmosphere is as intimate as it gets in Spring Training. To get a clear sense of baseball's appeal north of the border, check out the license plates in the parking lot: they're mostly from Quebec and Ontario.

## Getting to the Stadium

Take **Alternate Route 19** (coast road) into Dunedin, turn east onto Main Street, and take the next right on Douglas Street. Grant Field is at the next light. The Engleberg minor league training complex is 10 minutes northeast. To get there, take **Route 19** to Belcher, and Belcher to Solon Avenue. The complex is on the corner of Belcher and Solon.

*Parking:* The stadium lot has only 300 spots, but there is some additional parking at the shopping mall next door.

## Tickets

Toronto Blue Jays
P.O. Box 957
Dunedin, FL 34698
(813) 733-9302

The printed schedule is made available by the Blue Jays on December 1. The Blue Jays do not offer a season-ticket package. Single-game tickets may be purchased by check through the mail beginning in February. The tickets will be held at the box office, which opens early in Spring Training. Checks received before the schedule is made up will be mailed back. The Blue Jays sold out their small stadium nine times in 1987.

*Prices:* Reserved seats are $5 or $4, depending on location.

## Team Hotel
   Ramada Inn Countryside
   2560 U.S. 19 North
   Clearwater, FL 33515
   (813) 796-1234
   Only a few players stay at the hotel; most have condominiums. There are no fan-oriented activities at the hotel, although phone-in talk shows and morning radio shows are sometimes broadcast from there.

## Players' Favorite Leisure Spots
In their off hours, the Jays hang out at Penrod's, a disco-bar, Sabels's, a four-star and rather expensive restaurant, and Molly Goodhead's, which specializes in seafood.

## Previous Spring Training Locations
The Blue Jays have played their Spring Training games in Dunedin since entering the American League in 1977.

## Hottest Prospects
In 1977 the Blue Jays opened their first Spring Training camp with a roster made up mostly of veterans and draftees from other AL squads. Predictably, they finished last in their first season and would do the same for five more before finally attaining a winning record. However, unlike other expansion teams, they were building the superb minor league system that now stands them in good stead for seasons to come.

   Of the first-year players, only two remain. Jim Clancy has pitched his entire career for the Blue Jays, his close-to-.500 record a tribute to his determination as he had little support in the early years. Ernie Whitt, drafted from the Red Sox, occasionally caught Clancy and others until he became a regular in 1980.

   Two rookies named Woods, Gary and Al, were expected to add punch to the attack in 1977. The previous year, Gary hit .309 at Tucson, and his .291 spring average gave everyone hopes for a fine season, though it turned disappointing, and Gary was traded to Houston after the 1978 season. The consistent Al Woods, who had been on the Twins' 1976 spring roster, hit .284 that year at Tacoma. The next year, he hit .289 in the Grapefruit League and .284 for the Jays in the 1977 season. He played five more years for the Blue Jays before being traded to Oakland for big slugger Cliff Johnson.

Willie Upshaw's career began in 1978, mostly in the outfield; he moved permanently to first base in 1982 and has been a fixture there ever since. However, the unsung Victor Cruz, a nonroster pitcher picked up from the Cards, was the surprise of the 1978 spring camp. He was 3–8 the previous year at Arkansas and was not expected to stick. But he had a nifty 1.50 ERA over 12 innings in the spring and continued his fine pitching during the regular season, going 7–3 with a brilliant 1.71 ERA and nine saves. That performance made him attractive trade bait, and the Blue Jays quickly traded him to Cleveland for a young player they had scouted well who would cement their infield and inspire their performance. Alfredo Griffin was a highly touted rookie when camp opened in 1979. He had been up briefly with the Indians in 1976, 1977, and 1978 and had hit .291 at Portland during the 1978 season. He stepped right in as the Jays' shortstop, and the infield was built around him. Ace pitcher Dave Stieb, who launched his career as a strong-armed outfielder, also arrived in 1979.

Another infielder snagged from the AL Eastern division was Damaso Garcia, who came to the Jays in a six-player trade in December of 1979. Garcia had played 30 games in Yankee pinstripes, but the Yanks, with Willie Randolph established at second base, could afford to trade him. He and Griffin quickly formed a dynamic combination. The hard-hitting Lloyd Moseby, with a .332 average at Dunedin, was another prospect to make the jump in 1980, and he cemented the middle of the finest outfield in baseball today. Jesse Barfield came up at the end of 1981; possessing one of baseball's strongest arms, he was a regular in right field a year later.

The slick-fielding Tony Fernandez was promoted to the AAA team at Syracuse at the end of 1981 and responded by hitting .275. The Blue Jays could afford to develop his wondrous talent slowly as Griffin was solid at shortstop. Fernandez made heads turn in the springs of 1982 and 1983 but spent both years at Syracuse, hitting .300 and .302. He finished the 1984 season at Toronto, and by mid-1985 even Griffin could no longer stand in his way. He is today, by most accounts, the finest shortstop in the game and yet another in the line of stars from the small Dominican town of San Pedro de Macoris.

George Bell, a hard-hitting outfield prospect also from San Pedro de Macoris, had caught the Jays' attention in the 1981 spring camp. He came up briefly at the end of the season and was counted on for the following year, but fell ill after starting the 1982 season with Syracuse. Played sparingly in 1983, he became the third piece in the brilliant Jays' outfield in 1984 and was the AL MVP in 1987.

The Jays also had high hopes for a remarkable athlete from Brigham Young University whose baseball talents were excelled by his talents on the basketball court. Danny Ainge was the Jays' starting third baseman in 1981. Big league pitching eluded him, however, and his .187 average surely prompted his decision to join the Boston Celtics for whom he has been a star in the back court ever since. Ainge is one of the very few who have played more than one sport at a professional level.

In 1984 the Jays had high hopes for Kelly Gruber. Obtained from Cleveland in the draft, he was on the Opening Day roster, the youngest player in the Majors. Early in the season, he went down to Syracuse, where he was named minor-league player of the month in June. He was back in camp in 1985 but again went to Syracuse, where he led the club in slugging and was on the All-Star team. Again the Jays could afford to wait for him, as Rance Mulliniks was most capable at third.

Less touted than Gruber was a nonroster pitcher, Mark Eichhorn, who had a combined 7–6 record with Knoxville and Syracuse in 1985, his first winning season since 1980. He perfected a sinkerball/sidearm delivery in the Florida Instructional League the next winter, which helped him post a 2–0 1986 Spring Training record to make the team. Eichhorn went on to wrack up 14 wins and 10 saves to accompany a glittering 1.72 ERA. This earned him *The Sporting News'* AL Rookie Pitcher of the Year award.

Mike Sharperson, the number one hopeful of 1987, was named the Southern League's top prospect by *Baseball America*. Apparently, the Blue Jays management agreed and traded veteran Damaso Garcia to Atlanta to make room at second base. Sharperson wasn't quite ready, however, and was sent to Syracuse early in the season.

## Top Rookies Each Spring

1977   Alvin Woods, outfield
1978   Victor Cruz, pitcher
1979   Alfredo Griffin, shortstop
1980   Damaso Garcia, second base
1981   George Bell, outfield
1982   Tony Fernandez, shortstop
1983   Tony Fernandez, shortstop

1984   Stan Clarke, pitcher
1985   Kelly Gruber, third base
1986   Kelly Gruber, third base; Mark Eichhorn, pitcher
1987   Mike Sharperson, second base

## AL Rookie of the Year
1979   Alfredo Griffin, shortstop
       (co-Rookie of the Year with John Castino, Minnesota)

## Prospects to Watch in 1988
*Todd Stottlemyre, pitcher.* Son of the former Yankee ace Mel Stottlemyre, Todd was considered the hardest thrower in the International League in 1987. The first-round selection in the June '85 draft is considered a pitch away from stardom.
*Nelson Liriano, second base.* The speedy Liriano was named the International League's All-Star second-sacker despite hitting just above .250. One of the fastest runners in the league, he came up to the Blue Jays in September 1987.

# CHAPTER 7

*Arizona Group*

Chicago Cubs *Mesa*
San Francisco Giants *Scottsdale*
Seattle Mariners *Tempe*
Oakland Athletics *Phoenix*
California Angels *Phoenix*
Milwaukee Brewers *Chandler*

PHOENIX

San Diego Padres *Yuma*

Cleveland Indians *Tucson*

ONE WAY OF sorting out the Spring Training destination choice is: beach, amusement parks, or mountains? If mountains and beautiful deserts are your idea of the perfect baseball backdrop, Arizona is the place to go.

Phoenix is the biggest city where Spring Training is held. It has professional basketball, a zoo, a planetarium, various museums, and golf courses galore. Most of the baseball action is clustered in the suburbs south and east of Phoenix, near the airport. The Giants occupy an old wooden stadium in Scottsdale, just east of Phoenix and around the corner from some of the snappiest shopping east of Beverly Hills. Less than 10 minutes south are the Oakland A's, within Phoenix itself, and less than 10 minutes east are the Cubs in HoHoKam Park in Mesa. The Seattle Mariners are 10 minutes south of the A's in Tempe, the Brewers a 15-minute hop down the freeway from the Mariners, in Chandler. The proximity of these teams makes it easy to catch parts of two ballgames within an afternoon, with only an inning lost to travel time.

The bad news about the Indians' location in Tucson is that it is a two-hour drive south from Phoenix. The good news is that the drive is over a breathtaking stretch of rugged, mountainous desert, and the setting when you get to Tucson is among the most beautiful of all. The Indians' facility is housed within a large city park that is also home to the Tucson Zoo. The entire complex stands in the shadow of a starkly beautiful mountain.

In close proximity to the other Phoenix teams, the California Angels' facility, Gene Autry Park, is five miles east of the Cubs' site. They don't actually play big-league exhibition games there (no real stadium), but the club is based and plays intra-squad games there until the last two weeks before the regular season. They then move to Palm Springs, California, to play a game each day for the last two weeks.

The Padres' facility in Yuma is across a vast expanse of desert west of Phoenix, on the California border. The Padres set up in Yuma, base in Phoenix for the first two weeks of games (in a hotel, no practice facilities), and then go back to Yuma.

During the first two weeks of Spring Training games, therefore, all the teams are playing in Phoenix and Tucson. For the last two weeks, the Padres and Angels require "road trips" by the other teams. Except when the Padres and Angels are playing each other, two of the other Arizona teams are out of town, cutting the Phoenix baseball action nearly in half.

A bar/restaurant called The Pink Pony in Scottsdale has established quite a reputation as a baseball people's hangout, thanks to articles in *The New Yorker* by Roger Angell and in *Sports Illustrated* by Ron Fimrite. The insiders have discovered a new place called Don & Charlie's about a mile away.

Don & Charlie's is loaded with baseball memorabilia, and signatures of many ballplayers from all sports are magic-markered right onto the walls. Co-owner Don Carson arranges with a local cartoonist to do a caricature of the player himself near the spot on the wall the player has signed. Over this ad hoc wall covering (always in development; Carson says he tries to add "something" every week), are uniform jerseys, old scorecards (one completely filled in from a Cubs-Dodgers game at Wrigley Field in 1952), bats, team pictures, and other memorabilia.

On top of the fact that one could spend several hours studying the walls, Don & Charlie's serves fantastic barbecued ribs. While you are eating yours, a few faces off the baseball cards of your past are also eating theirs. Don discourages interrupting a ballplayer's dinner to get an autograph, but "sometimes you can do it politely when they are on their way out."

Don & Charlie's creates special memorabilia anchored in place; technology will have to advance somewhat to move its walls intact to the Hall of Fame. But the ballplayers want to appear in this little niche of baseball history. Chili Davis of the Giants asked Don when he could sign the wall. When he was shown to his spot, he wrote, "Now this will be complete when you get a picture up here, Charles 'Chili' Davis."

## Batting Cages

Tempe: The Batter's Edge, Mill & Baseline, inside Kiwanis Park, (602) 820-2757; six baseball cages, four softball cages, open 4 P.M. to 10 P.M. Monday to Friday, 9 A.M. to 10 P.M. Saturday and Sunday.

Tempe: Casey at the Bat, 1605 North Hayden Road, (602) 990-7742; six baseball cages, four softball cages, open 12 to 11 P.M. daily.

## Phoenix

### Sunny-Day Alternatives

*Phoenix Zoo:* 1,000 animals on 125 acres; children's zoo. 5810 East Van Buren, Phoenix. (602) 273-1341.
*Desert Botanical Garden:* Thousands of desert plants. 1201 North Galvin Parkway, Phoenix. (602) 941-1225.

***Pueblo Grande Ruins and Museum:*** Local Indian ruins.
4619 East Washington, Tempe. (602) 275-3452.
***Big Surf:*** Make waves, big ones, in an artificial ocean.
1500 North Hayden Road, Tempe. (602) 947-7873.
***Rawhide:*** Wild West atmosphere with stagecoach rides, burros,
mock gunfights, copies of frontier buildings.
23023 North Scottsdale Road, Phoenix. (602) 563-5111.
***Heritage Square:*** Victorian mansions, museums, shops.
127 North Sixth Street, Phoenix. (602) 262-5071.

## ARIZONA AIRPLAY

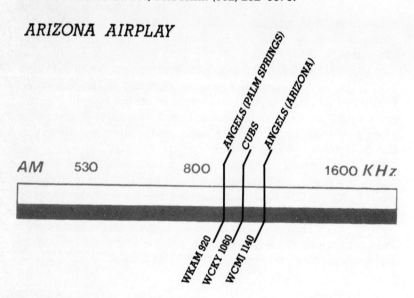

## Rainy-Day Activities

***Arizona Museum:*** Pioneer artifacts, Indian art, historic exhibits.
1002 West Van Buren, Phoenix. (602) 253-2734.
***Heard Museum:*** Indian arts, crafts.
22 East Monte Vista Road, Phoenix. (602) 252-8848.
***Taliesin West:*** Once Frank Lloyd Wright's home, the architec-
ture school (free admission) stands as a dramatic example of
the desert style, on 108th Street off Shea Boulevard, Phoenix.
(602) 948-6674.

## Day Trips

To the north, **The Grand Canyon**, though a long drive, is worth it.
For information: Superintendent, Grand Canyon National Park,
Arizona 86023. (602) 638-7888.

## Tucson

### Sunny-Day Alternatives
*Reid Park Zoo*, Randolph Way at East 22nd Street, Tucson.
(602) 791-4002.
*Tucson Botanical Garden*, 2150 North Alvernon Way, Tucson.
(602) 326-9255.
*Old Tucson:* Old West reenactments on preserved movie set,
with tours, costumes, shops, restaurants. Next to Arizona-Sonora
Desert Museum in Saguaro National Monument, about eight
miles west of downtown at 201 South Kinney Road, Tucson.
(602) 883-0100.

### Rainy-Day Activities
*Arizona-Sonora Desert Museum:* World-renowned exhibits of
desert flora and fauna. Route 9, Box 100, Tucson. (602) 883-1380.
*Tucson Museum of Art*, 140 North Main Avenue, Tucson.
(602) 624-2333.
*Arizona State Museum and Mineral Museum:* Both on University
of Arizona campus. For State Museum, whose exhibits portray
the cultural history of the Southwest, call (602) 621-6302; for
Mineral Museum, (602) 621-4227.

## Yuma

### Sunny-Day Alternative
*Yuma Territorial Prison State Park.* (602) 783-4771.

### Rainy-Day Activity
*Century House Museum*, Arizona Historical Society, 240 South
Madison Avenue, Yuma. (602) 782-1841.

# CALIFORNIA ANGELS

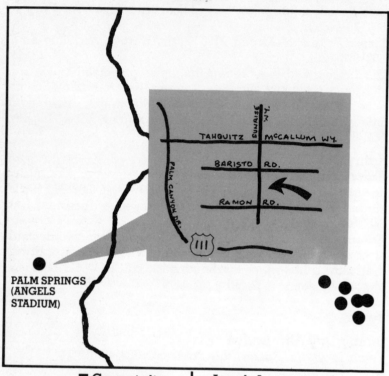

TAHQUITZ    SUNRISE WY.    McCALLUM WY.

BARISTO RD.

RAMON RD.

PALM CANYON DR.

111

PALM SPRINGS
(ANGELS
STADIUM)

■ **Current sites:**
Gene Autry Complex
4125 East McKellips
Mesa, AZ 85206
(602) 830-4137
Angels Stadium
Sunrise and Baristo Roads
Palm Springs, CA 92263
(619) 323-3325
■ **Dimensions:**
(Angels Stadium)
365' left and right;
408' center
■ **Seating:** 5,200
■ **Built:** 1963
■ **Off-season use:**
Arizona: California

Angels Instructional
League team, adult and
Little League teams;
California: Palm Springs
Angels, California
League (Class A)
■ **Practice site:** Arizona:
at the complex throughout
the day; California: at the
stadium daily at
10:00 A.M.
■ **Game time:** California,
1:00 P.M.
■ **Most convenient airport:**
Phoenix (1st 2 weeks),
Los Angeles or Palm
Springs (2nd 2 weeks).

Less than five miles down the road from the Cubs' HoHokam Stadium, in Mesa, is the Gene Autry Complex, where the Angels spend the first month of Spring Training. The entire organization — Major and minor leaguers alike — works out together, and the Angels' big-league squad plays road games at the many nearby parks through the middle of March.

Resembling a college campus somewhat more than a baseball training camp, the complex surrounds a low-slung modern building housing Angel offices. Several diamonds — unfenced and unpoliced — stretch out to the right of the headquarters building. A couple of the diamonds have sets of bleachers behind a cyclone fence. There are occasional "B" and intrasquad games played by Major League players on these fields. Nowhere in Arizona or Florida is there less competition for conversation with or autographs from players, but fans have to identify them by sight as there are no programs for sale.

When the Angels move to Angels Stadium in Palm Springs in mid-March, they play home games daily (except for an occasional quick hop to play the Padres in Yuma). Each of the Arizona teams returns the Angels' visits from the first two weeks of March by coming to Palm Springs for successive two-game series.

Angels Stadium is an excellent place to watch a game. The grandstand holds about half of the 5,200 capacity, while bleachers extend down both lines. Additional bleachers are in right field. All the seats have good sight lines.

Batting cages are down the left-field line, and they are accessible to fans. The Angels' clubhouse is under the grandstand, and the players emerge behind home plate; if you haven't gotten an autograph off the railing of the box seats, you can try outside the park after the game.

## Getting to the Stadium

Gene Autry Complex: Take **Interstate 10 South** through Phoenix to **Highway 360 East**, then north on **Greenfield Drive** to **McKellips**, and a half mile west on McKellips.

*Parking* is plentiful.

Angels Stadium: Take **Highway 10** to the 111 off-ramp, go east on the **Tahquitz-McCallum** to **Sunrise**, then go north to **Barristo**.

*Parking:* There is not much parking at the stadium, which is in a public park. There is, however, street parking in the residential area nearby, as well as on dirt fields in the neighborhood.

## Tickets
California Angels
Angels Stadium
Sunrise and Barristo Roads
P.O. Box 609
Palm Springs, CA 92263
(619) 325-4487

The schedule will be available on January 1. Beginning mid-February, all tickets go on sale at Ticketron and Teletron outlets nationwide, and at Palm Desert Town Center mall kiosk. No mail orders are accepted. The box office opens on March 16. The Angels sold out six times in 1987.

*Prices:* Reserved $4; general admission $3.

## Team Hotel
In Mesa:
Rodeway Inn
5700 East Main Street
Mesa, AZ 85205
(602) 985-3600
       and
Radisson Hotel
200 North Centennial Way
Mesa, AZ 85201
(602) 898-8300
In Palm Springs:
Gene Autry Hotel
4200 East Palm Canyon Road
Palm Springs, CA 92264
(619) 328-1171

## Players' Favorite Leisure Spots
While in Palm Springs the Angels usually spend their free time playing tennis or golf. Two night clubs attract them: Zelda's and The Red Onion.

## Previous Spring Training Locations
The Angels have used this arrangement since entering the American League as the Los Angeles Angels in 1961.

## Hottest Prospects
The Los Angeles Angels, as they parochially called themselves until they adopted the state of California, came into existence at baseball's annual December meeting in 1960 when the

American League awarded a franchise to Gene Autry and his associates. A week later, the new manager, Bill Rigney, and General Manager Fred Haney picked 28 players out of a pool of available talent.

An indication of their early prospects could be gleaned by their first selection, pitcher Eli Grba, off the Yankees' roster. To his credit, Grba did win 20 games over the next three years but was never an important part of the Angels' rotation. Ken McBride fared better, winning 36 from 1961–63 before suddenly going downhill. *The Sporting News* tabbed Gene Lock a likely starter before the Angels' first year, but he foiled the experts and never appeared in the Majors.

The 1962 season was altogether different, and the Angels finished 10 games over .500, a remarkable record for a second-year team. Maybe it was the shift from a minor league park to Dodger Stadium (which the Angels called Chavez Ravine); maybe it was the presence of rookie pitcher and irrepressible flake  Bo Belinsky. He had been a journeyman pitcher with six straight losing minor league seasons, but he took to the bright lights of Los Angeles as a moth to a flame. Belinsky called a poolside press conference his second day in Spring Training. Taking a look at the halo on his new Angels' cap, he remarked, "This is the closest I'll ever get to Heaven." Bo squired some of the prettiest women in Hollywood, but that didn't seem to interfere with his pitching the first two months of the season; he was simply marvelous, topping off a great run with a May 5 no-hitter, the first by a rookie since 1953. It was, however, downhill from there, though Belinsky would play parts of seven more seasons.

Another leading rookie in camp in 1962 was Dean Chance, taken from the Orioles' organization in the expansion draft. The young Chance threw 18 no-hitters in high school, and went 14–10 in his first full year. He would win 20 two years later, leading the Angels back over .500 for the second time in their brief history. Jim Fregosi was also snagged from the pool of unprotected players, and he came up toward the end of the 1962 season in preparation for his starting role the next year.

Costen Shockley was the Pacific Coast League Rookie of the Year in 1964, and the Angels sent Belinsky to the Phils for him over the winter. Shockley had a good spring in 1965 and was expected to platoon with veteran Joe Adcock at first base, but he hit less than his weight and lasted only 40 games for the Angels. Rudy May, a throw-in in the deal, became a solid starter in the years to come. Also debuting in 1965 was Marcelino

Lopez, the "player to be named later" when the Angels sold Vic Power to the Phillies. He came to camp with a 6–10 record at Chattanooga but surprised everyone by posting a 14–13 record with a 2.93 ERA for the Angels. He finished second behind Baltimore's Curt Blefary in the balloting for Rookie of the Year honors and was named the AL's top rookie pitcher by *The Sporting News.*

Rick Reichardt's first hit in the spring of 1966 was a massive home run. Reichardt had been up with the Angels for part of 1964 and 1965, and the fine young outfielder went on to hit .288 in his first full season, with 16 homers. That year also marked the beginning of Jay Johnstone's long career. Platooned in the outfield for three years, he became a starter in 1969, was traded to the White Sox in 1970, and has since played for six other teams.

The Angels had no further outstanding rookies until Mickey Rivers came to camp in 1971, after tearing up the minors the year before. The fleet centerfielder had to wait until 1974 before starting. The Angels gave up on him a little quickly, trading him to the Yankees for Bobby Bonds after the 1975 season. Rivers starred in The Big Apple, and in Texas after that, and left as his legacy some of the greatest one-liners the game has ever heard, fully rivalling those of Yogi Berra and Casey Stengel.

After the 1971 season, the Angels traded Fregosi to the Mets for young Nolan Ryan, who was expendable on the pitching-rich New York squad. Ryan fulfilled all his promise in California, winning 19, 21, and 22 his first three years there, while striking out an astounding 1,079 batters. Leroy Stanton came along in the Ryan deal and was an immediate starter in the outfield.

Frank Tanana, a former first draft pick, was considered a "can't-miss" prospect in 1974. The Angels were so sure of him that they traded away Clyde Wright, who had won almost 70 games the previous four years, to make room in the rotation. Tanana went 14–19 with a splendid 3.11 ERA, and he and Ryan were a dynamic pair through the decade. Tanana led the league in strikeouts in 1975, the only year Ryan did not do so from 1972–79. Dave Chalk, in his first full season with California, was selected to the All-Star team by his manager, Dick Williams, who remarked nepotistically, "he deserves it."

Jerry Remy was just hoping to make the jump to AAA when he came to camp in 1975. But he had an outstanding spring, making Denny Doyle expendable. Manager Williams called him "the best rookie I've had since Reggie Smith (in Boston) in

1967." Remy was the Angels' second-baseman for three years and then wound up in Boston himself, traded for pitcher Don Aase.

Danny Goodwin was the prize rookie in 1977. The number one pick in the draft by the White Sox some years before, he chose to attend Southern University. On graduation, the Angels again made him the top draft pick, the only player so sought-after. Goodwin, however, never measured up to expectations; bothered by injuries, he played no more than 59 games in any of his seven Major League seasons. Mark Clear honed his world-class curve ball in California, opening in 1979 with an 11–5 mark and following with 11 more wins the next year. He then joined Remy in Boston in 1981, traded with Carney Lansford and Rick Miller for Rick Burleson and Butch Hobson.

The Angels held on to their promising young pitcher, Mike Witt, who won eight games in 1981 and improved each year thereafter, winning 18 in 1986 and the recognition as one of the league's toughest pitchers. Tom Brunansky racked up some impressive numbers at Salt Lake City in 1981: 22 homers and a .332 average. But the Angels weren't that impressed with him in the spring of 1982 and traded him to Minnesota in May. He took a liking to the Twins' domed stadium and banged out more than 20 homers in each of his first six seasons there. The year after Brunansky's brief California experience, 1983, Mike Brown arrived in camp sporting a .355 minor league average. He got his chance when Ellis Valentine and Bobby Clark were hurt during Spring Training, and took full advantage, hitting three homers and driving home 11 in 12 exhibition games. But he couldn't crack the starting line-up once the season started and ended up going to the Pirates.

Golden glover Gary Pettis became a starter in center field in 1984, as adept on defense as he is on the bases. He lost the position to top rookie Devon White in 1987 as his bat went silent. Kirk McCaskill had to choose between professional baseball and hockey. The first collegian chosen in the 1981 National Hockey League draft (by Winnipeg) after an All-America year at the University of Vermont, the righthander decided to do his work on the mound, not the ice, and won 12 games his rookie year in 1985.

Fans were surprised the next spring when the Angels made no effort to sign Rod Carew and handed his first-base job to a young man up from Waterbury. But the Angels had followed Wally Joyner carefully; he had won the Puerto Rican League triple crown the winter before and quickly dispelled any doubts of Angels' followers. Soon nicknamed "Wallyworld," he was the starting first baseman in the All-Star game as a write-in, hit 22 home runs and drove in 100, and was runner-up to the A's Jose Canseco for Rookie of the Year. His illness just before the AL Divisional playoff with the Red Sox may well have been the overlooked reason Boston won that series. Joyner continued his excellent play in 1987, driving in more than 100 runs, and looks to be a fixture in California.

## Top Rookies Each Spring

| | |
|---|---|
| 1961 | Gene Lock |
| 1962 | Dean Chance, pitcher;  Bob Rodgers |
| 1963 | Ed Kirkpatrick, catcher |
| 1964 | Bobby Knoop, second base |
| 1965 | Costen Shockley, first base |
| 1966 | Rick Reichardt, outfield |
| 1967 | Aurelio Rodriguez, third base |
| 1968 | Jarvis Tatum, outfield |
| 1969 | none |
| 1970 | Dave LaRoche, pitcher |
| 1971 | Mickey Rivers, outfield |
| 1972 | Leroy Stanton, outfield |
| 1973 | Bill Gilbreth, pitcher |
| 1974 | Frank Tanana, pitcher |
| 1975 | Jerry Remy, second base |
| 1976 | Sid Monge, pitcher |
| 1977 | Danny Goodwin, first base |
| 1978 | Chris Knapp, pitcher |
| 1979 | Mark Clear, pitcher |
| 1980 | Bobby Clark, outfield |
| 1981 | Mike Witt, pitcher |
| 1982 | Tom Brunansky, outfield |
| 1983 | Mike Brown, outfield |
| 1984 | Gary Pettis, outfield |
| 1985 | Urbano Lugo, pitcher |
| 1986 | Wally Joyner, first base |
| 1987 | Mark McLemore, second base |

## Prospect to Watch in 1988

Jim Eppard, *first base.* The Pacific Coast League All-Star first baseman at Edmonton, Eppard was hitting .370 when he was called up to the Majors at the end of August.

# CHICAGO CUBS

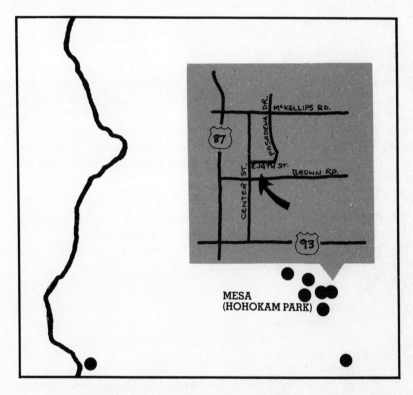

**■ Current site:**
HoHoKam Park,
1235 North Center Street,
Mesa, AZ 85201
(602) 964-4467
**■ Dimensions:** 365' left
and right, 400' center
**■ Seating:** 8,000
**■ Built:** 1976

**■ Off-season use:**
Little League games and
local baseball
tournaments
**Practice site:** At the Park
daily at 10:00 A.M.
**■ Game time:** 1:00 P.M.
**■ Most convenient airport:**
Phoenix

Run by a group of local businessmen known as the HoHoKams, HoHoKam Park opened in March 1977 as the Spring Training home of the Oakland A's. The Cubs moved in for the 1979 season, switching locations with the A's.

This is one of the largest, most active, and best run of the Spring Training parks. A Kachina dancing Indian statue welcomes you at the entrance. Inside, the field is beautifully manicured, and the stands are always neat. Seven rows of box seats and 16 rows of reserved grandstand seats behind them extend to the edge of the infield dirt down both lines. The bleachers extend from the edge of the regular stands to about 100 feet from the outfield walls. Note that the left-field bleachers are set back with standing room in front of them. During games with big crowds, which are frequent, you might choose to sit down the right-field line.

The players take batting practice in cages down the right-field line, where the clubhouse is also located. Autographs can be had off the box seat and bleacher railings and outside the clubhouse after the games.

## Getting to the Stadium
From **Route 10,** go to **Country Club Drive,** north to **Brown Avenue.** Go east on Brown Avenue to the ballpark.

*Parking:* Near the park there are several small lots and soccer fields.

## Tickets
Chicago Cubs
HoHoKam Park
1235 North Center Street
Mesa, AZ 85201
(602) 964-4467

The printed schedule is available on December 1. Season tickets may be ordered by mail, with payment made by check, beginning December 1. Single-game seats, which go on sale in early February, also may be purchased through the mail with a check, or at the box office. HoHoKam Park was sold out six times in 1987.

*Prices:* Reserved $4; general admission $2.50; children $1.

## Team Hotel
Mezona Motor Inn
250 West Main Street
Mesa, AZ 85201
(602) 834-9233

There are usually a few remote radio broadcasts from the lobby.

## Players' Favorite Leisure Spots
The players chow down at Harry & Steve's, owned by broadcaster Harry Carey and former pitcher Steve Stone; Rick's Café American, specializing in steaks; and Don & Charlie's, a rib joint in Scottsdale.

## Previous Spring Training Locations
| | |
|---|---|
| 1901–02 | Champaign, IL |
| 1903–04 | Los Angeles, CA |
| 1905 | Santa Monica, CA |
| 1906 | Champaign, IL |
| 1907 | New Orleans, LA |
| 1908 | Vicksburg, MS |
| 1909–10 | Hot Springs, AR |
| 1911–12 | New Orleans, LA |
| 1913–16 | Tampa, FL |
| 1917–21 | Pasadena, CA |
| 1922–42 | Catalina Island, CA |
| 1943–45 | French Lick, IN |
| 1946–47 | Catalina Island, CA |
| 1948–49 | Los Angeles, CA |
| 1950–51 | Catalina Island, CA |
| 1952–65 | Mesa, AZ |
| 1966 | Long Beach, CA |
| 1967–78 | Scottsdale, AZ |
| 1979–present | Mesa, AZ |

## Hottest Prospects
The Cubs opened their 1960 Spring Training camp under new manager Charlie Grimm, the last in a series of ex-Cubs to pilot the team through the '50s. Phil Cavarretta, the only manager fired during Spring Training, Stan Hack, and Bob Scheffing had preceded him, without notable success, as the Cubs remained mediocre at best. Grimm wasn't new to the Cubs, having skippered them 13 years in the '30s and '40s. This time he lasted just 17 games, switching places with announcer Lou Boudreau in a bizarre move by owner Phil Wrigley. Perhaps this set the owner's creative juices flowing, for he came up with an even stranger scheme in 1961 and 1962: a series of seven revolving managers called the "College of Coaches" headed the Cubs in those years. Were it not for the extraordinarily

inept play of the Phillies and Mets those years, the Cubs would have finished dead last. Not until 1967 would they finish as high as third place.

Sweet Lou Johnson was the prime rookie in Grimm's 1960 camp, but he lasted just the year and was traded at the end of Spring Training the next season. That camp welcomed a truly talented young outfielder who had been up briefly in 1959–60:Billy Williams would star in left field the next 14 years, averaging almost .300 and hitting most of his 426 career homers for Chicago. He had hit .323 in AA ball and, as a starter replacing George Altman, hit .278 with 25 home runs, 7 triples, and 20 doubles. This earned him the Rookie of the Year award; he was the first Cub ever to earn this honor. Ron Santo also began his long career in Chicago in 1960, starting over half the games at third and averaging more than 160 games per year the rest of the decade.

The second Rookie of the Year came quickly. Ken Hubbs, the likeable young second-baseman, hit only .260 in 1962 but won the award with his sharp fielding. He went through 78 straight games (418) chances without an error, breaking Bobby Doerr's record. Hubbs had another solid year in 1963 but was killed in a plane crash in February 1964 at the age of 22.

Nelson Mathews was finally recognized in 1963, after appearing in 21 games the previous three years. He would manage 64 appearances in 1963 but soon moved on to Kansas City where he led the league in strikeouts in his only full season.

The Cubs gained a keystone combination in Spring Training 1965. Glenn Beckert and Don Kessinger would play beside each other at second and short for the next nine years, their names almost as familiar in the Windy City as those of Joe Tinker and Johnny Evers 60 years earlier. The following year, in 1966, the Cubs would add their battery of the '60s: catcher Randy Hundley, and pitchers Ken Holtzman, Ferguson Jenkins, and Bill Hands, the latter two acquired in trades. Each took a couple of years to get started, but by the mid-'60s they were a formidable trio and a major reason the Cubs challenged hard at the end of the decade and into the '70s.

They never won a pennant, though it certainly looked as though they would in 1969. Leading the soon-to-be Amazin' Mets by a comfortable margin into August, they slumped a little as New York surged and finished eight games back. Don Young was a useful rookie that year, playing 100 games in the outfield. He had been up for a short time in 1965 and in his first game faced Sandy Koufax, who threw a perfect game. Perhaps that trauma pushed him back to the minors the intervening seasons; in any event, 1969 would be his last year in the Majors. Two young rookies up briefly that season, outfielder Oscar Gamble and pitcher Jim Colborn, would have their best years in the American League, as would top 1970 prospect Joe Decker, who had no chance to make the pitching rotation and was dealt to Minnesota, where he promptly won 26 games in two seasons.

The Cubs let two other leading rookies in the 1972–73 crop get away as well. Bill North had 74 games with the Cubs before going to Oakland, while Andre Thornton moved north to Montreal in 1976. Chicago had the good sense to nurture pitcher Rick Reuschel, and the portly righthander responded with a solid winning percentage throughout the '70s.

Surprisingly, Tony LaRussa was the top prospect in camp in 1973. He had first emerged 10 years earlier in Kansas City. Then, like Lou Piniella, he would spend the following four years in the minors, surfacing in Oakland. He would appear in only one game with the Cubs, as a pinch runner (he scored), and that would be his Major League swan song as a player. Though he never enjoyed Piniella's success, he shared the long minor league experience, and that has doubtless stood him in good stead as the manager of the White Sox and A's.

Bill Madlock was the prize from the Rangers when the Cubs sent Jenkins to Texas in the winter of 1973. Madlock hit .313 his first year in Chicago, when he replaced Ron Santo. Then he led the league in hitting the next two seasons. Astonishingly, the Cubs traded him to San Francisco for Bobby Murcer just before Spring Training in 1977, and he has since moved to Pittsburgh, Los Angeles, and Detroit, always wielding a superior bat.

Bruce Sutter was the best of the lot in 1976. He started the season in the minors but came up to the Cubs in May to save his first 10 games. His split-fingered fastball became the envy of opposing pitchers, the scourge of batters. In 1977 Sutter was named to the All-Star team, and two years later he won the Cy Young Award, leading the league with 37 saves, something he would do five of the following six years. Three of those were with the Cardinals after he was traded in December 1980.

His presence in the bullpen was soon filled by Lee Smith, the imposing fireballer who would lead the league in saves in 1983, the only year in six that Sutter didn't. Smith was a six-year minor leaguer in 1980, with more walks than strikeouts when the Cubs brought him up at the end of the season. But that ratio quickly changed in the Majors, and when Sutter's shoulder gave way soon after his trade to Atlanta, Smith became the league's top fireman.

Pat Tabler was tabbed the second baseman of the future after playing 35 games for the Cubs in 1981. That changed rapidly when the Cubs traded Ivan DeJesus to the Phillies just before Spring Training in 1982 for an aging Larry Bowa and a young infielder who would prove a remarkable catch. Ryne Sandberg played his first season mostly at third but moved across the diamond to second on occasion. He hit a solid .271, scored 103 runs and just missed the Rookie of the Year award. Two years later, he was named the league's MVP.

The sure-handed, but cranky, Bowa would hold down the shortstop spot until Shawon Dunston, the nation's number one draft pick in 1982, was ready three years later. Meantime, the Cubs returned to their practice of trading promising rookies, sending Joe Carter and Mel Hall to Cleveland for pitcher Rick Sutcliffe in June 1984. To say Sutcliffe was inspired by the move is a gross understatement: he went 16–1 in his 20 starts with the Cubs, leading them into the playoffs for the first time in decades, and within one game of the NL pennant. But Sutcliffe stumbled after that, shouldering a heavy new contract, and the benefit of the trade switched to Cleveland's side as Carter and Hall became stars. Carter led the American League in RBI in 1986.

Greg Maddux, an AAA All-Star with a 10–1 record, was counted on as one of the pitching starters in 1987, but the spring raves went to Rafael Palmeiro, up from Pittsfield where he had hit .306. *Baseball America* named him the top rookie in Spring Training in 1987.

## Top Rookies Each Spring

1960    Lou Johnson, outfield
1961    Billy Williams, outfield
1962    Ken Hubbs, second base
1963    Nelson Mathews, outfield
1964    Billy Cowan, outfield
1965    Glenn Beckert, second base
1966    Byron Browne, outfield; Ken Holtzman, pitcher
1967    Clarence Jones, outfield
1968    none
1969    Don Young, outfield
1970    George "Joe" Decker, pitcher

1971    Ray Newman, pitcher
1972    Bill North, outfield; Rick Reuschel, pitcher
1973    Tony LaRussa, second base
1974    Bill Madlock, third base
1975    Pete LaCock, outfielder/first base
1976    Bruce Sutter, pitcher
1977    Ed Putnam, catcher
1978    none
1979    Scot Thompson, outfield
1980    Karl Pagel, first base
1981    Lee Smith, pitcher; Pat Tabler, second base
1982    Ryne Sandberg, third base
1983    Joe Carter, outfield
1984    Don Schulze, pitcher
1985    Shawon Dunston, shortstop
1986    Jay Baller, pitcher
1987    Rafael Palmeiro, outfield

## NL Rookies of the Year
1961    Billy Williams, outfield
1962    Ken Hubbs, second base

## Prospects to Watch in 1988
**Drew Hall,** *pitcher.* The number three pick overall in the 1984 draft, he has been up with the Cubs on several occasions. Called up at the end of 1987 after a fine year at AAA Iowa, the Cubs are hoping he'll stay this time.

**Rafael Palmeiro,** *outfield.* For several years tabbed by *Baseball America* as a rookie to watch, he had a solid year at Iowa after starting the season with the Cubs. He is expected to stick in 1988.

# CLEVELAND INDIANS

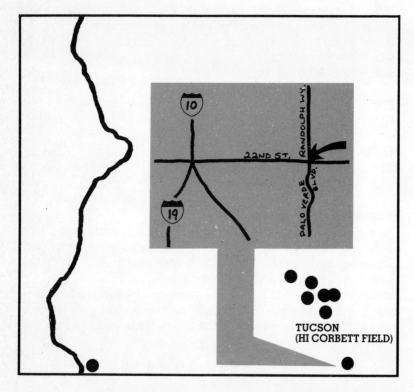

**TUCSON
(HI CORBETT FIELD)**

■ **Current site:**
Hi Corbett Field
Randolph Park
Tucson, AZ 85726
(602) 325-2621
■ **Dimensions:** 366' left,
348' right, 392' center
■ **Seating:** 9,500
■ **Built:** 1937

■ **Off-season use:** Tucson
Toros, Civic Coast League
(Class AAA, owned by
Houston Astros)
**Practice site:** At the field
daily at 9:00 A.M.
■ **Game time:** 1:00 P.M.
■ **Most convenient airport:**
Tucson

Built in the '20s, Hi Corbett Field is named after Hiram Corbett, a local baseball booster who was president of the Old Pueblo Baseball Club (Border Conference, Arizona-Texas League).

Set at the foot of a beautiful mountain and within a large city park that houses the Tucson Zoo, the Indians' facility is one of the loveliest sites for spring games. The stadium is also among the most capacious of the spring ballparks, but it is still intimate and charming. There are only four rows of boxes and 19 rows of covered reserves ringing the field to a point 30 feet beyond first and third bases. Bleachers extend on both sides from the permanent stands to the outfield corners.

Beyond the right-field fence are four more diamonds where the Indians are often found taking batting practice before a game, while the visiting team works out on the Corbett Field diamond.

Policing of the practice field is minimal; fans can enter through a gate in the field's outfield fence and dodge batting-practice line drives as they make their way to a safer area behind the batting cage. One of the best autograph-collecting opportunities in spring baseball comes when the Indians move from the practice field to the stadium about 100 yards away.

## Getting to the Stadium

Take **Interstate 10,** then go north on **6th Avenue.** From there, travel east on **22nd Street** to **Randolph Way.** Hi Corbett Field is on the left.

*Parking:* Despite the large capacity of the stadium, the parking lots can hold only 550 vehicles. There are, however, other lots within walking distance, one at a nearby golf course and another at a local mall.

## Tickets

Hi Corbett Field
P.O. Box 27577
Tucson, AZ 85726
(602) 325-2621

Printed schedules are available on New Year's Day. Season and single-game tickets can be ordered starting March 1, by mail or by phone. Payment may be made by MasterCard or Visa. Tickets can also be purchased locally at Picard's outlets. Single-game tickets can be ordered by phone, with payment made by credit card, as late as game day. Tickets so ordered will be held at the "will-call" window. There were no sell-outs in 1987.

**Prices:** Box $5; reserved $4; grandstand $3.50; general admission $2; children under 14, $1.

## Team Hotel
Sheraton Pueblo Hotel
350 South Freeway
Tucson, AZ 85745
(602) 622-6611

In past springs, two weeks of broadcasts from the hotel lobby have been carried on WWWE, the Cleveland radio station that carries Indians' games.

### Players' Favorite Leisure Spots
The Indians seem to enjoy sports when they're not playing baseball, especially at their two favorite hangouts: Tucson Greyhound Park and the Tucson Health & Fitness Center.

### Previous Spring Training Locations
| | |
|---|---|
| 1902–03 | New Orleans, LA |
| 1904 | San Antonio, TX |
| 1905–06 | New Orleans, LA |
| 1907–09 | Macon, GA |
| 1910–11 | Alexandria, LA |
| 1912 | New Orleans, LA |
| 1913 | Pensacola, FL |
| 1914 | Athens, GA |
| 1915 | San Antonio, TX |
| 1916–20 | New Orleans, LA |
| 1921–22 | Dallas, TX |
| 1923–27 | Lakeland, FL |
| 1928–39 | New Orleans, LA |
| 1940–42 | Ft. Myers, FL |
| 1943–45 | Lafayette, IN |
| 1946 | Clearwater, FL |
| 1947–present | Tucson, AZ |

### Hottest Prospects
Those who have followed the Indians for many years will remember they were world champs in 1948; perennial contenders throughout the '50s with one of the greatest pitching staffs ever assembled (Early Wynn, Bob Lemon, Mike Garcia, and

the aging Bob Feller); and winners of 111 games in 1954. That was surely the Indians' heyday: they have finished above .500 only six times since 1959 and have frustrated their fans by fielding talented teams that seem to find a way to lose and often trading away talented youngsters only to see them develop elsewhere.

Despite the arrival of three excellent pitchers, the major problem throughout the '60s was a dearth of new blood to replace the aging stars. The Indians opened the decade with one of the top minor league prospects in 6'7" Walter Bond. The big outfielder/first baseman had hit .318 at Vancouver but was a bust in Cleveland, enjoyed one good season in Houston, and was quickly out of baseball. Though possessing none of Bond's credentials, Mike de la Hoz began his useful and much longer utility career in 1960.

Sudden Sam McDowell began his storied career the next year by starting one game at the end of the season. He struck out five in six innings, a preview of things to come; in his 15 seasons, he averaged barely less than one strikeout an inning, twice fanning more than 300 in a season, and five times leading the league. Trouble was, Sam also led in walks five times, and though his career ERA was a fine 3.17, his record was just over .500.

Ty Cline and Max Alvis were the hopefuls in 1962. Cline had batted .290 at Salt Lake City the previous season but hit only .248 for the Indians and was traded after the season to Milwaukee for aging first-baseman Joe Adcock. Alvis spent most of the year at Salt Lake City, batting .319, and became the Tribe's third-baseman the next year, lasting the rest of the decade.

Diminutive Vic Davalillo was a part-time starter his rookie year in 1963, batting .292 in the first of his 16 big league seasons. He ended with one more triple (37) than he had home runs and one of the finest pinch-hitting records in baseball history. The year after Vic made the club, rookie pitcher Sonny Siebert joined the staff and went 7–9, but with an excellent ERA predicting his future success. Siebert won 16 and lost 8 each of the next two seasons and stayed in Cleveland until he was traded to Boston just after the 1969 season had started, in exchange for flamboyant Ken Harrelson.

But it was Luis Tiant who made the biggest impression in 1964, winning 10 with a 2.83 ERA. Four times thereafter he would win 20 games, including the remarkable 1968 campaign when he went 21–9 with a league-leading ERA of 1.60! Tiant's unique motion, especially with runners on base, and his vast repertoire of pitches served him well over 19 seasons.

After a decade-long dearth of young hitters, the Indians looked to outfielder Roy Foster to reverse the trend in 1970. Coming off 92 RBI in the International League, he spent most of Spring Training that year with Milwaukee; just before the season started, the Indians picked him up for Alvis. Foster hit a promising .268 with 23 home runs and was named Rookie of the Yeear by *The Sporting News.* He slipped the following season and was traded to Texas in December 1971, only to be reacquired by the Tribe four months later for his last Major League season.

Chris Chambliss changed the Tribe's rookie fortunes in 1971. The AA Rookie of the Year at Wichita in 1970, with a .342 average, Chambliss started 1971 in the minors but was called up in May. He went on to hit a solid .275 and earned AL Rookie of the Year honors, only the second Indian to do so (Herb Score in 1955 was the first). The Tribe had another AA Rookie of the Year in camp in 1972. Buddy Bell was faced with the problem of beating out Graig Nettles at third and was switched to the outfield for his rookie season. The son of excellent Reds' outfielder Gus Bell hit well enough to prompt the Tribe to trade Nettles to the Yankees right after the season. Dick Tidrow also emerged in 1972, winning 14 games each of his first two seasons. Then, just after the 1974 campaign began, he was packaged with Chambliss in a big trade with the Yankees, one that benefited New York to a much greater degree than the Indians.

Coming off a league-leading 14–3 record at San Antonio in 1972, Dennis Eckersley impressed everyone in the 1975 camp. Just 20 years old, he quickly became the ace of the staff with a 13–7 record and stingy 2.60 ERA, third best in the league. Eckersley was named the AL's best rookie pitcher by *The Sporting News,* though the Baseball Writers honored Fred Lynn's magnificent rookie year in Boston. Eckersley became yet another traded young mound star when he was dealt to Boston during Spring Training, 1978 for four young players. He promptly won 20 games for the Red Sox and was a mainstay of their staff well into the '80s.

Infielder Alfredo Griffin was in camp in 1976 but had never hit over .275 in the minors and was sent down for seasoning. He improved to .291 in 1978 and was rewarded by being traded to Toronto for pitcher Victor Cruz, another ill-fated swap as far as the Indians were concerned. Griffin became the Blue Jays' infield leader, but Cruz could never come close to the splendid rookie season that had attracted Cleveland's attention.

The Tribe hoped Eric Wilkins would be another McDowell. His 94-MPH fastball made him the top rookie two years running, but the promise arising from successive minor league records of 9–1 and 15–5 didn't pan out as injuries cut down on his effectiveness.

It is hard to believe that Joe Charboneau played only one full season in the Majors, but what a year it was and what an impression he left. The Indians obtained him from the Phillies for Cardell Camper, and he came to camp in 1980 straight off batting averages of .350 and .352 in the minors. He captivated Cleveland fans with his style and .289/23 homer/87 RBI rookie season, to become the third Indian to capture AL Rookie of the Year honors. Alas Charboneau, like Mark Fidrych, fell victim to injuries; his back acting up, he could play only 70 games the next two years and was forced into premature retirement.

A sentimental favorite in the 1981 camp was Steve Narleski, whose father, Ray, had been a top Indian pitcher of the '50s. Despite his 11–12 record at Tacoma, Steve did not make the team. Neither did nonroster outfielder Von Hayes, who was sent back to Charleston despite his .329 average in the minors the year before. He again impressed at .314, came up at the end of 1981, and was the leading rookie in camp in 1982. This time he stuck as a regular outfielder, but he, too was quickly traded, though this time the Indians received a bountiful package in return: among the five players sent by the Phillies was the excellent shortstop Julio Franco.

Four years later the Indians had another gem. Cory Snyder hit .281 at Waterloo in 1985, and started the '86 season with the Maine Guides of the International League. His .302 average prompted his promotion to the big club where he was something of a phenomenon: joining the line-up on June 13, he tripled in his second at-bat and belted 24 homers with 69 RBI the rest of the way, to place fourth in the top rookie balloting. Big lefthander Greg Swindell was the top prospect in 1987, based on his five victories at the end of the '86 season. Victimized by the Tribe's poor showing and by an arm injury, he nonetheless showed flashes of brilliance and could be a future stopper.

## Top Rookies Each Spring
1960    Walter Bond, outfield
1961    Jack Kubiszyn, shortstop

1962　Ty Cline, outfield
1963　Tony Martinez, shortstop
1964　Tom Kelley, pitcher
1965　none
1966　Tom Kelley, pitcher
1967　Steve Bailey, pitcher
1968　Harold Jurtz, pitcher
1969　none
1970　Steve Mingori, pitcher
1971　Rich Hand, pitcher
1972　Buddy Bell, third base
1973　Charlie Spikes, outfield
1974　Rick Sawyer, pitcher; Tommy Smith, outfield
1975　Jim Kern, pitcher
1976　Vassie Gardner, outfield
1977　Jim Norris, outfield
1978　Eric Wilkins, pitcher
1979　Eric Wilkins, pitcher
1980　Joe Charboneau, outfield
1981　Von Hayes, outfield
1982　Von Hayes, outfield
1983　Will Culmer, outfield
1984　Jerry Willard, catcher
1985　Jeff Barkley, pitcher
1986　Cory Snyder, outfield
1987　Greg Swindell, pitcher

## AL Rookies of the Year
1971　Chris Chambliss, first base
1980　Joe Charboneau, outfield

## Prospect to Watch in 1988
**Dave Clark,** *outfield.* Among the top five American Association hitters for all of the second half of the season before being called up by the Tribe, Clark hit .344 with 26 home runs through the end of August.

# MILWAUKEE BREWERS

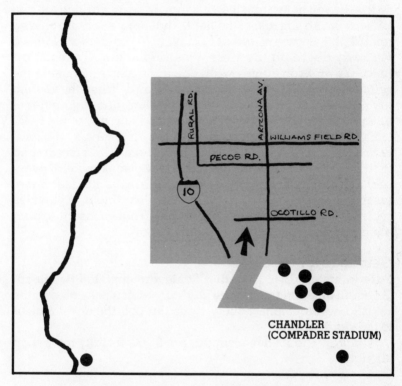

CHANDLER
(COMPADRE STADIUM)

■ **Current site:**
Compadre Stadium
1425 West Ocitillo Road
Chandler, AZ 85248
(602) 821-2200
■ **Dimensions:** 340′ left
and right, 440′ center;
■ **Seating:** 5,000,
plus on grass down the
the left-field line

■ **Built:** 1985
■ **Off-season use:** No
baseball is played there,
and the stadium is used
for concerts and
special events.
■ **Practice site:** At the
stadium daily at 10:00 A.M.
■ **Game time:** 1:00 P.M.
■ **Most convenient airport:**
Phoenix

Compadre Stadium (Spanish for "friend"), which opened in 1986, was built by a group of local businessmen, Chandler Baseball Stadium Limited Partners, and the Brewers are the primary tenant. The stadium is also the site of concerts and high school and college games. The facility is run by the Compadres, a local civic group.

This brand-new stadium in Chandler is dug into the ground, so that as you enter from the vast ground-level parking lot, you walk around a rim above the field. That unique feature offers a remarkable degree of access to players. A concrete arc forms a walkway above all the seats from third to first. To reach the field, players sometimes walk down the steps alongside the seats and, consequently, through the crowd. When the visiting team arrives to play the Brewers, it often runs a gauntlet of autograph seekers as the players make their way to the field.

The seven rows of box seats, two rows of reserves, and fourteen rows of general admission extend from third base around to first and have no cover. Because of the sunken field, every seat has a clear view. A grassy hill, about 100 feet wide, extends beyond the stands on the left-field line and provides seating when all other seats are sold. That pleasant setting almost makes you wish for a sellout.

## Getting to the Stadium

Take **Interstate 10** to **Chandler Boulevard** east, to **Price Road.** Go south on Price right to the stadium, which is located in the Ocitillo development. Follow signs through the development to the stadium.

*Parking:* The lot has a capacity of 3,000, usually more than enough.

## Tickets

Milwaukee Brewers
3800 South Alma School Road, Suite 300
Chandler, AZ 85248
(602) 899-9111

The schedule is available in November. In addition to home games in Chandler, the Brewers arrange for fans to go on road trips to Palm Springs and Yuma. Those interested can contact the Brewers at the above address.

Season and single-game tickets can be ordered beginning in December. Payment should be made by check. Ticket requests are filled in the order in which they are received. Tickets are held at the "will-call" window and can be picked up beginning three weeks before the first game.

*Prices:* Grandbox $6; box $5; grandstand $3.50.

## Team Hotel

> The Dobson Ranch Inn
> 1666 South Dobson Road
> Mesa, AZ 85202
> (602) 831-7000

There are two radio shows regularly broadcast over Milwaukee radio from the hotel. WKTI broadcasts a morning show and WISN's Pat Sheridan hosts talk shows several times during the exhibition season.

## Players' Favorite Leisure Spots

The Brewers spend most of their evenings at the local clubs, such as Bobby McGhee's, a restaurant and disco, TGIF, Bennigan's and the Lunt Avenue Marble Club. They also frequent two restaurants, Riccardo's, a Mexican eatery, and Steven's Chop House, owned by former pitcher Steve Stone and broadcaster Harry Carey.

## Previous Spring Training Locations

> *Seattle Pilots (1969)*
> *Milwaukee Brewers (1970 – present)*

1969–72    Tempe, AZ
1973–85    Sun City, AZ
1986–present    Chandler, AZ

## Hottest Prospects

The Brewers were actually born in Seattle as the Pilots in 1969, part of the American League's expansion. Made up mostly of castoffs, the Pilots finished in last place and drew only 678,000 fans. The absentee owners announced the team was for sale, and when a number of Seattle suitors were rejected by the other AL owners, a group of Wisconsin buyers rushed in just before Spring Training in 1970 and brought Major League baseball back to Milwaukee.

The newly christened Brewers won one more game than the Pilots the year before. Tommy Harper starred at third and in the outfield, hitting 31 runs, but was traded part way into the next season. Prospect Roy Foster was dealt to Cleveland just before the 1970 season commenced, as Max Alvis came to the Brewers.

John Morris, 9–1 at Indianapolis, was the best of the new pitchers, and Skip Lockwood showed promise despite his 5–12 record.

Mound help arrived in 1971 in the person of Jim Slaton, whose 10–8 rookie mark anticipated the solid seasons he would produce the next 13 years. The turn-around began for certain in 1973. Ed Rodriguez joined the bullpen and won 23 while saving 16 over three seasons. Darrell Porter took over behind the plate, and Gorman Thomas — destined to be the Brewers' leading slugger in coming years — hit his first two homers toward the end of the 1973 season. Robin Yount was the team's number one draft pick in June, and the 18-year-old with the "can't miss" label moved in at shortstop in 1974. Thirteen years later, he is still a Brewers regular. A scratch golfer, Yount threatened to pursue a career on the PGA tour when his elbow forced him onto the disabled list early in 1978, but he recovered to play most of the season.

Bill Castro pitched his first few games late in the 1974 season and shared the bullpen with Rodriguez for several years. Alliterative outfielder Sixto Lezcano followed a similar path, making a modest showing in late 1974 but earning a starting role the next spring. His rifle arm kept baserunners wary from the beginning, but his bat developed more slowly; finally in 1979 he came into his own, posting a .321/28 homer/101 RBI season. He slumped badly in 1980 and was a key figure in the big winter trade with St. Louis, which brought Pete Vuckovich, Rollie Fingers, and Ted Simmons north to Milwaukee.

The Brewers expected Lenn Sakata to push his way into the starting infield in 1978, but his anemic bat kept him on the bench. Instead, it was Paul Molitor, with just 64 games of AAA ball as the sum total of his pro experience, who made the line-up. When Yount went on the disabled list, Molitor filled in at shortstop and moved to second after Yount's return. Molitor hit a solid .273 that year, winning Rookie of the Year honors from *The Sporting News*, though losing the Baseball Writers' award to the Tigers' Lou Whitaker. Injuries have plagued him, so that he has played only two complete seasons in his 10-year career. But his presence in the Brewers line-up makes an astonishing difference: Milwaukee is way over .500 with Molitor and well under that level without him. In 1987 Molitor toyed with Joe Dimaggio's 56-game hitting streak, stopped only after he had hit in 39 straight, the longest such streak since Pete Rose's 44-game mark in 1978.

Jim Gantner apprenticed three years before becoming a part-timer at third and second in 1979. The hard-nosed infielder took over at second in 1981 when Molitor's injuries kept him on the shelf or in the outfield, and he has been there since. Mike Henderson made a strong impression in the 1980 camp. Henderson had received Yount's scholarship at Arizona State University when the teenage shortstop signed with the Brewers in '73; on graduation in 1977, Henderson was signed in his turn, though in the end he never did make it to the Majors.

The Brewers' first pick in the 1980 draft was slender outfielder Dion James, who made his way through the minor leagues to arrive in camp in 1984 sporting a .336 AAA mark. He promptly found himself starting in center field and hit a robust .295. But he never fully developed for Milwaukee and was traded in the spring of 1987 to Atlanta for Brad Komminsk, whom the Braves had given up on. James had a marvelous season in Atlanta, hitting over .300 and energizing the Braves' attack. Komminsk had another excellent minor league season, though he has yet to prove he can hit in the Majors.

The 1985 camp welcomed a number of players up from the minors, among them Billy Joe Robidoux and Mike Felder. Felder had hit .314 at Vancouver the previous year and brought his hot bat with him to Chandler in 1986, hitting a team-high .409. Sent back to Vancouver, he came up at the end of that season and made his mark in 1987. B.J. Surhoff also arrived in 1987. All eyes were on the talented catcher in Spring Training, though he was not even on the roster. The AAA All-Star catcher the year before according to *Baseball America*, Surhoff had been picked by *The Sporting News* as the best candidate for Rookie of the Year. That pressure notwithstanding, Surhoff had a splendid season and, had it not been for remarkable performances by a couple of other rookies, he might well have been named the top AL rookie.

## Top Rookies Each Spring

1969  Dick Baney, pitcher
1970  Roy Foster, outfield
1971  Bill Parsons, pitcher
1972  Darrell Porter, catcher
1973  John Vuckovich, third base
1974  Robin Yount, shortstop
1975  Bill Castro, pitcher; Sixto Lezcano, outfield
1976  Kevin Kobel, pitcher
1977  Danny Thomas, outfield
1978  Paul Molitor, second base
1979  Jim Gantner, third base

1980   Bob Galasso, pitcher; Mike Henderson, outfield
1981   Frank DiPino, pitcher
1982   Rich Olson, pitcher
1983   none
1984   Dion James, outfield
1985   Bill Wegman, pitcher
1986   Mike Felder, outfield
1987   B.J. Surhoff, catcher

## Prospects to Watch in 1988

*Steve Kiefer*, *third base*.  Considered one of the two best prospects in the American Association, Kiefer had reached the 30 home run mark for Denver by his eighty-third game. He was named the league's All-Star third baseman and was hitting .331 when he was injured at the end of the year.

*Lavell Freeman*, *outfield*.  A Texas League All-Star, Freeman hit .400 through the end of August while stroking 24 home runs.

*Joey Meyer*, *designated hitter*.  The 263-pound Meyer's only problem seems to be weight. An All-Star at Denver, he has hit some titanic home runs: there are painted seats as much as 583 feet from home plate in Mile High Stadium to show where six of his 29 home runs landed.

# *OAKLAND* *ATHLETICS*

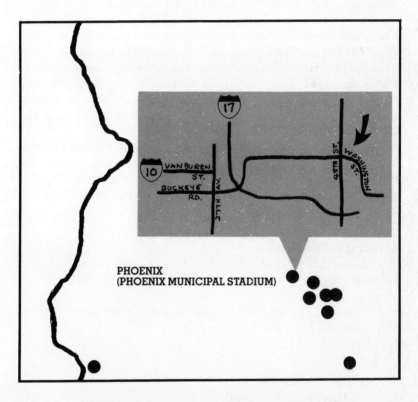

**PHOENIX
(PHOENIX MUNICIPAL STADIUM)**

■ **Current site:**
Phoenix Municipal Stadium
5999 East Van Buren
Phoenix, AZ 85008
(602) 275-0500
■ **Dimensions:**
375' left and right;
410' center
■ **Seating:** 8,000
■ **Built:** 1965

■ **Off-season use:**
Phoenix Firebirds,
Pacific Coast League
(Class AAA, farm team of
San Francisco Giants)
■ **Practice site:** At the
stadium daily at 10:00 A.M.
■ **Game time:** 1:00 P.M.
■ **Most convenient airport:**
Phoenix

Phoenix Municipal Stadium opened in 1966. It is also used by the Phoenix Firebirds, the Giants' AAA team, and until four years ago it was used by the Giants for Spring Training. The A's and Giants have since swapped stadiums, with the Giants going to Scottsdale.

This large (for Spring Training) stadium looks more like a Major League facility than most. With reasonably comfortable bleachers (with backs) extending past the fixed stands to both outfield corners, good views are available no matter what the size of the crowd. The only drawback to the vast, adjacent parking lot is the distance you'll have to walk to and from your car.

There is a practice field behind the right-field wall, and you can sometimes get autographs there. Failing that, the front rows of the box seats and bleachers afford good opportunities, and you can also wait for the players to emerge from the clubhouse on the third-base side.

The stadium itself sits as a hub of activity: 10 minutes west is the airport, 10 minutes north are the Giants, 10 minutes east are the Cubs, and 10 minutes south are the Mariners. This is a good place to make a second stop if you want to catch bits of two games in one day.

## Getting to the Stadium
Take **Interstate 10** to **44th Street** and drive north several blocks. Make a right turn on **Van Buren**, and follow it to the stadium, which is on the right.

*Parking:* They virtually never run out of spaces, but for convenience, park early on busy days.

## Tickets
Oakland Athletics
Phoenix Municipal Stadium
5999 East Van Buren
Phoenix, AZ 85008
(602) 275-0500 (information)
(602) 829-5555 (credit card orders)

The schedule is available on January 1. Season and single-game tickets go on sale in early February. Tickets may be ordered by phone or mail, using either a check or a credit card, although no credit card orders are taken within 24 hours of the game. There is a service charge of 50 cents per ticket or a minimum of $1.30 per order on all phone orders. Any orders received before February will be returned. Only twice were the A's sold out in 1987.

*Prices:* Box $5; reserved $3.50; general admission $2.50.

## Team Hotel
Gateway Park Hotel
320 North 44th Street
Phoenix, AZ 85005
(602) 225-0500

## Players' Favorite Leisure Spots
The management personnel usually hang out at the Pink Pony, while the players prefer the reasonably priced Italian cuisine at Riazzi, the steaks at What's Your Beef, and the Mexican food at Garcia's.

## Previous Spring Training Locations
*Philadelphia Athletics (1901–54)*
*Kansas City Athletics (1955–67)*
*Oakland Athletics (1968–present)*

| | |
|---|---|
| 1901 | Philadelphia, PA |
| 1902 | Charlotte, NC |
| 1903 | Jacksonville, FL |
| 1904 | Spartanburg, SC |
| 1905 | Shreveport, LA |
| 1906 | Montgomery, AL |
| 1907 | Dallas, TX |
| 1908–09 | New Orleans, LA |
| 1910 | Atlanta, GA |
| 1911 | Savannah, GA |
| 1912–13 | San Antonio, TX |
| 1914–18 | Jacksonville, FL |
| 1919 | Philadelphia, PA |
| 1920–21 | Lake Charles, LA |
| 1922 | Eagle Pass, TX |
| 1923–24 | Montgomery, AL |
| 1925–36 | Fort Myers, FL |
| 1937 | Mexico City, Mexico |
| 1938–39 | Lake Charles, LA |
| 1940–42 | Anaheim, CA |
| 1943 | Wilmington, DE |
| 1944–45 | Frederick, MD |
| 1946–62 | West Palm Beach, FL |

1963–68    Bradenton, FL
1969–78    Mesa, AZ
1979–83    Scottsdale, AZ
1984–present   Phoenix, AZ

## Hottest Prospects

Kansas City fans could justifiably have been frustrated by the departure of the Athletics to Oakland in 1968. The team had finished last four times (including the final year in Kansas City) and next-to-last twice since 1960, and here it was winning 82 games in its first year in Oakland. To add insult to injury, the splendid players developed in the Kansas City farm system all arrived just as the team was leaving and would soon be leading Oakland to three consecutive World Series victories, 1972–74. Only Dick Green and Rick Monday, of the Kansas City rookies from 1960–67, would have an impact in Oakland. And on top of it all, the Oakland fans didn't seem to care that much about their team during the regular season, showing up in droves only when the playoffs began.

Justice ultimately prevailed, however, in the eyes of Kansas City supporters. When the A's fell prey to free agency in 1976 and dropped to the bottom a year later, the Royals — poor replacement for the A's in their glory years — were ready, winning four of five pennants from 1976–80.

Those first-year Oakland fans were graced by an excellent pitching staff, sporting two of the modern era's best nicknames: Jim "Catfish" Hunter and John "Blue Moon" Odom. After four straight 20-win seasons, the last three during the World Series triple, and a Cy Young Award, Hunter jumped ship to Steinbrenner's Yankees, the first of the A's players to leave town. He then hit the 20-win mark for a fifth year in a row. Recently, he was elected to the Hall of Fame. Odom was solid into the '70s but slumped after the first championship.

Complementing the 1968 staff was a quartet of future stars in their first or second full years. Celebrated outfielder Rick Monday was the most experienced. The 1965 College Player of the Year, he was the first player selected in the draft and had started the 1967 season in Kansas City. He missed the championship years, however, dealt to the Cubs for lefty Ken Holtzman in a move that cemented the A's staff. Holtzman won 59 games in Oakland from 1972–74.

Reggie Jackson and Sal Bando became starters in 1968. Possessing a tremendous arm, speed, and great power, Jackson had been in 35 games in Kansas City, but he blossomed his first full year, hitting 29 homers and finishing second in the AL in outfield assists. The A's traded him to Baltimore in 1976 to avoid another free agent defection, as the championship team was dismantled. The 1987 season was Jackson's twenty-first and last, and it was fitting he played it back in Oakland. The drama and flair he has brought to the game cannot be replaced. For him it has usually been all or nothing at the plate. Sixth on the all-time home run list, he is also first in career strikeouts.

Bando had also played briefly in 1967, and regular play definitely suited him. His leadership abilities were a big part of the glue holding the championship teams together, and his bat and glove were essential ingredients. The 1968 season was also Joe Rudi's first year, but the fourth in the remarkable quartet was unable to crack the line-up until 1970. He, too, became a free agent in 1976, signing with the Angels, but his best years were with the A's.

The best of the young pitchers in 1969 were Rollie Fingers and George Lauzerique, whose careers moved in opposite directions. Fingers became the dominant relief pitcher in baseball and has more saves than any other reliever. Lauzerique spent two nondescript years in Oakland and was soon out of baseball. Catching them in spring 1969 was a rookie up from the Carolina League, where he had hit 21 home runs. Gene Tenace would not be a regular until 1973, and then mostly at first base as Dave Duncan and Ray Fosse were behind the plate. Tenace was a major factor in the championship years but, like so many, opted out of Oakland as a free agent after the 1976 season.

Who will ever forget Vida Blue's first full year, 1971? He literally exploded on the American League, going 24–8 with an astonishing 1.82 ERA. Blue won the Cy Young Award that year. Perhaps it happened too fast to the youngster, for though he won 20 games twice more, he was never quite the same as in that first year.

The 1974 spring season featured two good rookies from Tucson: infielder Manny Trillo and pitcher Glenn Abbott. Charlie Finley tried to put Trillo on the roster for the 1973 World Series after he sent Mike Andrews home for committing a crucial error. Finley's creativity grated on everyone and continued next spring with the experiment of Herb Washington as a designated base runner. The Olympic sprinter never got to bat during the year but stole 28 bases and scored 29 runs as the A's won again. Another

Washington, Claudell, came up in August 1974 after hitting an impressive .365 at Birmingham and was put on the 1975 spring roster. He was joined by rookie Phil Garner, replacing the retired Dick Green at second base. Both Washington and Garner had solid seasons in 1975–76, and both were caught in Finley's trading frenzy as the team disintegrated, going to Texas and Pittsburgh respectively during Spring Training 1977.

But the sensation of the 1975 spring was young pitcher Mike Norris, who made the squad as the number three starter, replacing the departed Catfish Hunter. Norris threw a shutout against the White Sox but then developed arm trouble and finished the regular season with a 1–0 record and 0.00 ERA. It would take him several years to come back; he finally won 22 games in 1980 on Billy Martin's staff that finished almost every game it started. A number of physical and personal problems combined to finally derail Norris's promising career.

The 1977 season marked the changing of the A's guard. Only one starter, Bill North, from Opening Day of 1976 was in the line-up the first game next year, and the house-cleaning showed. The A's finished last in the AL West. But it was a good opportunity for rookies. Wayne Gross, called up the previous year when Claudell Washington was injured, was the best of the newcomers in Spring Training until Mitchell Page showed up on March 15. Page tore up the league, hitting .307 during the regular season. He couldn't sustain that level of play, however, and declined steadily through 1983. Gross was the regular at third in those years.

The 1979 season marked Rickey Henderson's debut. He came into camp with three years of minor league ball under his belt, having been named his league's player of the year each time. He had a strong spring, was farmed out until June, and came back to be the starting left fielder. Dwayne Murphy, too, became a starter in 1979, in center, joining Henderson and incumbent Tony Armas, acquired in the Garner deal, to form one of baseball's best outfields. They and the durable staff of Norris, Rick Langford, Matt Keough, and Steve McCatty, developed mostly in the A's system, led Billy Martin's club back into contention for a brief period in 1980–81. They slumped thereafter and played indifferently until 1986.

Jose Canseco, the 1985 Southern League MVP and *Baseball America*'s Minor League Player of the Year despite playing just 58 games, came into the 1986 camp as the most heralded rookie in years. *Sports Illustrated* heaped more attention on the young slugger by making him its choice for Rookie of the Year. And he delivered, finishing fourth in home runs and second in RBI, winning the Baseball Writers' rookie award, and reigniting baseball fever in Oakland. He started slowly in 1987, over-shadowed perhaps by Mark McGwire's entry into baseball, but by season's end his stats were impressive again.

McGwire was nothing short of a phenomenon in his 1987 rookie season. The A's first round pick in 1984 hit .300+ both years in the minors, and his home run total in 1987 set a new Major League mark for rookies, far eclipsing the mark of 38 held jointly by Wally Berger and Frank Robinson. McGwire won the Baseball Writers' Rookie of the Year award in a landslide. Modest and self-effacing, he seems to have an attitude success won't spoil. He and Canseco in the same line-up assure that the A's will be contenders even with merely decent pitching.

## Top Rookies Each Spring

1960  Lou Klimchock, second base
1961  Dick Howser, shortstop
1962  Joe Azcue, catcher
1963  Hector Martinez, outfield
1964  Dick Green, second base
1965  Tom Reynolds, outfield
1966  Ron Stone, outfield
1967  Rick Monday, outfield
1968  Reggie Jackson, outfield
1969  Rollie Fingers, pitcher
1970  Bobby Brooks, outfield
1971  Gonzalo Marquez, first base
1972  none
1973  Gonzalo Marquez, first base
1974  Manny Trillo, second base
1975  Claudell Washington, outfield
1976  Mike Norris, pitcher
1977  Wayne Gross, third base
1978  Dave Revering, first base
1979  Rickey Henderson, outfield
1980  Jeff Cox, second base
1981  none
1982  Dave Beard, pitcher
1983  Mike Warren, pitcher
1984  Mickey Tettleton, catcher
1985  Steve Kiefer, shortstop

1986   Jose Canseco, outfield
1987   Mark McGwire, first base

## AL Rookies of the Year
1986   Jose Canseco, outfield
1987   Mark McGwire, first base

## Prospect to Watch in 1988
*Eric Plunk*, *pitcher*. Rated one of the top 10 prospects in the Pacific Coast League by *Baseball America*, the hard-throwing Plunk had an ERA of 1.59 through mid-August for Tacoma. He is expected to provide bullpen help in 1988.

# SAN DIEGO PADRES

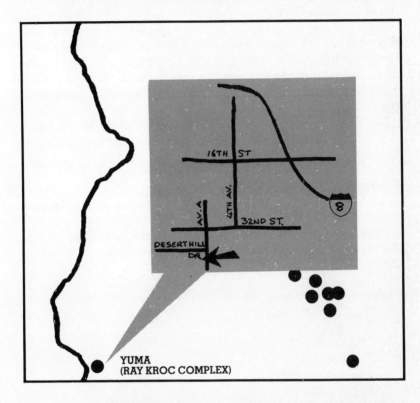

16TH ST

4TH AV.

32ND ST.

DESERT HILL DR.

8

YUMA
(RAY KROC COMPLEX)

■ **Current site:**
Desert Sun Stadium
1440 Desert Hills Drive
Yuma, AZ 85364
(602) 782-2567
■ **Dimensions:** 350′ left
and right; 420′ center
■ **Seating:** 6,874
■ **Built:** 1973
■ **Off-season use:**
Japan's Yakult Swallows
train there in February;

high school and college
games are also played
there.
■ **Practice site:** At the
stadium daily at 10:00 A.M.
■ **Game times:**
1:00 P.M.(day),
7:00 P.M. (night)
■ **Most convenient airport:**
Phoenix (1st 2 weeks)
San Diego or Yuma
(2nd 2 weeks)

The Padres' Complex was gradually improved in the '70s and evolved into the Ray A. Kroc Baseball Complex, named after the late Padres owner. Set in the midst of a recreational oasis, and surrounded by a green belt of golf course, playing fields, and park, the complex consists of four playing fields in a cloverleaf shape, with the Padre offices located at the center.

The box seats and grandstand extend to the bases, and bleachers reach down both lines. The front rows of the boxes and bleachers are the best place to get autographs, though one can also wait for the players to leave the field along the third-base line. The batting cages in the complex are accessible to the public.

The Padres' Spring Training home is far from the others in the Cactus League. Fans should be sure tickets are secured before traveling to Yuma to see a game.

## Getting to the Stadium
From **Interstate 8**, go west on **32nd Street**, then south on **Avenue A** to Desert Hills Drive. The stadium is at the intersection.

*Parking:* The stadium lot can hold 1,200 vehicles. The complex shares parking facilities with the Yuma Civic and Convention Center, which is next door.

## Tickets
San Diego Padres
Caballeros de Yuma
Chamber of Commerce
P.O. Box 230
Yuma, AZ 85364
(602) 782-2567

The printed team schedule is available on January 1. Season-ticket holders from the previous season have the right of first refusal. No orders for season tickets are accepted before these people are contacted, and any checks received by the Padres will be returned. Single-game tickets may be ordered in advance only with the team's official order form, which may be obtained from the Padres spring-ticket office in early November. Payment for advance tickets should be in the form of a check accompanying the order form. The Padres were sold out four times in 1987.

*Prices:* Reserved $5; general admission $2. Box seats are sold on a seasonal basis.

## Team Hotel
Stardust Hotel
2350 South 4th Street
Yuma, AZ 85364
(602) 783-8861

In the past, KSON radio in San Diego has broadcast from the lobby.

## Players' Favorite Leisure Spots
In addition to golf at Mesa Del Sol, and the Yuma Golf and Country Club, the players enjoy attending the races at Yuma Greyhound Park. Favorite restaurants are Hungry Hunter, Jack & Rosie's, and Arroyo Dunes, all for steaks, as well as the Mandarin Palace for Chinese cuisine.

## Previous Spring Training Locations
The Padres have played their exhibition games in Yuma since their first spring in 1969.

## Hottest Prospects
San Diego joined the National League in the expansion year of 1969. Unlike many of their expansion predecessors, the Padres opted for youth. Fifteen rookies got a shot that first year, and in short order the team had a power base. Nate Colbert had had cups of coffee with Houston in '66 and '68, but the open air in California obviously agreed with him and he quickly became one of the NL's top sluggers, belting 163 homers the next six years. Ollie Brown had hit modestly in San Francisco, but his marks shot up when he moved south. Cito Gaston came from the Braves and had a career year in 1970, at .318, with 29 homers and 93 RBI.

The best of the new pitchers was Clay Kirby, who lost 20 games in the Padres' maiden season but nonetheless managed a respectable 3.79 ERA. Two years later he became the Padres' first winning starter, at 15–13. Dave Roberts and Steve Arlin were also among the initial 15 rookies. Winless their first years, they quickly posted notable records. Roberts was 14–17 in 1971 but held his ERA to an astonishing 2.10, indicative of the lack of support he received. As a reward, the Padres sent him to Houston for a trio of players in December 1971. This eliminated the possibility of a Dave Roberts battery, for a third baseman/sometime catcher by that name made the Padres the next year. Steve Arlin had originally been signed by the Phillies in 1966 but skipped the next two Spring Trainings to attend dental school. Each June found him in the minors. Picked up by the Padres after the 1968 season, he threw a shutout in his second start. But he eventually picked up where Kirby left off, losing a combined 40 games in 1972–73, despite an ERA around 3.50 that would make many big winners proud.

Mike Caldwell signed in June 1971 and joined the rotation the next year. His 12–15 record over two years impressed the Giants, if not San Diego, and they traded aging star Willie McCovey to the Padres for Caldwell right after the 1973 season. The Giants were right. Given support, Caldwell went 14–5 with a 2.95 ERA. But the Giants, too, gave up on Caldwell too quickly. In 1978 he led the Brewers at 22–9 and starred in Milwaukee the next five years.

Johnny Grubb looked impressive in the spring of 1973. A first-round draft choice two years earlier, he led the Padres with a .311 batting average while holding down center field. Thirteen years later his bat was still a valuable commodity. But the most significant arrival of 1973 was pitcher Randy Jones. He would lose 22 the next year, but that was a prelude to consecutive years at 20–12 and 22–14, the latter winning the Cy Young Award in 1976.

After jumping camp in 1973, Mike Ivie returned the following spring as a promising catching prospect. He injured his hand during Spring Training and was told he might develop a permanent impairment if he continued catching. Ivie was sent to AA to learn to play the infield and outfield. This he did well enough to start at first and third, but the Padres weren't impressed and reacquired Derrel Thomas from the Giants for Ivie just before Spring Training in 1978.

Dave Winfield was in Spring Training for the first time in 1974, though by then he was no longer a rookie. Winfield had been in the College World Series for Minnesota the previous year and then went right into the Padres' starting line-up. He remained there through 1980, opting that December for free agency and signing with George Steinbrenner's Yankees for $23 million over 10 years.

Butch Metzger, a throw-in when the Padres acquired Tito Fuentes from San Francisco, was a bullpen surprise in 1976. His 11–4 record and 16 saves earned him NL Rookie of the Year honors, which he shared with the Reds' Pat Zachry. It marked the first time the Baseball Writers had split their vote. Metzger could never repeat his first season, bouncing to St. Louis and the Mets his last two years in the Majors.

Bill Almon, the number one draft pick in the country in 1974, finally arrived in '77 and teamed with Mike Champion as an all-rookie keystone combination. Pitcher Bob Owchinko was also on the spring 1977 roster but was sent down to Hawaii before the season started. His 5–1 record convinced San Diego to bring him back, and he finished the year at 9–12 to win *The Sporting News'* award as the NL's top rookie pitcher.

Ozzie Smith wasn't even on the roster in spring 1978 — and with reason. With just one minor league season under his belt, nobody expected him to make the jump. But it was the last time anyone underestimated the Wizard of Oz, who almost fielded his way to Rookie of the Year honors. The only more impressive young shortstop in the late '70s was the Cardinals' Garry Templeton, who hit well over .300 his first six years. Hoping to add punch, the Padres traded Smith for Templeton after the '81 season, a deal that has only favored the Cards. Smith's bat has come alive, and his brilliance in the field makes him one of the all-time finest at his position. Templeton, on the other hand, has struggled in San Diego, no longer the hitter he was.

Journeyman minor leaguer Randy Bass, picked up in a trade with the Expos, was expected to make a push for the first base job in 1978. He had hit 37 homers and driven in 143 runs at Denver the year before. But could manage only nine round-trippers in three years and had little impact. At the end of Spring Training in 1980, the Padres acquired Juan Bonilla, the best defensive infielder in the Pacific Coast League, from Cleveland. He showed he could hit as well, batting .290 in 1981. But he sulked when Alan Wiggins replaced him in 1984 and has bounced from team to team ever since. The class of 1980 is noteworthy as well for a name. Juan Tyrone Eichelberger, born in St. Louis, will not make the Hall of Fame with his pitching arm, but his ethnic diversity is world class.

Tony Gwynn brought some amazing minor league stats to the 1983 camp — .331 and .462 with two teams in his first year. Sent down to Hawaii in the Pacific Coast League, he hit .328 and was brought up in midseason to hit .309. A year later he led the league at .351 and has been the NL's best hitter since, over-shadowed though not outperformed by Wade Boggs and Don Mattingly, the AL leaders. Kevin McReynolds joined Gwynn in the outfield in 1984, and his powerful rookie season helped propel the Padres to their first league championship. San Diego fell on hard times the following two seasons, and when the Mets offered minor league stars Stanley Jefferson and Shawn Abner, McReynolds was on his way to New York before the '87 season started.

The top prospect in 1987 was rifle-armed catcher Benito Santiago, who hit .287 in the Pacific Coast League while nailing 49 percent of the runners attempting to steal on him. *Sports Illustrated* selected Santiago as its choice to win the Rookie of the Year, and he has lived up to his billing. On September 26, 1987, he hit in his twenty-eighth straight game, surpassing the modern-day rookie record set by Pittsburgh's Jimmy Williams way back in 1899. His streak extended to 34 games and was still alive as the season ended. Santiago won the Baseball Writers' Rookie of the Year award.

## Top Rookies Each Spring

1969   Clay Kirby, pitcher
1970   Rafael Robles, shortstop
1971   Steve Arlin, pitcher
1972   Mike Caldwell, pitcher
1973   Johnny Grubb, outfield
1974   Joe McIntosh, pitcher
1975   Randy Elliott, outfield
1976   Butch Metzger, pitcher
1977   Bill Almon, shortstop; Bob Owchinko, pitcher
1978   Ozzie Smith, shortstop
1979   Jim Beswick, outfield
1980   Juan Eichelberger, pitcher
1981   Randy Bass, first base
1982   Alan Wiggins, outfield
1983   Mark Thurmond, pitcher
1984   Kevin McReynolds, outfield
1985   Ed Wojna, pitcher
1986   Leon Roberts, second base
1987   Benito Santiago, catcher

## NL Rookie of the Year

1976   Butch Metzger, pitcher
       (co-Rookie of the Year with Pat Zachry, Cincinnati)
1987   Benito Santiago, catcher

## Prospects to Watch in 1988

*Shawn Abner*, outfield.  Abner seems about ready to fulfill the expectations that the Mets had for him when they made him

the number one pick in the 1984 draft. He came to the Padres
when San Diego traded Kevin McReynolds to the Mets.

*Rob Nelson, first base.* The Padres acquired him at the tail end
of the 1987 season. He had been expected to be the Athletics'
first baseman in 1987 instead of Mark McGwire. But Nelson lost
the job in the spring of 1987 and spent the year at Tacoma.
He got a measure of revenge because it was his name — not
McGwire's — that appeared on the AL All-Star ballot in 1987!

# SAN FRANCISCO GIANTS

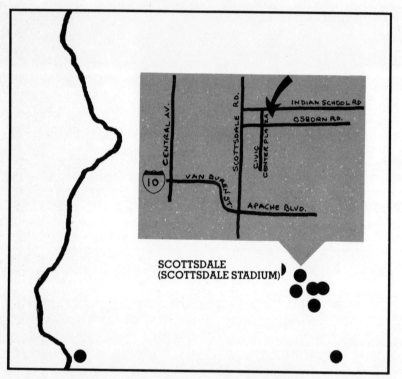

SCOTTSDALE
(SCOTTSDALE STADIUM)

■ **Current site:**
Scottsdale Stadium
7408 East Osborne Road
Scottsdale, AZ 85251
(602) 994-5123
■ **Dimensions:** 360′ left,
390′ right, 430′ center
■ **Seating:** 4,721
■ **Built:** 1951

■ **Off-season use:**
Giants Instructional
League teams
■ **Practice site:**
At the stadium daily
at 10:00 A.M.
■ **Game time:** 1:00 P.M.
■ **Most convenient airport:**
Phoenix

Scottsdale Stadium was built in 1951, and before the Giants moved in, was used by the Oakland A's. The ballpark is city-owned and is leased by the Scottsdale Charros, a civic organization that takes care of ticket sales, promotions, advertising, and concessions. The field itself is good sized, though not symmetrical: the charming redwood stadium has a hand-operated scoreboard that harks back to a bygone era. It is set within the upscale bedroom suburb of Scottsdale with plenty of good shopping, good restaurants, and Western-style tourist attractions nearby.

The grandstand, with boxes and reserves, extends to the bases, and bleachers reach down both lines. Each seat offers an excellent view. The bullpens are next to the bleachers and are an excellent place for autographs. Batting cages down each line are accessible to fans. The clubhouses are by the third- and first-base stadium entrances, and players emerge here after games, affording another autograph opportunity.

## Getting to the Stadium
Take **Interstate 10**, to **Scottsdale Road** heading north, then turn east onto **Osborne Road**. Take Osborne all the way to the stadium.

To get to the minor league practice field at Indian School Park, go north on **Scottsdale Road** for one mile beyond Osborne. Then travel east on **Camelback** for two blocks until **Hayden Road**. Take Hayden to Indian School Park.

*Parking:* There is no stadium parking and virtually no street parking, but nearby public lots provide space for several hundred vehicles.

## Tickets
San Francisco Giants
Scottsdale Stadium
7408 East Osborne Road
Scottsdale, AZ 85251
(602) 994–5123

The printed team schedule is available on January 1. Season and single-game tickets go on sale on January 1. Tickets can be purchased through the mail, with payment by check, or at the box office, using cash. The Giants sold out Scottsdale Stadium three times in 1987.

*Prices:* Reserved box $5; grandstand $4; general admission $3.

## Team Hotel

Sheraton Scottsdale Resort
7200 North Scottsdale Road
Scottsdale, AZ 85252
(602) 948-5000

In the past, Dave Newhouse of KNBR, the team's flagship station, has broadcast live-remotes from the hotel lobby.

## Players' Favorite Leisure Spots

For action, the Giant players head for the Greyhound Track in Phoenix and local clubs in the area, especially West L.A. and Studebakers. There are also several good eateries in the area, including the Pink Pony, Vito's and Scampi for Italian cuisine, Garcia's for Mexican, Don & Charlie's for ribs, What's Your Beef, and Armenia, a family-oriented restaurant.

## Previous Spring Training Locations

| | |
|---|---|
| 1901–02 | New York, NY |
| 1903–05 | Savannah, GA |
| 1906 | Memphis, TN |
| 1907 | Los Angeles, CA |
| 1908–18 | Marlin Springs, TX |
| 1919 | Gainesville, FL |
| 1920–23 | San Antonio, TX |
| 1924–27 | Sarasota, FL |
| 1928 | Augusta, GA |
| 1929–31 | San Antonio, TX |
| 1932–33 | Los Angeles, CA |
| 1934–35 | Miami Beach, FL |
| 1936 | Pensacola, FL |
| 1937 | Havana, Cuba |
| 1938–39 | Baton Rouge, LA |
| 1940 | Winter Haven, FL |
| 1941–42 | Miami, FL |
| 1943–45 | Lakewood, NJ |
| 1946 | Miami, FL |
| 1947–50 | Phoenix, AZ |
| 1951 | St. Petersburg, FL |
| 1952–83 | Phoenix, AZ |
| 1984–present | Scottsdale, AZ |

## Hottest Prospects

There was a lot of pressure on Joey Amalfitano, *The Sporting News*' pick as the Giants' best rookie in the spring of 1960. He was following two mighty tough acts. It had never happened before, and hasn't since, but the Rookie of the Year awards the two previous years had gone to players on the same team playing the same position. First-baseman Orlando Cepeda was the Writers' unanimous choice in 1958, when he hit .312 with 96 RBI. Then along came Willie McCovey in 1959 to take over the first-base job and push Cepeda to the outfield. McCovey hit .354 to be named the loop's top rookie.

Amalfitano was an original bonus baby with the New York Giants, forced to stay on the Major League roster because his signing bonus was so high. Consequently, Amalfitano was in 45 games for the 1954–55 Giants, before being sent to the minors. When he finally got his chance in 1960, he responded with a .277 average and was a starter at second in 1961. But Chuck Hiller also showed promise in that, his rookie year, and Amalfitano was left unprotected over the winter. Drafted by the expansion Houston Colt .45s, he missed the pennant year of 1962. The Giants got him back for the 1963 season, by trading one of their young outfielders, Manny Mota, to Houston. Amalfitano was released after the 1963 season, but Mota turned out to be a gem. Rarely a regular, he would play 20 years as a pinch hitter extraordinaire, batting .300 in that capacity and .304 for his career.

Perhaps the most significant newcomer in 1960, however, was pitcher Juan Marichal, who came up in mid-season to go 6–2 and unveil his dramatic leg kick and pitching repertoire. No pitcher was more dominant in the '60s than Marichal, a decade in which he won 191 games. His lifetime winning percentage of .631 is one of the best in history, and he was selected to the Hall of Fame in 1983. Red Sox fans often forget that Marichal's last five wins came in Boston, in 1974.

Another future Hall of Fame pitcher made his debut in 1962. Gaylord Perry developed slowly, his first big season coming in 1966 when he won 21 games. He would break the 20-win mark four more times in his long career. He and his brother, Jim, held the record for the most wins (529) by a brother combination when they retired. That record has since been broken by Phil and Joe Niekro.

After five years in the minors, never batting lower than .324, Jesus Alou was ready to join his two brothers, Felipe and Matty, in the outfield in 1964. They had been together for 16 games in

**237**

1963, when Jesus was recalled from the minors. Picked by *The Sporting News* as the NL's top prospect, Jesus hit .274 in 115 games in 1964 but found himself the only Alou in the Giants' outfield. Felipe was traded to Milwaukee over the winter, and Matty spent most of the year as a pinch hitter. Matty was dealt to Pittsburgh after the 1965 season, and Jesus to Houston early in 1969, thus breaking up another of baseball's best brother acts.

Two other good rookies joined Jesus in 1964: third-baseman Jim Ray Hart and shortstop Hal Lanier. Hart was the only rookie in the Opening Day line-up that year, and he would be there each Opening Day for the rest of the '60s. His 31 home runs in 1964 were the most ever hit by a Giant rookie. Lanier started at second and eventually moved to short in 1964. His light bat was more than offset by his glove, and he, like Hart, was a regular through the '60s. The best of the new pitchers in 1964 was Ron Herbel, who went 9–9. But he got little attention compared to that accorded Masanori Murakami. The 20-year-old hurler came over from Japan to pitch brilliantly in relief at the end of the season. He was a mainstay in the 1965 bullpen, winning four and saving eight, and then he returned to Japan.

Frank Linzy turned in an impressive 1965 rookie season at 9–3 with 21 saves and a 1.43 ERA. *The Sporting News* recognized him as the NL's top rookie pitcher at the end of the season, and he turned in four more solid seasons in the Giants' bullpen, winning 14 in 1969.

Bobby Bonds was the top prospect in 1968. Starting the season at Phoenix, he pounded the ball at a .370 clip before the Giants brought him back up and installed him in the outfield. In his first game he hit a grand slam, the only rookie in this century to accomplish that feat. Bonds hit .254 in 80 games his first year. That most rare combination of raw power and speed, he stole 30 or more bases while hitting 30 or more home runs five times in his career. He would stay with the Giants through 1974 and was then traded seven times in the next seven years. Now the batting coach of the Indians, he can take pride in his son, Barry, a prize young outfielder with the Pirates.

None of the 1969 rookies would have an impact on the Giants, but one put up some amazing numbers elsewhere. George Foster played just nine games for San Francisco in both 1969 and 1970 before the Giants shipped him to Cincinnati in May 1971 for two inconsequential players. The Reds had more patience than the Giants and let Foster develop slowly. By 1975 he was their left fielder; two years later he was the leader of the Big

Red Machine and had one of the finest seasons ever produced: 52 home runs, 149 RBI, 124 runs scored, and a .320 average.

Ron Bryant joined the pitching staff in 1969 and also took time to come into his own. He won 14 in 1972, and then astounded baseball by going 24–12 in 1973. That may have worn him out: he was 3–15 the following year, one of the most precipitous falls ever taken, and quickly exited from baseball.

Big Dave Kingman was looked over in the spring of 1971 and then sent out to hammer Pacific Coast League homers for a while longer. He came back to hit a grand slam in his second game for the Giants and wielded his big stick for the Giants through 1974. He couldn't cut down on his swing, however, and strikeouts were for him more prevalent than hits. Because of this, the Giants sold Kingman to the Mets in early 1975. The year 1977 was truly an odyssey for Kingman. He began with the Mets, who traded him to San Diego in June. The Padres sold him to the Angels in September; the Angels in turn sold him a week later to the Yankees, for whom he finished the season. A free agent, he then signed with the Cubs in November, his fifth team of the year. He had his best years in Wrigley Field, disciplining himself at the plate and raising his average dramatically in the process. The Cubs eventually traded him back to the Mets, and he ended his career in Oakland, in 1986. One can only imagine what it would have been like to face Kingman, Canseco, and McGwire in the same line-up!

Meanwhile, Willie Mays was traded in Kingman's second year, and Gary Maddox replaced the legend in center field. The rookie hit .266 in 1972 and played solid outfield. Dave Rader provided good catching and was named the NL's Rookie of the Year by *The Sporting News*. Gary Matthews had a fine 1972 in Phoenix, setting a club record for RBI with 108 while hitting .313. He hit an even .300 for the Giants in 1973, his first full year, and won the Baseball Writers' Rookie of the Year award. Maddox was traded early in the 1975 season for Phillies' first-baseman Willie Montanez; Matthews left as a free agent in 1977. They were reunited in the Philadelphia outfield in Spring Training 1981.

The 1974 season also featured two good-looking prospects. John D'Acquisto, who came up in September of 1973 and had a team-high 11 strikeouts against the Padres, was expected to contribute, and did. He won 12 games and was named *The Sporting News'* NL rookie pitcher of the year. Steve Ontiveros, the 1973 Pacific Coast League batting champion in 1973 (.357) and minor league Player of the Year, hit .265 in '74 and would go to the Cubs after two more years of unfulfilled promise. Always a good hitter, he never generated the power expected of third basemen.

The Giants came up with a gem in 1975. "The Count," brash John Montefusco, had been called up at the end of 1974, winning three games and stroking two homers. In 1975 he came on strong, striking out 215 batters in his first full year, the most by a rookie since Grover Cleveland Alexander had 227 in 1911. Montefusco was named the National League's Rookie of the Year and won 16 the next season. But his personality got in the way of his performance, and the Giants traded him to Atlanta in December 1980, in an exchange of malcontented pitchers: Doyle Alexander went to San Francisco.

Catcher Gary Alexander was the Topps player of the year in two leagues. But he and Jack Clark, teammates on four teams, were hurt by the strike that shortened the 1976 spring and both were sent to Phoenix for the season. Both hit well there, but Alexander slipped when he got to the Giants. Clark, meanwhile, hit .252 for the big club in 1977 and was named to the All-Rookie team by *Baseball Digest*. He produced seven more excellent seasons in San Francisco, though never rewarded by postseason play. Traded to St. Louis before the 1985 season for a quartet of promising youngsters, his bat has led the Cardinals, and despite injuries, he has been as productive as any National League hitter.

While Alexander and Clark labored in the minors, the best rookie for the Giants in 1976 was Larry Herndon. Acquired from the Cardinals for Ron Bryant, Herndon hit just .269 for Phoenix in 1975 and started the 1976 season there. But he was brought up after 14 games, hit .288, and was named *The Sporting News*' Rookie of the Year. It was the fifth year in a row that the magazine had honored a Giants' rookie.

Al Holland was a real bullpen find for the Giants in 1980. Acquired with Ed Whitson when Bill Madlock went to Pittsburgh, Holland had a 0.90 ERA at the end of June, and finished the year at 1.76, with a 5–3 record. The Giants let him go too soon, to Philadelphia the winter of 1982; Holland promptly saved 25 and 29 games for the Phillies the next two years.

Chili Davis got a close look in the spring of 1981. The young power hitter had led each of his teams in homers his three years in the minors. He seemed ready to make the jump after hitting .408 in the spring but was optioned out in May. He hit .350 in the Pacific Coast League and came back the next year to make the

Topps All-Rookie team. Davis remains a Giants' starter in the outfield, though the superstardom some predicted for him has never materialized.

Chris Brown made the Topps All-Rookie team in 1985 when he led the Giants with a .271 batting average. But Brown did not get on with Giants' management and was dealt to San Diego midway through the 1987 season, in a trade many credit for launching the Giants' divisional pennant victory. Kevin Mitchell and Dave Dravecky went north in return for Brown.

The Giants came up with a genuine star in 1986. Will Clark was the 1985 winner of the Golden Spikes award as the best collegiate player in the country. He hit a homer in his first at-bat in AA ball, playing just 65 games before making the jump to the Majors. He promptly hit a home run off Nolan Ryan in his first big league at-bat. Named by *Sports Illustrated* as the likely 1986 rookie award winner, he made a pretty good effort to prove them right. Clark hit .297 in the spring, and a solid .287 during the regular season, despite missing 47 games while on the disabled list. His 1987 stats suggest he will only improve, giving the Giants an infield anchor for the future.

Kelly Downs was the outstanding spring rookie in 1987. His 10 wins during the season also augur well for the Giants, whose return to the top of the NL West in 1987 had been long-awaited in the Bay Area.

## Top Rookies Each Spring

1960  Joey Amalfitano, second base
1961  Charles Miller; Matty Alou, outfield
1962  Cap Peterson, outfield
1963  Bob Bishop
1964  Jesus Alou, outfield; Jim Ray Hart, third base
1965  Frank Linzy, pitcher
1966  none
1967  Dick Dietz, catcher
1968  Bobby Bonds, outfield
1969  Ron Bryant, pitcher
1970  Alan Gallagher, third base
1971  Chris Speier, shortstop
1972  Garry Maddox, outfield; Dave Rader, catcher
1973  Gary Matthews, outfield
1974  John D'Acquisto, pitcher
1975  John Montefusco, pitcher
1976  Larry Herndon, outfield

1977    Jack Clark, outfield
1978    Skip James, first base
1979    Joe Strain, second base
1980    Al Holland, pitcher
1981    Chili Davis, outfield
1982    Chili Davis, outfield
1983    Mike Chris, pitcher
1984    Frank Williams, pitcher
1985    Chris Brown, third base
1986    Will Clark, first base
1987    Kelly Downs, pitcher

## NL Rookies of the Year
1973    Gary Matthews, outfield
1975    John Montefusco, pitcher

## Prospect to Watch in 1988
*Matt Williams*, *third base*. A top fielder, Williams can play
short and second as well. He hit less than .280 for most of the
year at Phoenix, but the former Giants' first pick in the June '86
draft is considered the best infield prospect in the organization.

# SEATTLE MARINERS

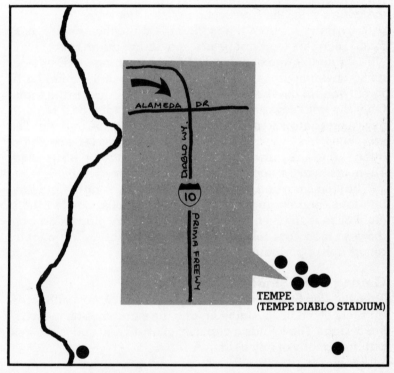

ALAMEDA DR

DIABLO WY.

10

PRIMA FREEWY

**TEMPE
(TEMPE DIABLO STADIUM)**

■ **Current site:**
Diablo Stadium
2200 West Alameda
Tempe, AZ 85282
(602) 731-8381
■ **Dimensions:** 360' left
and right; 410' center
■ **Seating:** 5,400
■ **Built:** 1968
■ **Off-season use:**

Arizona state high
school championships;
local baseball leagues;
Mariners' Instructional
League
■ **Practice site:** At the
stadium daily, at 9:30 A.M.
■ **Game time:** 1:00 P.M.
■ **Most convenient airport:**
Phoenix

Tempe's Diablo Stadium (Diablo is Spanish for devil) was completed in 1968 and was used by the Seattle Pilots and Milwaukee Brewers for Spring Training from 1969 to 1972. It has been the Mariners' only Spring Training home, and they are the primary users of the complex, which includes two-and-a-half diamonds for baseball and two recreational fields. It is owned and operated by the City of Tempe Parks and Recreation Department.

The Mariners' stadium sits under a picturesque butte, around the corner from the intersection of two freeways. Across the wide parking lot from the stadium is a practice field, where Major Leaguers work out before and during the games.

The stands are extensive as Spring Training stadiums go, going down the lines 100 feet past the edge of the infield dirt. Twenty-one of the 28 rows of stands have no backs to the seats. Only the front seven rows, the boxes, are individual seats. A new scoreboard and message center lights up the outfield. The park becomes very crowded when more than 4,000 spectators attend, and the view from certain areas may be obstructed. There is always a free seat on the butte behind left field.

A batting cage and the bullpen are down the right-field line, and fans congregate there to seek autographs. The Mariners' clubhouse is under the grandstand, and the players go from there to their cars in front of the stadium, affording another autograph opportunity.

## Getting to the Stadium

Take the **48th Street South** exit off **Interstate 10**, go south three-quarters of a mile to **Alameda**, and the stadium is on the left.

*Parking:* The lot has a capacity of over 1,000 and is the best parking facility of any field in Arizona.

## Tickets

Tempe Diablo Stadium
2200 West Alameda
Tempe, AZ 85282
(602) 731-8381

The printed schedule is available on January 1. Beginning January 10, the Mariners accept credit card orders for season and single-game tickets. Orders may be made by phone or through the mail. The Mariners have never sold out Diablo Stadium.

*Prices:* Box $5; reserved $4; general admission $3.

## Team Hotel

Ramada Hotel Airport East
1600 South 52nd Street
Tempe, AZ 85281
(602) 967-6600

There are usually a few remote broadcasts from the lobby of the hotel. Dave Niehaus, the team's broadcaster, usually does at least one three-hour talk show from the lobby.

## Players' Favorite Leisure Spots

The players often go to Phoenix for the racing at Greyhound Park on Van Buren Street. For dinner, you can find them at Don & Charlie's for ribs or at Rustlers' Roost. In Tempe, as well as Phoenix, they frequent the Szechuan Inn. Finally, players, managers, and scouts from all the teams in the area are often at the Pink Pony in Scottsdale.

## Previous Spring Training Locations

Diablo Stadium has been the Mariners' Spring Training base since they joined the League in the 1977 expansion season.

## Hottest Prospects

The city of Seattle had a brief fling with professional baseball in 1969 but gave so little support to the first-year Pilots (only 678,000 fans went through the turnstiles) that the owners quickly sold the team to a group in Milwaukee. Yet Seattle yearned for a second chance, and when the league expanded again in 1977, the Mariners were born.

The first group of Mariner rookies included a couple of highly coveted players. One was Ruppert Jones, Seattle's first choice in the draft. The flycatcher played 28 games with Kansas City after hitting 19 homers at Omaha in 1976, so the Mariners had high hopes. They were immediately raised when Jones hit 24 over the fence and, two years later, another 21; but Jones was then dealt to the Yankees for a quartet of youngsters, chief among them pitcher Jim Beattie.

The other 1977 prospect was Carlos Lopez, a .350 hitter at Salt Lake City. After a useful first year he, too, was traded, to Baltimore for pitching prospect Mike Parrott. Parrott's next three seasons were the epitome of a rollercoaster. He was 1–5 his rookie year, blossomed into the staff leader at 14–12 in 1979, only to fall to 1–16 in 1980.

Towards the end of the 1977 season, Julio Cruz moved in at second base to pair with fellow rookie Craig Reynolds. Both had superlative 1978 campaigns, Reynolds batting .292, and Cruz stealing 59 bases. But the combination was quickly broken up in the Mariners' search for pitching, Reynolds going to Houston for promising lefty Floyd Bannister.

The 1978 season also featured the debut of pitcher Shane Rawley, whose live arm impressed more than his losing minor league record. Rawley turned in four solid seasons in the bullpen before the Yankees dangled Bill Caudill in front of the Mariners, and the trade was made as the 1982 season began. It couldn't have worked out better for Seattle. Caudill had been poised for stardom and saved 52 while winning another 14 in his two Seattle seasons. But he was frustrated in Seattle, and the Mariners made the best deal they could, sending Caudill to Oakland and foregoing the 36 saves and 9 victories he produced in 1984.

Rodney Craig became the first Seattle farmhand to make it to the Mariners when he came up at the end of the 1979 season and hit .385. He played sparingly in 1 980, his average dropping precipitously. He then fell victim to Seattle's revolving door, dealt to Cleveland for Wayne Cage who, in turn, never made it back to the Majors.

Dave Henderson had been Seattle's first draft choice in 1977, like Craig, plucked out of the Kansas City system. He was brought up late in 1981 and turned in five productive, if unspectacular, years in the Mariners' outfield. But Henderson was, nonetheless, destined for one glorious moment. Traded to Boston for the Red Sox' pennant drive in August 1986, he batted under .200 until called on to replace injured Tony Armas in center in the AL playoffs. Henderson hit one of the most dramatic home runs in baseball history to keep the Sox alive against the Angels and was unstoppable through the World Series. His moment in the sun over, he was a back-up again in 1987 as rookie Ellis Burks arrived.

University of Texas shortstop Spike Owen came up midway through 1983 to claim that role with the Mariners. His Texas team had one of the finest college pitching rotations in history: three of them — Roger Clemens, Calvin Schiraldi, and Joe Johnson — quickly made the big leagues. Owen soon joined Clemens and Schiraldi in Boston as part of the Henderson trade, which delivered shortstop Rey Quinones to Seattle. He may prove the sleeper in the deal: since moving west, he has displayed all the talents for which the Red Sox had been waiting.

The Seattle farm system delivered in spades in 1984. Alvin Davis came into camp that year with the "can't miss" tag on his bat. Recalled from Salt Lake City the first week of the season when starter Ken Phelps broke his hand, he has been at first base ever since. Davis won his first game with a homer, hit 26 more and drove in 116 runs, and was named the American League's Rookie of the Year by the Baseball Writers. Just behind him in the voting was Mark Langston, who won 17 games and became only the fourth rookie to lead the league in strikeouts. Phil Bradley, up briefly in '83, took over in left field and has hit .300 ever since; Bradley had been an All-Big Eight option quarterback at Missouri before opting for baseball. And powerful Jim Presley was, by season's end, the Mariners' third baseman.

Danny Tartabull, son of former Major Leaguer Jose Tartabull, almost equalled Davis's rookie stats in 1986. Chosen in the 1983 compensation pool when Seattle lost free agent Floyd Bannister, the 19-year-old Tartabull hit .301 at Chattanooga that year and was tabbed by *Baseball America* as the league's second best prospect. In 1985 he was the Pacific Coast League's player of the year, leading all professional baseball with 43 homers at Calgary. Danny was the Opening Day second baseman in 1986 but soon moved to right field and knocked in 96 runs with 25 homers. Had Jose Canseco not had his remarkable rookie season, Tartabull would have been a leading Rookie of the Year candidate. The opinionated Tartabull wanted out of Seattle, however, and the Mariners obliged, sending him to Kansas City for several young arms in a deal that frustrated the Seattle faithful.

In 1987 the Mariners had another hot-hitting prospect in camp. Brick Smith led the Southern League in batting the previous year with a .344 average. He was expected to challenge for the first-base job because of the combined 22 errors committed there by Davis and Phelps in 1986. But he was sent down for more experience.

## Top Rookies Each Spring

1977  Carlos Lopez, outfield; Ruppert Jones, outfield
1978  Shane Rawley, pitcher
1979  Charlie Beamon, first base; Steve Burke, pitcher
1980  Rodney Craig, outfield
1981  Dave Henderson, outfield

1982   Paul Serna, shortstop
1983   Terry Bulling, catcher
1984   Alvin Davis, first base
1985   Ivan Calderon, outfield
1986   Danny Tartabull, second base
1987   Brick Smith, first base

## AL Rookie of the Year
1984   Alvin Davis, first base

## Prospect to Watch in 1988
*Mike Campbell*, *pitcher*. Campbell was the consensus top prospect in the Pacific Coast League in 1987 in a poll of league managers. By mid-August he had posted an oustanding 15–2 record. Seattle's number one pick in the '85 draft, Campbell had more trouble with big league hitters after being brought up, going 0–4 in his first four starts late in 1987.

# APPENDIX A

## Final Standings Since 1960

On the following pages are the combined Grapefruit and Cactus League Spring Training standings since 1960. These do not include ties or records against non-Major League competition, but they do include split squad games.

Along with the standings for Spring Training there are the won-lost records and league standings for that season so you can determine the correlation, or lack thereof. Note that the number of games played in a season jumped from 154 to 162 in the American League in 1961 and in the National League in 1962.

# 1960

| AMERICAN LEAGUE | Spring | Reg Season | | NATIONAL LEAGUE | Spring | Reg Season | |
|---|---|---|---|---|---|---|---|
| Baltimore | 16–13 | 89–65 | 2 | St. Louis | 18– 8 | 86–68 | 3 |
| Boston | 17–14 | 65–89 | 7 | Pittsburgh | 15–10 | 95–59 | 1 |
| Chicago | 16–15 | 87–67 | 3 | Mil. Braves | 14–11 | 88–66 | 2 |
| Cleveland | 16–15 | 76–78 | 4 | Los Angeles | 12–10 | 82–72 | 4 |
| Detroit | 14–14 | 71–83 | 6 | Chicago | 13–13 | 60–94 | 7 |
| Washington | 13–16 | 73–81 | 5 | San Francisco | 13–13 | 79–75 | 5 |
| KC Athletics | 14–18 | 58–96 | 8 | Cincinnati | 11–14 | 67–87 | 6 |
| New York | 11–21 | 97–57 | 1 | Philadelphia | 7–13 | 59–95 | 8 |

Unfazed by the Major Leagues' worst spring record, the Yankees went on to win 97 games, tops in baseball, before losing the World Series to the Pirates in seven games.

# 1961

| AMERICAN LEAGUE | Spring | Reg Season | | NATIONAL LEAGUE | Spring | Reg Season | |
|---|---|---|---|---|---|---|---|
| Washington | 15–10 | 61–100 | 10 | Pittsburgh | 18–11 | 75– 79 | 6 |
| Boston | 14–11 | 76– 86 | 6 | St. Louis | 16–10 | 80– 74 | 5 |
| Minnesota | 15–14 | 70– 90 | 7 | San Francisco | 15–11 | 85– 69 | 3 |
| KC Athletics | 15–14 | 61–100 | 9 | Philadelphia | 14–11 | 47–107 | 8 |
| Detroit | 16–15 | 101– 61 | 2 | Chicago | 14–13 | 64– 90 | 7 |
| Chicago | 12–14 | 86– 76 | 4 | Los Angeles | 13–15 | 89– 65 | 2 |
| Baltimore | 12–16 | 95– 67 | 3 | Mil. Braves | 12–15 | 83– 71 | 4 |
| Cleveland | 10–14 | 78– 83 | 5 | Cincinnati | 12–17 | 93– 61 | 1 |
| LA Angels | 7–10 | 70– 91 | 8 | | | | |
| New York | 10–19 | 109– 53 | 1 | | | | |

Both last-place spring clubs won pennants, the Yankees turning the trick for the second year in a row with 109 wins behind Mantle and Maris, followed by a World Series triumph over the Reds. The expansion Senators started fast, winning the AL spring flag, but went on to lose 100 games during the regular season. American League jumped to 162 games.

# 1962

| AMERICAN LEAGUE | | | | NATIONAL LEAGUE | | | |
|---|---|---|---|---|---|---|---|
| | Spring | Reg Season | | | Spring | Reg Season | |
| New York | 17–10 | 95– 66 | 1 | St. Louis | 18– 8 | 84– 78 | 6 |
| Chicago | 17–11 | 85– 77 | 5 | Chicago | 18– 9 | 59–103 | 9 |
| KC Athletics | 16–11 | 72– 90 | 9 | Houston Colts | 17–11 | 64– 96 | 8 |
| LA Angels | 16–13 | 86– 76 | 3 | Los Angeles | 18–12 | 102– 63 | 2 |
| Washington | 12–10 | 60–101 | 10 | San Francisco | 13–13 | 103– 62 | 1 |
| Baltimore | 13–11 | 77– 85 | 7 | Pittsburgh | 9–11 | 93– 68 | 4 |
| Minnesota | 12–13 | 91– 71 | 2 | New York | 12–15 | 40–120 | 10 |
| Boston | 10–18 | 76– 84 | 8 | Cincinnati | 11–18 | 98– 64 | 3 |
| Detroit | 8–17 | 85– 76 | 4 | Mil. Braves | 10–18 | 86– 76 | 3 |
| Cleveland | 9–20 | 80– 82 | 6 | Philadelphia | 7–14 | 81– 80 | 7 |

The Yankees played well in March for a change, edging the White Sox for the American League lead, and followed with their third straight pennant in the regular season. In the NL, the original Mets showed flashes of competence with a 12–15 spring slate but fooled no one the rest of the summer, losing a Major League record 120 games. National League jumped to 162 games.

# 1963

| AMERICAN LEAGUE | | | | NATIONAL LEAGUE | | | |
|---|---|---|---|---|---|---|---|
| | Spring | Reg Season | | | Spring | Reg Season | |
| LA Angels | 18–10 | 70– 91 | 9 | Houston Colts | 16–11 | 66– 96 | 9 |
| Baltimore | 17–10 | 86– 76 | 4 | Mil. Braves | 16–12 | 84– 78 | 6 |
| KC Athletics | 15–11 | 73– 89 | 8 | New York | 15–12 | 51–111 | 10 |
| Cleveland | 16–12 | 79– 83 | 5 | St. Louis | 15–14 | 93– 69 | 2 |
| Detroit | 16–12 | 79– 83 | 6 | Cincinnati | 14–16 | 86– 76 | 5 |
| Chicago | 16–12 | 94– 68 | 2 | Pittsburgh | 11–13 | 74– 88 | 8 |
| Washington | 13–14 | 56–106 | 10 | Los Angeles | 12–15 | 87– 75 | 4 |
| New York | 12–17 | 104– 57 | 1 | Chicago | 11–16 | 82– 80 | 7 |
| Minnesota | 7–20 | 91– 70 | 3 | San Francisco | 10–17 | 88– 74 | 3 |

The Los Angeles Angels looked like contenders after an 18–10 spring showing, but it was the crosstown Dodgers who impressed when it counted, winning 99 games after a below - .500 preseason. The Yankees reverted to form, copping their fourth consecutive AL flag after another dismal spring.

# 1964

| AMERICAN LEAGUE | Spring | Reg Season | | NATIONAL LEAGUE | Spring | Reg Season | |
|---|---|---|---|---|---|---|---|
| Minnesota | 16–10 | 79– 83 | 7 | Mil. Braves | 19– 6 | 88– 74 | 5 |
| Baltimore | 16–12 | 97– 65 | 3 | San Francisco | 25– 8 | 90– 72 | 4 |
| LA Angels | 14–13 | 82– 80 | 5 | Chicago | 23–11 | 76– 86 | 8 |
| Washington | 12–13 | 62–100 | 9 | St. Louis | 17–10 | 93– 69 | 1 |
| New York | 12–15 | 99– 63 | 1 | Pittsburgh | 16–10 | 0– 82 | 7 |
| Chicago | 12–16 | 98– 64 | 2 | Houston Colts | 13–12 | 66– 96 | 9 |
| Detroit | 10–16 | 85– 77 | 4 | Cincinnati | 14–13 | 92– 70 | 2 |
| KC Athletics | 8–18 | 57–105 | 10 | Philadelphia | 12–14 | 92– 70 | 3 |
| Cleveland | 10–24 | 79– 83 | 6 | New York | 10–17 | 53–109 | 10 |
| Boston | 8–22 | 72– 90 | 8 | Los Angeles | 9–16 | 80– 82 | 6 |

The NL race looked to be a thriller after seven clubs headed north with above –.500 records, and it was, as the Cards rallied to edge the Reds and Phillies by a single game. The Yankees finished a half game in front of Chicago in the middle of the AL exhibition standings and nosed out those same White Sox by one game in October for their fifth consecutive trip to the Series.

# 1965

| AMERICAN LEAGUE | Spring | Reg Season | | NATIONAL LEAGUE | Spring | Reg Season | |
|---|---|---|---|---|---|---|---|
| Chicago | 17–13 | 95– 67 | 2 | Cincinnati | 20–10 | 89– 73 | 4 |
| Cleveland | 14–13 | 87– 75 | 5 | Pittsburgh | 16–10 | 90– 72 | 3 |
| Boston | 11–12 | 62–100 | 9 | Los Angeles | 17–11 | 97– 65 | 1 |
| Washington | 11–13 | 70– 92 | 4 | Houston Astros | 15–10 | 65– 97 | 9 |
| Baltimore | 12–16 | 94– 68 | 3 | San Francisco | 12– 8 | 95– 67 | 2 |
| New York | 13–18 | 77– 85 | 6 | Mil. Braves | 16–13 | 86– 76 | 5 |
| Minnesota | 11–16 | 102– 60 | 1 | St. Louis | 15–13 | 80– 81 | 7 |
| Detroit | 11–17 | 89– 73 | 4 | Chicago | 13–12 | 72– 90 | 8 |
| LA Angels | 9–14 | 75– 87 | 7 | Philadelphia | 13–13 | 85– 76 | 6 |
| KC Athletics | 7–17 | 59–103 | 10 | New York | 11–15 | 50–112 | 10 |

The Indians were the only AL squad with a winning spring record, but it was the Twins who unseated the Yankees as American League champs. The Dodgers fell a game short of the Pirates in Florida but edged the Giants to win their second pennant in three years.

# 1966

| AMERICAN LEAGUE | Spring | Reg Season | | NATIONAL LEAGUE | Spring | Reg Season | |
|---|---|---|---|---|---|---|---|
| Chicago | 21– 7 | 83–79 | 4 | St. Louis | 18– 9 | 83– 79 | 6 |
| New York | 17–11 | 70–89 | 10 | New York | 14–10 | 66– 95 | 9 |
| Baltimore | 15–11 | 97–63 | 1 | San Francisco | 15–11 | 93– 68 | 2 |
| KC Athletics | 14–12 | 74–86 | 7 | Houston | 14–14 | 72– 90 | 8 |
| California | 15–13 | 80–82 | 6 | Atlanta | 13–13 | 85– 77 | 5 |
| Minnesota | 15–13 | 89–73 | 2 | Pittsburgh | 13–13 | 92– 70 | 3 |
| Detroit | 13–12 | 88–74 | 3 | Chicago | 13–14 | 59–103 | 10 |
| Cleveland | 11–16 | 81–81 | 5 | Los Angeles | 10–16 | 95– 67 | 1 |
| Washington | 8–17 | 71–88 | 8 | Philadelphia | 10–16 | 87– 75 | 4 |
| Boston | 8–19 | 72–90 | 9 | Cincinnati | 10–20 | 76– 84 | 7 |

The Mets put together their best spring yet (14–10) and promptly climbed out of the National League cellar for the first time in their history, finishing ninth. The White Sox won a whopping 21 exhibition games but could do no better than fourth in the regular season.

# 1967

| AMERICAN LEAGUE | Spring | Reg Season | | NATIONAL LEAGUE | Spring | Reg Season | |
|---|---|---|---|---|---|---|---|
| Chicago | 16–10 | 89–73 | 4 | San Francisco | 17– 9 | 91– 71 | 2 |
| Washington | 14–12 | 76–85 | 7 | Pittsburgh | 17–10 | 81– 81 | 6 |
| Baltimore | 14–13 | 76–85 | 6 | Cincinnati | 17–12 | 87– 75 | 4 |
| Detroit | 14–13 | 91–71 | 2 | St. Louis | 16–12 | 101– 60 | 1 |
| Boston | 14–13 | 92–70 | 1 | Houston | 15–14 | 69– 93 | 9 |
| Cleveland | 13–14 | 75–87 | 8 | New York | 13–13 | 61–101 | 10 |
| California | 11–14 | 84–77 | 5 | Chicago | 12–13 | 87– 74 | 3 |
| New York | 13–17 | 72–90 | 9 | Atlanta | 12–13 | 77– 85 | 7 |
| Minnesota | 12–17 | 91–71 | 3 | Los Angeles | 11–16 | 73– 89 | 8 |
| KC Athletics | 11–16 | 62–99 | 10 | Philadelphia | 9–20 | 82– 80 | 5 |

After finishing ninth the year before, the Red Sox showed signs of improvement in the spring of '67 with a 14–13 mark before embarking on the road to the Impossible Dream. The White Sox won their third straight spring title, and for the second straight season finished fourth.

# 1968

| AMERICAN LEAGUE | Spring | Reg | Season | NATIONAL LEAGUE | Spring | Reg | Season |
|---|---|---|---|---|---|---|---|
| Washington | 17– 8 | 65–96 | 10 | Cincinnati | 16– 9 | 83–79 | 4 |
| Oakland | 15–12 | 82–80 | 6 | St. Louis | 17–11 | 97–65 | 1 |
| California | 13–12 | 67–95 | 8 | Pittsburgh | 16–11 | 80–82 | 6 |
| Baltimore | 12–12 | 91–71 | 2 | Atlanta | 13–12 | 81–81 | 5 |
| Detroit | 14–15 | 103–59 | 1 | Los Angeles | 14–13 | 76–86 | 7 |
| Chicago | 13–14 | 67–95 | 9 | Philadelphia | 14–14 | 76–86 | 8 |
| New York | 11–13 | 83–79 | 5 | San Francisco | 14–14 | 88–74 | 2 |
| Cleveland | 12–17 | 86–75 | 3 | Chicago | 13–13 | 84–78 | 3 |
| Minnesota | 11–16 | 79–83 | 7 | Houston | 13–14 | 72–90 | 10 |
| Boston | 9–18 | 86–76 | 4 | New York | 9–18 | 73–89 | 9 |

St Louis looked ready to defend its World Championship title after a 17–11 spring and had no trouble winning the National League flag by nine games. In the AL, the Tigers burst from the middle of the Spring Training pack to win the pennant, while the Senators, exhibition champs, finished last.

# 1969

| AMERICAN LEAGUE<br>East | Spring | Reg | Season | NATIONAL LEAGUE<br>East | Spring | Reg | Season |
|---|---|---|---|---|---|---|---|
| Baltimore | 19– 5 | 109–53 | 1 | St. Louis | 16– 9 | 87– 75 | 4 |
| New York | 18–11 | 80–81 | 5 | New York | 14–11 | 100– 62 | 1 |
| Cleveland | 18–12 | 52–99 | 6 | Montreal | 13–11 | 52–110 | 6 |
| Boston | 11–15 | 87–75 | 3 | Philadelphia | 14–12 | 63– 99 | 5 |
| Detroit | 9–17 | 90–72 | 2 | Chicago | 13–15 | 92– 70 | 2 |
| Washington | 8–19 | 86–76 | 4 | Pittsburgh | 10–16 | 88– 74 | 3 |

*Standings since 1960*

| West | Spring | Reg Season | | West | Spring | Reg Season | |
|---|---|---|---|---|---|---|---|
| Chicago | 14–12 | 68–94 | 5 | San Francisco | 19– 7 | 90– 72 | 2 |
| Minnesota | 12–12 | 97–65 | 1 | Houston | 14–13 | 81– 81 | 5 |
| California | 13–14 | 71–91 | 3 | Cincinnati | 13–14 | 89– 73 | 3 |
| Kansas City | 11–15 | 69–93 | 4 | Atlanta | 12–13 | 93– 69 | 1 |
| Oakland | 10–14 | 88–74 | 2 | Los Angeles | 12–16 | 85– 77 | 4 |
| Sea. Pilots | 10–15 | 64–98 | 6 | San Diego | 10–15 | 52–110 | 6 |

In the first season of divisional play, the Mets' 14–11 Florida record was far better than the 9–18 slate they had posted a year earlier but gave little indication of the Amazin' season that was to follow. The Orioles looked awesome with a 19–5 spring tally, and were, winning 109 games and the AL flag before stumbling in the Series.

# 1970

| AMERICAN LEAGUE East | Spring | Reg Season | | NATIONAL LEAGUE East | Spring | Reg Season | |
|---|---|---|---|---|---|---|---|
| New York | 18– 9 | 93–69 | 2 | Chicago | 19–11 | 84–78 | 2 |
| Washington | 13–10 | 70–92 | 6 | Philadelphia | 17–10 | 73–88 | 5 |
| Boston | 14–12 | 87–75 | 3 | Pittsburgh | 13–10 | 89–73 | 1 |
| Baltimore | 11–12 | 108–54 | 1 | New York | 13–13 | 83–79 | 3 |
| Detroit | 12–17 | 79–83 | 4 | St. Louis | 10–13 | 76–86 | 4 |
| Cleveland | 12–17 | 76–86 | 5 | Montreal | 9–14 | 73–89 | 6 |

| West | Spring | Reg Season | | West | Spring | Reg Season | |
|---|---|---|---|---|---|---|---|
| Oakland | 14–15 | 89– 73 | 2 | Los Angeles | 17– 9 | 87–74 | 2 |
| Chicago | 11–13 | 56–106 | 6 | Atlanta | 17–12 | 76–86 | 5 |
| Milwaukee | 14–17 | 65– 97 | 5 | Houston | 16–12 | 79–83 | 4 |
| California | 10–16 | 86– 76 | 3 | San Francisco | 9– 7 | 86–77 | 3 |
| Kansas City | 7–16 | 65– 97 | 4 | San Diego | 14–12 | 63–99 | 6 |
| Minnesota | 7–20 | 98– 64 | 1 | Cincinnati | 14–14 | 102–60 | 1 |

The Twins rebounded from a 7–20 spring performance to capture their first American League Western Division title but were swept by Baltimore in the AL Championship Series. Despite a .500 record, the Reds were last in the NL West in March but earned a place in the World Series with 102 regular-season wins.

# 1971

| AMERICAN LEAGUE | | | | NATIONAL LEAGUE | | | |
|---|---|---|---|---|---|---|---|
| *East* | | | | *East* | | | |
| | Spring | Reg | Season | | Spring | Reg | Season |
| Baltimore | 13–13 | 101– 57 | 1 | Pittsburgh | 18– 8 | 97–65 | 1 |
| Boston | 13–14 | 85– 77 | 3 | Chicago | 18– 9 | 83–79 | 3 |
| Washington | 12–14 | 63– 96 | 5 | New York | 15–12 | 83–79 | 4 |
| Detroit | 13–16 | 91– 71 | 2 | Montreal | 14–12 | 71–90 | 5 |
| Cleveland | 10–14 | 60–102 | 6 | St. Louis | 15–14 | 90–72 | 2 |
| New York | 8–21 | 82– 80 | 4 | Philadelphia | 11–13 | 67–95 | 6 |
| *West* | | | | *West* | | | |
| | Spring | Reg | Season | | Spring | Reg | Season |
| Chicago | 18–10 | 79–83 | 3 | Los Angeles | 13– 9 | 89– 73 | 2 |
| Milwaukee | 16– 9 | 69–92 | 6 | San Francisco | 15–11 | 90– 72 | 1 |
| Oakland | 12–15 | 101–60 | 1 | Houston | 14–13 | 79– 83 | 5 |
| Minnesota | 11–15 | 74–86 | 5 | Cincinnati | 15–14 | 79– 83 | 4 |
| Kansas City | 10–16 | 85–76 | 2 | Atlanta | 13–14 | 82– 80 | 3 |
| California | 9–15 | 76–86 | 4 | San Diego | 10–15 | 61–100 | 6 |

The Pirates and Orioles paced the Eastern divisions with exhibition records of 18–8 and 13–13 respectively, and went on to meet in the World Series. The White Sox posted the AL's best spring mark for the fourth time in seven years but finished the regular season below .500.

# 1972

| AMERICAN LEAGUE | | | | NATIONAL LEAGUE | | | |
|---|---|---|---|---|---|---|---|
| *East* | | | | *East* | | | |
| | Spring | Reg | Season | | Spring | Reg | Season |
| Detroit | 16– 9 | 86–70 | 1 | New York | 15– 9 | 83–73 | 3 |
| Baltimore | 10– 8 | 80–74 | 3 | Pittsburgh | 15–10 | 96–59 | 1 |
| Milwaukee | 11–10 | 65–91 | 6 | Montreal | 10– 7 | 70–86 | 5 |
| Cleveland | 11–12 | 72–84 | 5 | Chicago | 13–10 | 85–70 | 2 |
| Boston | 12–15 | 85–70 | 2 | Philadelphia | 9–11 | 59–97 | 6 |
| New York | 11–15 | 79–76 | 4 | St. Louis | 6–14 | 75–81 | 4 |

| | West | | | | West | | |
|---|---|---|---|---|---|---|---|
| | Spring | Reg Season | | | Spring | Reg Season | |
| Minnesota | 16– 9 | 77– 77 | 3 | San Francisco | 9– 6 | 69–86 | 5 |
| Oakland | 9–11 | 93– 62 | 1 | Los Angeles | 10– 7 | 85–70 | 3 |
| Texas | 11–14 | 54–100 | 6 | San Diego | 9– 8 | 58–95 | 6 |
| Kansas City | 8–11 | 76– 78 | 4 | Houston | 10– 9 | 84–69 | 2 |
| Chicago | 9–15 | 87– 67 | 2 | Cincinnati | 11–11 | 95–59 | 1 |
| California | 7–13 | 75– 80 | 5 | Atlanta | 8–12 | 70–84 | 4 |

The Oakland A's finished second in the AL West this spring despite an unimpressive 9–11 record but went on to win the first of three consecutive World Championships.

# 1973

**AMERICAN LEAGUE** — **NATIONAL LEAGUE**

| | East | | | | East | | |
|---|---|---|---|---|---|---|---|
| | Spring | Reg Season | | | Spring | Reg Season | |
| Cleveland | 17– 9 | 71–91 | 6 | Montreal | 14– 8 | 79–83 | 4 |
| New York | 18–12 | 80–82 | 4 | Chicago | 12–11 | 77–84 | 5 |
| Baltimore | 13–11 | 97–65 | 1 | St. Louis | 13–12 | 81–81 | 2 |
| Detroit | 14–14 | 85–77 | 3 | New York | 11–13 | 82–79 | 1 |
| Boston | 13–14 | 89–73 | 2 | Philadelphia | 11–13 | 71–91 | 6 |
| Milwaukee | 9–12 | 75–88 | 5 | Pittsburgh | 12–15 | 80–82 | 3 |

| | West | | | | West | | |
|---|---|---|---|---|---|---|---|
| | Spring | Reg Season | | | Spring | Reg Season | |
| Oakland | 15–10 | 94– 68 | 1 | Cincinnati | 17– 9 | 99– 63 | 1 |
| Chicago | 15–11 | 77– 85 | 5 | San Francisco | 13– 8 | 88– 74 | 3 |
| Minnesota | 15–14 | 81– 81 | 3 | Los Angeles | 15–12 | 95– 66 | 2 |
| Kansas City | 12–13 | 88– 74 | 2 | Houston | 11–14 | 82– 80 | 4 |
| California | 9–13 | 79– 83 | 4 | San Diego | 6–16 | 60–102 | 6 |
| Texas | 8–15 | 57–105 | 6 | Atlanta | 4–18 | 76– 85 | 5 |

Oakland and Cincinnati gave signs of a World Series rematch by capturing spring division titles, but the Mets upended the Reds in the playoffs after an 11–13 spring and the worst regular-season record ever for a division champion. In the AL East, the Indians took spring honors, then finished the regular season 26 games out of first place.

# 1974

| AMERICAN LEAGUE | | | | NATIONAL LEAGUE | | | |
|---|---|---|---|---|---|---|---|
| *East* | | | | *East* | | | |
| | Spring | Reg Season | | | Spring | Reg Season | |
| Boston | 16– 8 | 84–78 | 3 | Chicago | 14–11 | 66–96 | 6 |
| Cleveland | 12–10 | 77–85 | 4 | Philadelphia | 12–10 | 80–82 | 3 |
| Baltimore | 11–11 | 91–71 | 1 | Montreal | 13–11 | 79–82 | 4 |
| New York | 13–14 | 89–73 | 2 | St. Louis | 13–11 | 86–75 | 2 |
| Detroit | 12–15 | 72–90 | 6 | New York | 11–13 | 71–91 | 5 |
| Milwaukee | 10–13 | 76–86 | 5 | Pittsburgh | 10–15 | 88–74 | 1 |
| *West* | | | | *West* | | | |
| | Spring | Reg Season | | | Spring | Reg Season | |
| Kansas City | 13– 9 | 77–85 | 5 | Los Angeles | 17– 7 | 102– 60 | 1 |
| Texas | 13–10 | 84–76 | 2 | Houston | 14–10 | 81– 81 | 4 |
| California | 11–10 | 68–94 | 6 | San Francisco | 12– 9 | 72– 90 | 5 |
| Chicago | 11–16 | 80–80 | 4 | Cincinnati | 13–12 | 98– 64 | 2 |
| Oakland | 8–16 | 90–72 | 1 | San Diego | 10–10 | 60–102 | 6 |
| Minnesota | 5–22 | 82–80 | 3 | Atlanta | 10–13 | 88– 74 | 3 |

The Dodgers served notice that they were back with a 17–7 spring record, but the other three division champs all overcame unimpressive March showings. The Twins compiled one of the worst spring records ever but still finished a respectable third in the regular season.

# 1975

| AMERICAN LEAGUE | | | | NATIONAL LEAGUE | | | |
|---|---|---|---|---|---|---|---|
| *East* | | | | *East* | | | |
| | Spring | Reg Season | | | Spring | Reg Season | |
| Baltimore | 18– 9 | 90– 69 | 2 | Montreal | 19– 8 | 75–87 | 6 |
| Cleveland | 9– 8 | 79– 80 | 4 | Philadelphia | 15–10 | 86–76 | 2 |
| Milwaukee | 12–12 | 68– 94 | 5 | Pittsburgh | 18–15 | 92–69 | 1 |
| New York | 14–17 | 83– 77 | 3 | St. Louis | 11–15 | 82–80 | 4 |
| Detroit | 13–18 | 57–102 | 6 | New York | 8–18 | 82–80 | 3 |
| Boston | 10–20 | 96– 65 | 1 | Chicago | 6–16 | 75–87 | 5 |

| West | Spring | Reg Season | | | West | Spring | Reg Season | |
|---|---|---|---|---|---|---|---|---|
| California | 15- 9 | 72-89 | 6 | | Los Angeles | 19- 8 | 88-74 | 2 |
| Minnesota | 17-13 | 76-83 | 4 | | San Francisco | 12- 6 | 80-81 | 3 |
| Kansas City | 13-12 | 91-71 | 2 | | Cincinnati | 18-11 | 108-54 | 1 |
| Texas | 14-15 | 79-83 | 3 | | San Diego | 10-10 | 71-91 | 4 |
| Chicago | 14-19 | 75-86 | 5 | | Houston | 14-15 | 64-97 | 6 |
| Oakland | 7-11 | 98-64 | 1 | | Atlanta | 8-19 | 67-94 | 5 |

Both AL division winners finished last in March, with the Red Sox compiling a pathetic 10–20 mark. In the NL, the Reds' 18–11 spring record was only good for third in the West, but their 108 regular-season wins brought them a World Championship seven months later. The Expos tied the Dodgers for the best overall spring record but finished last in October.

# 1976

| AMERICAN LEAGUE East | Spring | Reg Season | | | NATIONAL LEAGUE East | Spring | Reg Season | |
|---|---|---|---|---|---|---|---|---|
| Boston | 9- 8 | 83-79 | 3 | | Montreal | 7- 5 | 55-107 | 6 |
| New York | 8- 7 | 97-62 | 1 | | Philadelphia | 8- 7 | 101- 61 | 1 |
| Detroit | 9- 8 | 74-87 | 5 | | Chicago | 7- 7 | 75- 87 | 4 |
| Cleveland | 6- 8 | 81-78 | 4 | | St. Louis | 6- 9 | 72- 90 | 5 |
| Milwaukee | 6- 9 | 66-95 | 6 | | Pittsburgh | 7-11 | 92- 70 | 2 |
| Baltimore | 4-11 | 88-74 | 2 | | New York | 4-11 | 86- 76 | 3 |

| West | Spring | Reg Season | | | West | Spring | Reg Season | |
|---|---|---|---|---|---|---|---|---|
| Minnesota | 10- 6 | 85-77 | 3 | | Los Angeles | 10-3 | 92-70 | 2 |
| Kansas City | 8- 5 | 90-72 | 1 | | San Diego | 8-7 | 73-89 | 5 |
| California | 7- 5 | 76-86 | 4 | | Atlanta | 8-8 | 70-92 | 6 |
| Texas | 7- 6 | 76-86 | 5 | | San Francisco | 7-7 | 74-88 | 4 |
| Chicago | 9- 8 | 64-97 | 6 | | Cincinnati | 7-7 | 102-60 | 1 |
| Oakland | 5-11 | 87-74 | 2 | | Houston | 7-8 | 80-82 | 3 |

With an abbreviated schedule in a strike year, the Yankees, Phillies, and Royals captured regular-season titles after winning only eight exhibition games each. The other division champ, Cincinnati, won only seven.

# 1977

| AMERICAN LEAGUE | | | |
|---|---|---|---|
| East | | | |
| | Spring | Reg Season | |
| Milwaukee | 17– 9 | 67– 95 | 6 |
| Detroit | 17–10 | 74– 88 | 4 |
| Boston | 16–10 | 97– 64 | 3 |
| Baltimore | 13–10 | 97– 64 | 2 |
| New York | 11–14 | 100– 62 | 1 |
| Cleveland | 11–14 | 71– 90 | 5 |
| Toronto | 8–14 | 54–107 | 7 |

| | | | |
|---|---|---|---|
| West | | | |
| | Spring | Reg Season | |
| Kansas City | 17– 9 | 102–60 | 1 |
| California | 15–12 | 74–88 | 5 |
| Texas | 12–10 | 94–68 | 2 |
| Minnesota | 10–15 | 84–77 | 4 |
| Oakland | 11–14 | 63–98 | 7 |
| Seattle | 9–15 | 64–98 | 6 |
| Chicago | 11–20 | 90–72 | 3 |

| NATIONAL LEAGUE | | | |
|---|---|---|---|
| East | | | |
| | Spring | Reg Season | |
| Philadelphia | 17– 9 | 101–61 | 1 |
| Chicago | 13–12 | 81–81 | 4 |
| Montreal | 14–13 | 75–87 | 5 |
| St. Louis | 12–12 | 83–79 | 3 |
| New York | 11–14 | 64–98 | 6 |
| Pittsburgh | 10–17 | 96–66 | 2 |

| | | | |
|---|---|---|---|
| West | | | |
| | Spring | Reg Season | |
| Los Angeles | 17– 7 | 98– 64 | 1 |
| San Diego | 15–12 | 69– 93 | 5 |
| Houston | 12–12 | 81– 81 | 3 |
| Atlanta | 13–14 | 61–101 | 5 |
| Cincinnati | 12–13 | 88– 74 | 2 |
| San Francisco | 12–15 | 75– 87 | 4 |

Three spring champions, Kansas City, Philadelphia, and Los Ángeles, repeated during the regular season, but the Milwaukee Brewers collapsed after a 17–9 spring. Newcomers Toronto and Seattle showed their form early with 8–14 and 9–15 slates, followed by seventh and sixth place finishes.

# 1978

| AMERICAN LEAGUE | | | |
|---|---|---|---|
| East | | | |
| | Spring | Reg Season | |
| Boston | 18– 9 | 99– 64 | 2 |
| Detroit | 18– 9 | 86– 76 | 5 |
| Cleveland | 12–13 | 69– 90 | 6 |
| New York | 10–13 | 100– 63 | 1 |
| Milwaukee | 10–16 | 93– 69 | 3 |
| Toronto | 8–17 | 59–102 | 7 |
| Baltimore | 13–11 | 90– 71 | 4 |

| NATIONAL LEAGUE | | | |
|---|---|---|---|
| East | | | |
| | Spring | Reg Season | |
| Philadelphia | 14–11 | 90–72 | 1 |
| Montreal | 12–14 | 76–86 | 4 |
| St. Louis | 11–15 | 69–93 | 5 |
| New York | 10–15 | 66–96 | 6 |
| Pittsburgh | N/A | 88–73 | 2 |
| Chicago | 15–10 | 79–83 | 3 |

| | West Spring | Reg Season | | | West Spring | Reg Season | |
|---|---|---|---|---|---|---|---|
| California | 15–11 | 87– 75 | 2 | San Francisco | 18–0* | 89–73 | 3 |
| Kansas City | 12–12 | 92– 70 | 1 | Atlanta | 14–11 | 69–93 | 6 |
| Chicago | 14–14 | 71– 90 | 5 | Los Angeles | 10–14 | 95–67 | 1 |
| Texas | 13–10 | 87– 75 | 3 | Cincinnati | N/A | 92–69 | 2 |
| Minnesota | 15–10 | 73– 89 | 4 | San Diego | N/A | 84–78 | 4 |
| Seattle | N/A | 56–104 | 7 | Houston | N/A | 74–88 | 5 |

*There is a discrepancy regarding this record. The Giants claim they were undefeated, but other statistics suggest they actually lost a few games. For some reason, spring records were not available for several teams.

The Giants looked like world-beaters after a nearly flawless spring, but it was the Dodgers who were atop the standings once again when October arrived. In the AL East, the Red Sox tied the Tigers for the spring title, then lost the regular season title to the Yankees in a thrilling one-game playoff at Fenway.

# 1979

| AMERICAN LEAGUE East Spring | Reg Season | | | NATIONAL LEAGUE East Spring | Reg Season | | |
|---|---|---|---|---|---|---|---|
| Boston | 15–10 | 91– 69 | 3 | Chicago | 14– 9 | 80–82 | 5 |
| Detroit | 14–10 | 85– 76 | 5 | St. Louis | 13–10 | 86–76 | 3 |
| Toronto | 12–12 | 53–109 | 7 | Pittsburgh | 11–10 | 98–64 | 1 |
| Milwaukee | 11–11 | 95– 66 | 2 | Montreal | 12–11 | 95–65 | 2 |
| Cleveland | 12–14 | 81– 80 | 6 | Philadelphia | 11–12 | 84–78 | 4 |
| Baltimore | 8–14 | 102– 57 | 1 | New York | 10–12 | 63–99 | 6 |
| New York | 7–18 | 89– 71 | 4 | | | | |

| West Spring | Reg Season | | | West Spring | Reg Season | | |
|---|---|---|---|---|---|---|---|
| Texas | 13–10 | 83– 79 | 3 | Atlanta | 15–10 | 66–94 | 6 |
| Oakland | 12–10 | 54–108 | 7 | Los Angeles | 13– 9 | 79–83 | 3 |
| California | 13–11 | 88– 74 | 1 | San Francisco | 14–12 | 71–91 | 4 |
| Chicago | 14–12 | 73– 87 | 5 | San Diego | 9–11 | 68–93 | 5 |
| Minnesota | 11–11 | 82– 80 | 4 | Cincinnati | 10–13 | 90–71 | 1 |
| Kansas City | 11–13 | 85– 77 | 2 | Houston | 9–12 | 89–73 | 2 |
| Seattle | 9–13 | 67– 95 | 6 | | | | |

The Red Sox won their second straight AL East spring title, but the Orioles won 102 games after an 8–14 March. The Pirates, Reds, and Angels all grabbed pennants after mediocre springs, while the Braves finished last after snatching spring laurels in the NL West.

# 1980

| AMERICAN LEAGUE | | | | NATIONAL LEAGUE | | | |
|---|---|---|---|---|---|---|---|
| *East* | | | | *East* | | | |
| | Spring | Reg | Season | | Spring | Reg | Season |
| Toronto | 10– 7 | 67–95 | 7 | Philadelphia | 10– 9 | 91–71 | 1 |
| New York | 10– 8 | 103–59 | 1 | Montreal | 10– 9 | 90–72 | 2 |
| Boston | 11– 9 | 83–77 | 4 | St. Louis | 10– 9 | 74–88 | 4 |
| Cleveland | 10–10 | 79–81 | 6 | Chicago | 10–10 | 64–98 | 6 |
| Milwaukee | 10–10 | 86–76 | 3 | Pittsburgh | 9– 9 | 83–79 | 3 |
| Detroit | 10–13 | 84–78 | 5 | New York | 5–11 | 67–95 | 5 |
| Baltimore | 7–14 | 100–62 | 2 | | | | |
| *West* | | | | *West* | | | |
| | Spring | Reg | Season | | Spring | Reg | Season |
| Minnesota | 15– 6 | 77– 84 | 3 | San Francisco | 14– 7 | 75–86 | 5 |
| Kansas City | 15– 8 | 97– 65 | 1 | Los Angeles | 10– 7 | 92–71 | 2 |
| Oakland | 15– 7 | 83– 79 | 2 | Atlanta | 10– 9 | 81–80 | 4 |
| Chicago | 11–12 | 70– 90 | 5 | San Diego | 8–10 | 73–89 | 6 |
| Texas | 10–14 | 76– 85 | 4 | Cincinnati | 9–13 | 89–73 | 3 |
| California | 6–11 | 65– 95 | 6 | Houston | 6–11 | 93–70 | 1 |
| Seattle | 6–12 | 59–103 | 7 | | | | |

The young Blue Jays had their first winning spring ever but were back in the cellar at the end of the regular season. The Astros seemed destined to return to the second division after a 6–11 spring but rallied for their first division title before bowing to the Phillies in the playoffs.

# 1981

| AMERICAN LEAGUE | | | | NATIONAL LEAGUE | | | |
|---|---|---|---|---|---|---|---|
| *East* | | | | *East* | | | |
| | Spring | Reg | Season | | Spring | Reg | Season |
| Detroit | 23–11 | 60–49 | 4 | Montreal | 14–13 | 60–48 | 2 |
| Boston | 15–13 | 59–49 | 5 | New York | 13–13 | 41–62 | 5 |
| Cleveland | 16–14 | 52–51 | 7 | Pittsburgh | 13–13 | 46–56 | 4 |
| New York | 14–13 | 59–48 | 3 | Philadelphia | 9–15 | 59–48 | 3 |
| Toronto | 13–13 | 37–69 | 7 | Chicago | 11–19 | 38–65 | 6 |
| Baltimore | 12–13 | 59–64 | 2 | St. Louis | 9–17 | 59–43 | 1 |
| Milwaukee | 13–15 | 62–47 | 1 | | | | |

| | West | | | | West | | |
|---|---|---|---|---|---|---|---|
| | Spring | Reg Season | | | Spring | Reg Season | |
| California | 16– 9 | 51–59 | 5 | San Francisco | 14–13 | 56–55 | 4 |
| Chicago | 17–10 | 54–52 | 3 | Atlanta | 15–15 | 50–56 | 5 |
| Oakland | 17–10 | 64–45 | 1 | Cincinnati | 12–13 | 66–42 | 1 |
| Texas | 15–12 | 57–48 | 2 | San Diego | 12–13 | 41–69 | 6 |
| Kansas City | 12–11 | 50–53 | 4 | Los Angeles | 12–14 | 63–47 | 2 |
| Minnesota | 15–14 | 41–68 | 7 | Houston | 10–13 | 61–49 | 3 |
| Seattle | 11–18 | 44–65 | 6 | | | | |

The Tigers were the first team to win 20 spring games since 1966 but finished fourth in the AL East. Milwaukee and St. Louis were in the spring cellars but finished first in their respective divisions.

# 1982

| AMERICAN LEAGUE | | | | NATIONAL LEAGUE | | | |
|---|---|---|---|---|---|---|---|
| | East | | | | East | | |
| | Spring | Reg Season | | | Spring | Reg Season | |
| Cleveland | 16– 9 | 78–84 | 6 | Chicago | 14– 8 | 73–89 | 5 |
| Toronto | 15–12 | 78–84 | 7 | Pittsburgh | 16–10 | 84–78 | 4 |
| Baltimore | 14–12 | 94–68 | 2 | St. Louis | 13–11 | 92–70 | 1 |
| Milwaukee | 9–13 | 95–67 | 1 | Montreal | 14–12 | 86–76 | 3 |
| Boston | 11–16 | 89–73 | 3 | Philadelphia | 10–14 | 89–73 | 2 |
| Detroit | 11–16 | 83–79 | 4 | New York | 10–14 | 65–97 | 6 |
| New York | 9–16 | 79–83 | 5 | | | | |

| | West | | | | West | | |
|---|---|---|---|---|---|---|---|
| | Spring | Reg Season | | | Spring | Reg Season | |
| Texas | 15–10 | 64– 98 | 6 | Atlanta | 18– 7 | 89– 73 | 1 |
| Chicago | 13–10 | 87– 75 | 3 | San Diego | 15– 8 | 81– 81 | 4 |
| California | 12–12 | 93– 69 | 1 | Cincinnati | 14–12 | 61–101 | 6 |
| Kansas City | 10–11 | 90– 72 | 2 | Los Angeles | 12–12 | 88– 74 | 2 |
| Seattle | 10–12 | 76– 86 | 4 | San Francisco | 9–14 | 87– 75 | 3 |
| Minnesota | 9–16 | 60–102 | 7 | Houston | 7–14 | 77– 85 | 5 |
| Oakland | 8–15 | 68– 94 | 5 | | | | |

Atlanta won the NL West in the spring then opened the season 13–0 en route to the division title, while the Brewers' 9–13 spring gave no indication of their impending first-ever playoff season. Both the Indians and the Rangers, AL division champs in the spring, finished the regular season sixth, while the Cubs finished fifth after a 14–8 spring.

# 1983

| AMERICAN LEAGUE | | | | NATIONAL LEAGUE | | | |
|---|---|---|---|---|---|---|---|
| *East* | | | | | *East* | | |
| | *Spring* | *Reg Season* | | | *Spring* | *Reg Season* | |
| New York | 16– 8 | 91–71 | 3 | Montreal | 18–10 | 82–80 | 3 |
| Toronto | 16–10 | 89–73 | 4 | New York | 11–12 | 68–94 | 6 |
| Milwaukee | 15–10 | 87–75 | 5 | Philadelphia | 9–11 | 90–72 | 1 |
| Baltimore | 15–11 | 98–64 | 1 | Chicago | 12–16 | 71–91 | 5 |
| Detroit | 13–12 | 92–70 | 2 | St. Louis | 8–12 | 79–83 | 4 |
| Cleveland | 12–16 | 70–92 | 7 | Pittsburgh | 10–16 | 84–78 | 2 |
| Boston | 9–16 | 78–84 | 6 | | | | |
| *West* | | | | | *West* | | |
| | *Spring* | *Reg Season* | | | *Spring* | *Reg Season* | |
| Chicago | 20– 7 | 99– 63 | 1 | San Diego | 12–12 | 81–81 | 4 |
| Minnesota | 17– 6 | 70– 92 | 6 | Atlanta | 13–15 | 88–74 | 2 |
| California | 16– 8 | 70– 92 | 5 | San Francisco | 11–13 | 79–83 | 5 |
| Oakland | 15–11 | 74– 88 | 4 | Los Angeles | 11–17 | 91–71 | 1 |
| Texas | 11–12 | 77– 85 | 3 | Cincinnati | 9–14 | 74–88 | 6 |
| Seattle | 11–14 | 60–102 | 7 | Houston | 3–16 | 85–77 | 3 |
| Kansas City | 10–15 | 79– 83 | 2 | | | | |

The White Sox had another strong spring, and this time it carried over to the season as they won the AL West by a whopping 20 games. Both NL champs had losing springs, and the Red Sox 9–16 exhibition mark kicked off their first losing season since 1966.

# 1984

| AMERICAN LEAGUE | | | | NATIONAL LEAGUE | | | |
|---|---|---|---|---|---|---|---|
| *East* | | | | | *East* | | |
| | *Spring* | *Reg Season* | | | *Spring* | *Reg Season* | |
| Boston | 13–10 | 86–76 | 4 | Pittsburgh | 13– 7 | 75–87 | 6 |
| Cleveland | 13–10 | 75–87 | 6 | New York | 11–10 | 90–72 | 2 |
| Baltimore | 14–11 | 85–77 | 5 | Montreal | 12–14 | 78–83 | 5 |
| Milwaukee | 13–11 | 67–94 | 7 | Philadelphia | 12–14 | 81–81 | 4 |
| Toronto | 11–14 | 89–73 | 2 | St. Louis | 6–15 | 84–78 | 3 |
| Detroit | 10–15 | 104–58 | 1 | Chicago | 5–18 | 96–65 | 1 |
| New York | 9–15 | 87–75 | 3 | | | | |

| | West Spring | Reg Season | | | West Spring | Reg Season | |
|---|---|---|---|---|---|---|---|
| Chicago | 17– 9 | 74–88 | 5 | Houston | 17– 8 | 80–82 | 3 |
| California | 13– 9 | 81–81 | 2 | San Francisco | 16– 8 | 66–96 | 6 |
| Texas | 11– 9 | 69–92 | 7 | Atlanta | 12–11 | 80–82 | 2 |
| Kansas City | 12–10 | 84–78 | 1 | Cincinnati | 11–11 | 70–92 | 5 |
| Oakland | 13–11 | 77–85 | 4 | Los Angeles | 10–13 | 79–83 | 4 |
| Seattle | 11–12 | 74–88 | 6 | San Diego | 12–16 | 92–70 | 1 |
| Minnesota | 10–13 | 81–81 | 3 | | | | |

The first were last and vice-versa in the National League, as spring champions San Francisco and Pittsburgh finished in the basement, while spring (and perennial) cellar-dwellers Chicago and San Diego surprised everyone by grabbing division titles. In the AL, the Tigers' 10–15 spring mark belied their talent, as Detroit won 35 of its first 40, 104 overall, and the World Series.

# 1985

| AMERICAN LEAGUE | East Spring | Reg Season | | NATIONAL LEAGUE | East Spring | Reg Season | |
|---|---|---|---|---|---|---|---|
| Toronto | 18– 7 | 99– 62 | 1 | Philadelphia | 14– 9 | 75– 87 | 5 |
| Detroit | 17–12 | 84– 77 | 3 | Chicago | 17–12 | 77– 84 | 4 |
| New York | 14–12 | 97– 64 | 2 | New York | 13–11 | 98– 64 | 2 |
| Baltimore | 14–13 | 83– 78 | 4 | Montreal | 11–15 | 84– 77 | 3 |
| Milwaukee | 15–14 | 71– 90 | 6 | St. Louis | 7–14 | 101– 61 | 1 |
| Cleveland | 12–15 | 60–102 | 7 | Pittsburgh | 6–17 | 57–104 | 6 |
| Boston | 12–16 | 81– 81 | 5 | | | | |

| | West Spring | Reg Season | | | West Spring | Reg Season | |
|---|---|---|---|---|---|---|---|
| California | 14– 9 | 90–72 | 2 | Atlanta | 17–10 | 66– 96 | 5 |
| Chicago | 18–13 | 85–77 | 3 | Los Angeles | 14–10 | 95– 67 | 1 |
| Oakland | 12–12 | 77–85 | 5 | Cincinnati | 14–12 | 89– 72 | 2 |
| Kansas City | 12–15 | 91–71 | 1 | San Francisco | 13–13 | 62–100 | 6 |
| Seattle | 12–15 | 74–88 | 6 | San Diego | 12–14 | 83– 79 | 4 |
| Minnesota | 12–16 | 77–85 | 4 | Houston | 13–17 | 83– 79 | 3 |
| Texas | 9–14 | 62–99 | 7 | | | | |

The Blue Jays' 18–7 spring mark served notice they had finally arrived, and Toronto followed with its first division title. Atlanta looked strong again in the NL West with a 17–10 slate but tumbled to fifth, while St. Louis overcame a 7–14 spring to reach the World Series for the second time in four seasons.

# 1986

| AMERICAN LEAGUE | | | | NATIONAL LEAGUE | | | |
|---|---|---|---|---|---|---|---|
| *East* | | | | *East* | | | |
| | Spring | Reg Season | | | Spring | Reg Season | |
| Detroit | 18–11 | 87–75 | 3 | Philadelphia | 16–10 | 86–75 | 2 |
| New York | 17–11 | 90–72 | 2 | Pittsburgh | 16–10 | 64–98 | 6 |
| Milwaukee | 16–11 | 77–84 | 6 | New York | 13–13 | 108–54 | 1 |
| Toronto | 15–12 | 86–76 | 4 | St. Louis | 12–15 | 79–82 | 3 |
| Baltimore | 14–14 | 73–89 | 7 | Chicago | 13–20 | 70–90 | 5 |
| Cleveland | 14–16 | 84–78 | 5 | Montreal | 9–21 | 78–83 | 4 |
| Boston | 13–15 | 95–66 | 1 | | | | |
| *West* | | | | *West* | | | |
| | Spring | Reg Season | | | Spring | Reg Season | |
| Oakland | 17–12 | 76–86 | 4 | Atlanta | 18–11 | 72–89 | 6 |
| Texas | 15–13 | 87–85 | 2 | San Francisco | 15–12 | 83–79 | 3 |
| California | 14–14 | 92–70 | 1 | Cincinnati | 16–13 | 86–76 | 2 |
| Chicago | 15–15 | 72–90 | 5 | San Diego | 16–14 | 74–88 | 4 |
| Kansas City | 12–13 | 76–86 | 3 | Los Angeles | 12–16 | 73–89 | 5 |
| Seattle | 13–15 | 67–95 | 7 | Houston | 9–18 | 96–66 | 1 |
| Minnesota | 11–19 | 71–91 | 6 | | | | |

The Astros and Red Sox finished last in their spring divisions but coasted to division titles in September. The other two champs were .500 clubs in March, with the Mets' 13–13 mark giving no indication of the 108 wins that were to follow. The Braves won their second straight NL West spring crown but dropped another notch, to sixth, during the regular season.

# 1987

| AMERICAN LEAGUE | | | | NATIONAL LEAGUE | | | |
|---|---|---|---|---|---|---|---|
| *East* | | | | *East* | | | |
| | Spring | Reg Season | | | Spring | Reg Season | |
| Boston | 16–13 | 78– 84 | 5 | St. Louis | 17– 6 | 95–67 | 1 |
| Milwaukee | 16–17 | 91– 71 | 3 | Chicago | 19–14 | 76–85 | 6 |
| New York | 14–15 | 89– 73 | 4 | Philadelphia | 13–11 | 80–82 | 4 |
| Baltimore | 13–15 | 67– 95 | 6 | Pittsburgh | 13–13 | 80–82 | 4 |
| Cleveland | 13–15 | 61–101 | 7 | New York | 12–14 | 92–70 | 2 |
| Toronto | 9–11 | 96– 66 | 2 | Montreal | 11–16 | 91–71 | 3 |
| Detroit | 9–20 | 98– 64 | 1 | | | | |

| | West | | | | West | | |
|---|---|---|---|---|---|---|---|
| | Spring | Reg Season | | | Spring | Reg Season | |
| Minnesota | 14-10 | 85-77 | 1 | San Francisco | 20-10 | 90-72 | 1 |
| California | 15-15 | 75-87 | 6 | Cincinnati | 16- 9 | 84-78 | 2 |
| Chicago | 15-15 | 77-85 | 5 | Atlanta | 16-14 | 69-92 | 5 |
| Oakland | 14-15 | 81-81 | 3 | Houston | 13-15 | 76-86 | 3 |
| Kansas City | 12-13 | 83-79 | 2 | Los Angeles | 12-14 | 73-89 | 4 |
| Texas | 13-16 | 75-87 | 6 | San Diego | 13-16 | 65-97 | 6 |
| Seattle | 12-17 | 78-84 | 4 | | | | |

Minnesota and St. Louis showed their potential with easy spring flags, and the Giants put together a rare 20-win March. All won divisional pennants. Cleveland's 13-15 exhibition record indicated that *Sports Illustrated*'s high expectations were indeed out of line.

# APPENDIX B

*Chambers of Commerce*

## Florida

**Bradenton:** 222 10th Street West, P.O. Box 321, 33506
(813) 748-3411

**Clearwater (Greater Clearwater):** 128 North Osceola Avenue,
P.O. Box 2457, 33517 (813) 461-0011

**Clearwater (Pinellas Suncoast):** 3696 Ulmerton Road, 33520
(813) 576-2770

**Dunedin:** 434 Main Street, 33528 (813) 733-3197

**Fort Lauderdale (Fort Lauderdale – Broward County):**
208 Southeast 3rd Avenue, P.O. Box 14516, 33302 (305) 462-6000

**Kissimmee (Kissimmee/Osceola County):**
320 East Monument Avenue, 32741 (305) 847-3174

**Lakeland:** 35 Lake Morton Drive, P.O. Box 3538, 33802
(813) 688-8551

**Miami (Coconut Grove):** 3437 Main Highway, 33133
(305) 444-7270

**Miami (Greater Miami):** 1601 Biscayne Boulevard, 7th Level,
33132 (305) 350-7700

**Miami Beach:** 1920 Meridian Avenue, 33139 (305) 672-1270

**Orlando (East Orange):** 10111 East Colonial Drive,
P.O. Box 27027, 32867-7027 (305) 425-1234

**Plant City:** 303 North Warnell Street, P.O. Drawer CC, 33566
(813) 754-3707

**Port St. Lucie:** 1626 Southeast Port St. Lucie Boulevard, 33452
(305) 335-4422

**Saint Petersburg Beach:** 6990 Gulf Boulevard, 33706
(813) 360-6957
**Sarasota:** P.O. Box 5188, 33579  (813) 924-9696
**Tampa (North Tampa):** P.O. Box 8247, 33674  (813) 935-7200
**Tampa (West Tampa):** 3005 West Columbus Drive, 33607
(813) 870-3144
**Vero Beach:** 1216 21st Street, P.O. Box 2947, 32961 (305) 567-3491
**West Palm Beach:** 501 North Flagler Drive, P.O. Box 2931, 33401
(305) 833-3711
**Winter Haven:** 101 6th Street, Northwest, P.O. Box 1420,
33882-1420  (813) 293-2138

## Arizona

**State of Arizona:** 1366 East Thomas Road, Suite 202, Phoenix,
85012  (602) 248-9172
**State of Arizona (State Board of Tourism):** 3507 North Central
Avenue, Suite 506, Phoenix, 85012  (602) 255-3618
**Chandler:** 218 North Arizona Avenue, 85224  (602) 963-4571
**Mesa:** 120 North Center Street, P.O. Drawer C, 85201
(602) 969-1307
**Phoenix (Greater Paradise Valley):** 16042 North 32nd Street,
Suite D-18, 85032  (602) 482-3344
**Phoenix (Phoenix Metro):** 34 West Monroe Street, Suite 900,
85003  (602) 254-5521
**Scottsdale:** 7333 Scottsdale Mall, P.O. Box 130, 85251
(602) 945-8481
**Tempe:** 504 East Southern Avenue, 85282  (602) 967-7891
**Tucson:** P.O. Box 991, 85702  (602) 792-2250
**Yuma:** 377 South Main Street, P.O. Box 230, 85364
(602) 782-2567

# A FAN'S NOTES

# A FAN'S NOTES

# A FAN'S NOTES

# A FAN'S NOTES

# A FAN'S NOTES

# A FAN'S NOTES